THE LEGENDARY CADDIES
OF AUGUSTA NATIONAL

The Legendary Caddies of Augusta National

INSIDE STORIES
FROM GOLF'S GREATEST STAGE

Ward Clayton

— BLAIR —

Blair is an imprint of Carolina Wren Press.

The mission of Blair/Carolina Wren Press is to seek out, nurture,
and promote literary work by new and underrepresented writers.

We gratefully acknowledge the ongoing support of general operations by the
Durham Arts Council's United Arts Fund and the North Carolina Arts Council.

Some of the contents of this book appeared in a different form
in *Men on the Bag: The Caddies of Augusta National* (Ann Arbor,
Mich.: Sports Media Group, 2004).

Library of Congress Control Number: 2023949953

On the cover: Caddie Jariah Beard (right) guided Fuzzy Zoeller (left)
to the 1979 Masters Tournament title. They are pictured at the 1980 Masters.
Fuzzy Zoeller at the Augusta National Golf Course during the 1980
Masters. © The Augusta Chronicle - USA TODAY NETWORK

To Elizabeth, Monica, and Will,
and for all those who carry the bags
and burdens of others

CONTENTS

Foreword by Michael Croley ix

Prologue xi

Introduction 1

THE CADDIES

Nicknames:
From Baldy to Waynesboro 11

The First Caddie 19

Stovepipe 21

Pappy 29

Cemetery 45

A Caddie's Letter 53

Fireball 57

Iron Man 61

Snipes and E. B. 77

Cricket 85

Pete 89

Jariah 109

Carl Jackson 117

Burnt Biscuits 139

THE PLACE

The Neighborhood 149

The Caddie Masters 165

The Caddie Shack 177

The Jumpsuit 181

Picking the Numbers of a Masters Champion 193

THE END OF AN ERA

1982–1983 199

The First Female Caddies 211

The First White Caddie at the Masters 217

Today: Signs of the Times 221

Masters Champions and Caddies 241

Acknowledgments 243

Bibliography 249

FOREWORD

Off to the side but front and center is a good way to think of the caddie's role to the golfer. Even when the golfer is a hack, and the round has no stakes—and your two-dollar Nassau doesn't count as stakes—the caddie's job is to help you but never be in the way. And yet, when we tune into golf on television, we see these men and women on the screen before us, and though their actions are rarely detailed, what they do matters greatly to the person on which the camera and announcers are focused.

Caddying is a service position. Make no mistake. The chef is the star of the restaurant, but your server is the one who makes the experience. The same principle holds true in golf. On the rare occasions I've taken a caddie as a player, only two kinds of caddies stand out: the very good and the very bad. The very good have made my rounds memorable and me a better player. Handing a golfer their club and providing a yardage is easy. Reading putts is tougher. Managing a player's—a stranger's, no less—emotions is critical and most important. The best caddies I've had were excellent greens readers, but they also had excellent people skills. They knew when to talk, when to walk away, and when to come in and provide some knowledge.

Caddies, like therapists, see all kinds of personalities, and the best ones learn how to handle each situation with grace and, because it's golf, a little sense of style and moxie.

Ward Clayton's book is a testament to the merits of a good caddie, for sure. But to say it's simply a detailing of caddie attributes does both his book and the men he chronicles a disservice. Augusta National Golf Club is one of the game's greatest venues and host to one of the most exciting and dynamic professional golf tournaments every year: the Masters. And because it's in the Deep South and because in the Deep South service jobs often are held by African Americans, Clayton seeks to give the Black caddies of golf their rightful due by telling the stories of their lives both in and outside of the storied golf course.

Clayton doesn't shy away from the thorny racial politics of the South or the National, as it's known to locals, but he doesn't make it a centerpiece of this fine book of reporting. Golfers know the history of their sport and of the Masters, but what they may not know is that in those reels of black-and-white footage with the game's greatest heroes and champions, the forerunners of today's modern professional game, the men carrying the clubs were not abstractions for the plight of Black men or the long march toward equality that exists today. They were individuals with hopes, dreams, and struggles independent of racial classification but whose race intersected with their personal ambitions as well as their employment by the club.

Clayton lets us learn about them all with plenty of great nuggets of Masters lore sprinkled in. We learn about the men who taught the greats how to play their course—and those caddies thought of the National as their course—until the club relented and let the professionals bring their own caddies to work for them during the Masters. This change in policy shifted the value of the local caddies to the professional golfer and, as Clayton subtly shows us, chipped away at their mystique and value. But it's also true that for a good long while, the Black caddies of Augusta carried more than clubs. They carried the men who carried the Masters into the hearts and imaginations of every golfer who's ever loved this game. Such is the power of this singular golf event, and such was the depth of knowledge and grace these men brought to their profession.

—Michael Croley
Author, essayist, sports journalist, & creative writing professor

PROLOGUE

My favorite caddie story takes place on the fifteenth fairway at the Augusta National Golf Club, the same place where Stovepipe and Gene Sarazen contrived a miracle in 1935 and numerous Masters Tournaments have been won or lost coming down the stretch on Sunday. There are no famous names in this story, just an experienced Augusta National caddie handing out some simple, pertinent advice to the guest of a member during a casual round of golf.

Faced with a shot of approximately two hundred yards to the green on the downhill par-5 hole, the player was torn about which club to use for his next shot. He asked repeatedly, "Hit the easy 4-iron or the hard 5-iron?"

Finally, the caddie, an anonymous, veteran Black Augusta native, looked toward the player and answered: "It's the solid ball that'll carry," he said.

The player laughed and immediately realized he needed to focus on executing the shot in front of him and not overanalyzing.

I don't know the result, but that piece of advice from a half century ago tells the story of Augusta National caddies: Simple, to the point. Just strike the ball solidly and the club choice won't matter as much. Both strategic and psychological advice in one fell swoop.

Therein lies the intrigue of telling the story of these too-often-unnamed Black men who overcame long odds to become golf course whisperers or the hidden figures of Masters Tournament golf, in a similar time frame and notion to the heroic Black women who helped NASA become successful in the 1950s and 1960s and whose story finally has been told in full over the last decade.

My first sense that this book was necessary occurred in 1999 when I was the sports editor of the *Augusta (Ga.) Chronicle*, which covers the Masters inside and out each April. Early that spring, the phone rang in the newspaper office, and it was Vanessa Peterson-Fox, calling to report that her father, Willie Peterson, had died in New York. As we spoke for a news story, I quickly realized I had wondered through the years why I'd never heard the full back stories of

the men behind such great nicknames as Pappy and Iron Man. I was curious
not just about their given names but a full biographical treatment of the lives
and the personal touch behind the Augusta National jumpsuits. The caddies
were largely unknown and undocumented in media archives. That was the
goal at the outset of this project nearly twenty-five years ago.

As I researched material for the original edition and update of this book, I
also kept coming back to my youth in Durham, North Carolina, and a first,
small glimpse at the importance of caddies, later to be fully documented
with the Augusta caddies story. A summer staple in the Bull City, the *Herald-
Sun* Golf Classic was a weeklong match-play tournament that originated before World War II and concluded in 2018 in concert with the decline of local
newspapers. The *Durham Morning Herald* and its afternoon sister paper, the
Durham Sun, dedicated the entire sports front pages to the tournament, offering major play for, at best, a regional golf tournament, with multiple stories, features, and photos about a field of 224 players of varying abilities. The
event drew some of the top amateurs in the area and quite a few high handi-
cappers who simply enjoyed the camaraderie and head-to-head competition.
Previous winners and medalists included future PGA Tour winners Skip
Alexander, Mike Souchak, Jim Ferree, and Leonard Thompson.

For those who grew up in the Durham area, the tournament had a Masters feel because it drew an unusually large gallery of friends, family, and
the golf community, mainly because the newspaper treated the tournament
with widespread coverage that was usually reserved for such revered events
as Duke or University of North Carolina basketball. While learning to play
the game as a preteen, I would walk the six blocks to Hillandale Golf Course
and work as a forecaddie at the tournament, spotting tee shots on the par-4
twelfth hole for top regional amateurs who included Elbert Thorpe, the oldest brother of PGA Tour and Champions Tour player Jim Thorpe, one of
golf's most prominent Black golfers whose family started the game as caddies at nearby Roxboro (North Carolina) Country Club.

Years later, as a participant in the tournament, I learned the value of teamwork on the golf course. Young kids would volunteer to caddie for parents,
siblings, or friends just so they could be in the mix and experience the competition, which was even more of an unusual element in lower-level amateur
competition. When players were eliminated from match play, it wasn't unusual to see sidelined golfers take up the bag of a friend or relative and coax
them on to victory. If they couldn't play, caddying was as close to the com-

petitive fire as they could get. Caddying friends would brag to players that they couldn't win without the assistance.

I was fortunate enough to experience this on a higher level in 1986, the day after Jack Nicklaus won his sixth green jacket, as a part of the national media's one shot at walking the Augusta National fairways. I was a young sportswriter for the *Durham Morning Herald* when I rose at 5:30 a.m. on the Saturday of that tournament to get in line outside the media center for the privilege of signing up for Monday play. In those days, a first-come, first-served sheet was posted on the front door of the old Quonset hut media center at 8:15 a.m. sharp. Much to my despair, I ended up as the first alternate, only to jump out of my seat in the media center twenty-four hours later when I was informed that a German journalist was bumped because he had played on the Monday after the Masters a few years before. The day was reserved for first-timers or those who hadn't played in a predetermined number of years.

I shared the experience of playing the golf course with a young Augusta National caddie, David Chestnut, who noted that he had looped for Nicklaus in a couple of practice rounds the week before the tournament when Nicklaus's oldest son, Jack II, had yet to arrive to scout the course as a caddie and when the use of Augusta National's in-house caddie corps was required before and after the Masters. David redirected my putts on the tricky putting surfaces, was dead-on with his club selection, and kept me smiling with idle conversation about everything under the sun except golf, much like his Black Augusta National caddying forebears had offered to golfers since the club's founding in 1931.

"Play it here," he pointed to a spot on the fifth green as I eyed a rare birdie chance.

"You're kidding me?" I said from a crouch behind the ball, shaking my head while reading the twenty-five-foot putt. I figured that the putt would start left of the hole and break back.

"This is it ... trust me," David said.

His line guided me at least ten feet to the right of the back hole position. I followed his lead, at first uneasily because my back was nearly turned to the hole, and made a difficult two-putt par.

From tee to green, we talked about Michael Jordan's new NBA career; Augusta's own Godfather of Soul, James Brown; and where the best barbecue is served in Augusta. Golf strategy was a topic reserved for when we arrived at the next shot. I would estimate that 75 percent of my conversation that day was with David rather than with my two playing companions.

The camaraderie eased the tension of playing golf on such hallowed ground. Simply having a caddie made the day considerably more enjoyable.

As the years passed I had deeper discussions with Augusta National caddies, Masters participants, and golf experts and heard their stories of overcoming in the world of golf. These conversations painted a clearer picture that caddying involved much more than simply carrying a bag and passing out advice with friends or associates. They had such a rocky path simply to reach the course and caddie. Battling racism in the Deep South and its growing web of setting Black people aside was a much larger hurdle than any vital golf shot or ornery player, or any of the other trials of the white caddies who met lower barriers to caddie in the first place. Caddying was a job filled with great passion for these men, who became a team with various personalities and skill sets but still a band of men unified in perfecting their craft. What is so alarming is the amount of persistence it took just to reach the job site.

During the early days of Augusta National, in the mid-to-late 1930s, before on-property accommodations had been built there, an all-white group of club members was regularly entertained off-site at various Augusta hotels. According to David Owen's 2003 book, *The Making of the Masters*, which was written with Augusta National's blessing and archival access, club employees arranged for musical groups and dancers to perform when members requested. They also drafted area young men for an all-Black boxing brawl in front of members at a hotel ballroom. Such wagering contests for these all-Black fights were somewhat commonplace among private golf clubs throughout the country. The free-for-all was particularly rogue, demoralizing, and demeaning, with the boxers—most of whom caddied or worked in the kitchen or dining areas at Augusta National—often being blindfolded and asked to combat each other in groups comprised of six to ten fighters until a winner was determined by those dropping out or getting knocked out. Onlookers chided the fighters with taunts of "Black boy" or "Black bastard" during the fracas and eventually made contributions—some via coins or bills thrown onto the floor of the makeshift boxing area for the survivors to accumulate.

Most notable among those young fighters was Sidney Walker, an Augusta teenager and shoeshiner better known as "Beau Jack." While blindfolded, he learned to feel his way to a corner and flail away at any shadow or presence

An old Augusta National caddie badge from the 1930s at the
inception of the tournament. Caddies wore the badges to verify
their employment with Augusta National. *Courtesy of Fred Daitch*

that came his way, often becoming the last man standing. He worked in the
locker room and caddied at Augusta National until the early 1940s when a
group of Augusta National members, led by Augusta National cofounders
Bobby Jones and Clifford Roberts and sports writing legend Grantland Rice,
sent him to the Northeast to train and financed his boxing career. Jack's style
was ultra-aggressive, much like the battle royals he fought in as a teenager,
and his boxing career was starry, with two world lightweight titles during
the 1940s, a claim as "the greatest lightweight ever," and filling New York's
Madison Square Garden as the headliner a record twenty times, including
three bouts in one months' time. Jack was managed by Bowman Milligan,
the head steward at Augusta National who was also his guardian. Jack be-
friended singers Frank Sinatra and Dean Martin, comedian Jackie Gleason,
and heavyweight champion Rocky Marciano, and the boxing career set him
up for life even though the fisticuffs were harmful in his later life. Surely, the
youthful and abhorrent skirmishes in Augusta never left his mind.

Unfortunately, Jack's popularity and that of prominent players' caddie sidekicks was a rarity until the 1960s. The unsettling off-course racism in Augusta escalated further in early May 1970, just one month after the completion of the Masters where caddie Matthew "Shorty Mac" Palmer was credited with guiding Billy Casper, renowned as the world's best putter, to victory. "My caddie's name today was Matthew Palmer," Casper told the *New York Times*. "If it weren't for him, I wouldn't be here. He helped me read every green, one, two, three, right on through eighteen."

Inner-city Black communities were fed up that spring about how basic city services—such as repairing poor roads and water and sewer work—police brutality, and neighborhood violence were being overlooked. On May 9, 1970, Charles Oatman, an intellectually disabled sixteen-year-old Black boy, died in the Richmond County jail, Augusta's home county, with evidence of torture revealed over the next couple days, even though the police said his death had been an accident. On May 11, a three-day riot began with Black Augustans demanding justice as they marched through the city in what is touted as the largest urban uprising in the Deep South during the civil rights era. The riots came one week after student shootings and deaths at Kent State University (Ohio) and three days before student killings at Jackson State University (Mississippi).

More than two thousand people marched on Augusta government offices and law-enforcement facilities. The protesters also burned and looted businesses in downtown Augusta. White police officers were evidently given permission to fire on protestors. Six Black men were killed, all unarmed and shot in the back while running from Augusta police, the Georgia State Patrol, and the National Guard, and more than sixty protesters were injured.

The deceased men were forever labeled the "Augusta Six."

John Bennett, nineteen, was one of those killed on the tragic night of May 11. A neighborhood friend, Walter Newton, sixteen, lamented the lack of discussion about difficulties in the city. The 1970 riot wasn't documented in general history books for another fifty years, and the Department of Justice finally announced in May 2022 that the cold case would be reopened. Newton indicated that Bennett and his twin brother, James, were his 1970 role models simply by their job choices.

"They were both caddies at the Augusta National," Newton told the *Augusta Chronicle*. "They started at Augusta Country Club and graduated, that's what we called it, on to the National. That's what I intended to do."

Imagine just wanting to work for a living and having to climb a seemingly unscalable fence just to be there, plus the other put-downs they may have experienced on the job? Other accounts include the Avery family being shot at on the grounds of Augusta National a decade later. As a result, caddies with famous names such as Bennett, Jackson, Beard, and Avery strongly encouraged their relatives and descendants to pursue careers far from the caddying world.

I was also heartened and saddened—both at the same time—during the initial preparation of this book and now this second edition. I learned that many of these men who became fixtures at Augusta National had not received the notoriety and respect they deserved despite the numerous roadblocks to success that they faced. Too many lived hard lives and failed to benefit from their fame.

Augusta National caddies were not viewed as the most sophisticated caddies during their heyday, but simplicity may have been one of the keys to their success. They earned the moniker of the world's best caddie corps because of their work ethic, inherent knowledge of the course, and their ability to read people. A lack of equity within society prohibited many from gaining access to educational opportunities. Necessary mental, physical, and dental care were merely a dream for them because of long-standing racial barriers that led to hygiene difficulties, undereducation, and poverty. They had few alternatives but to loop at either Augusta Country Club (simply called "the country club") or "the National." As a result of lifelong challenges, too many of the top caddies didn't sustain their caddie association with top professional golfers or influential members, had minimal financial plans, and ended their days in poor health or some type of addiction. Others succeeded because of their associations with players and Augusta National members or due to their own inherent sense of determination.

Some weren't even the best at clubbing players or reading greens. Those rare birds, such as "Pappy" Stokes or Carl Jackson, who knew the course just by sight, go down in history as the great students of this storied course, keeping to themselves the "secrets" in reading the greens and figuring the swirling winds until their time was done. Arnold Palmer and Jack Nicklaus seldom relied on the advice of "Iron Man" Avery or Willie Peterson, respectively, in choosing clubs or reading putts, but these men knew how to get a player around the golf course in the least number of strokes by passing along their knowledge of the course's subtleties or knowing when to push the player's buttons. Who can forget the 1960 Masters when "Iron Man" inspired Arnie with his famous comment late on Sunday, "Are we chokin'?"

"Golf is not my game," Matthew Palmer once said of his playing ability. "Knowing about golf is my game."

"You can't just read these greens," said caddie Marion Herrington, who looped for winner Seve Ballesteros in 1980. "You've got to remember them."

Reading yardages and putts wasn't the limit for these men.

"You had to know the elements," Jariah Beard said. "It was more than telling somebody they had 130 yards to the pin. Nobody can be that exact. You had to know the conditions and get the feel of the player, see how he was feeling at that time. He might be pumped up a little. He might be hitting the ball solid; he might not be. It's not just how far it is to the hole or how far the putt breaks."

Ben Crenshaw, who won two Masters with Carl Jackson on the bag, saw the value of the historic intuition that the Augusta National caddies possessed.

"They knew the course like the back of their hand," Crenshaw said in 2017. "They were proud of it, proud of their caddie corps sort of speak, a very proud bunch. I got to know a bunch of them, and they were indispensable when you go out because there are always surprises when you play Augusta National."

Their standing as the game's most famous and respected caddie corps carries forward simply because they were a cast of characters who added a dimension to the Masters that no other golf tournament had. The U.S. Open, British Open, and PGA Championship, the game's other professional majors, all move from site to site annually. Until the caddie ranks were opened in the 1970s, these tournaments didn't have a consistent cast of loopers that the golf public and top players could latch on to every spring like the Masters had. Many times, kids at the local clubs reserved for the U.S. Open or PGA were forced into action, purely as someone to carry the bag around for eighteen holes. The British Open offered caddies, but they weren't always attached to the host club. The Masters was different. Where else could you see Willie Peterson every year whipping his towel toward a Nicklaus putt or Eddie McCoy and Gary Player walking arm in arm up to the eighteenth green in 1978?

Or look at the humor of Edward White, a former caddie who for years helped organize the caddie ranks and handful of golf carts at Augusta National. He walked around with a nickel in his ear. Why?

"I'm down to my last nickel," he would say with a sheepish grin as you laughed out loud despite the corny punch line.

Or listen to the late Leon McCladdie. The caddie for two-time Masters champion Tom Watson had the opportunity in 1979 to caddie for longtime *Atlanta Journal-Constitution* columnist Furman Bisher. A left-hander with a 14-handicap, Bisher was playing a casual round at Augusta National and kept noticing the grimace on McCladdie's face, especially when Furman severely hooked his tee shot on the par-3 twelfth hole over near Nelson Bridge in front of the thirteenth tee.

"Well, Tom Weiskopf took a thirteen here," Furman told McCladdie.

"You ain't through yet," McCladdie shot back.

These instances are the main reasons why the World Golf Hall of Fame in St. Augustine, Florida, for years had a display about caddies with a photo of the Augusta National caddies and a voice-over by former longtime caddie master Freddie Bennett. When the Hall of Fame moved to Pinehurst, North Carolina, in late 2023, Jackson's Number 1 caddie suit was still on display at the closing in St. Augustine.

They were and remain a proud group of men, still disturbed by the sudden change in policy in 1983 that allowed "outside" caddies to tote on their home turf. For every player who has stated he didn't rely on the caddie's input, that same caddie will respond that there were at least five key moments in the round when the player heeded his advice. Name a Masters champion before 1983—and even through forty years later—and I'll bet his caddie did something that week that inspired his victory, whether it involved strategy or simply being a part of the team.

The caddie comes closer than anyone in any sport to feeling the pulse of athletic competition on the highest level. Coaches and officials are on the same playing surface in other sports, but they don't consult at close range with the player just as a key play is being executed. They don't stand behind the quarterback while he reads the defensive alignment and awaits the snap in football. They cannot peer in at the catcher just as the pitcher goes into his motion against the power hitter. They can't hand the basketball to the forward just before he prepares for a last-second free throw against the backdrop of a hostile crowd.

Imagine standing on the twelfth tee at Augusta National on a Sunday afternoon, in the heat of the battle, with the CBS cameras focused on a do-or-die moment at Rae's Creek, as a swirling breeze and possible doom lurk. The

Carl Jackson's caddie uniform from the 1996 Masters Tournament, when Ben Crenshaw was the defending champion, and a caddie uniform description were on display at the World Golf Hall of Fame through late 2023. *Photo by Ward Clayton*

Amen Corner crowd covers the hillside and grandstands behind the par-3 tee and spreads toward the eleventh and thirteenth fairways, most people standing on tiptoes to get a glimpse. A hush comes over the gallery, enough to hear the birds sing and the wind rush through the tall pine trees. The green-and-white scoreboard on the opposite side of the eleventh green tells the story. There you stand, talking with a player about the wind's impact, the exact yardage, and what club to choose. One wrong move and the green jacket drowns in Rae's Creek.

I'm reminded of Johnny Miller and Mark Eubanks in this instance. "Banks" was such a worrier on the course while caddying for Miller that Johnny prohibited him from touching the grips of his clubs in fear that Eubanks's profuse sweating would make his grips slippery. Still, Miller found comfort in his caddie's nervous demeanor, perhaps because he realized he couldn't possibly be as torn up about a golf tournament as Eubanks.

Or take the case of Sam Snead and O'Bryant Williams, the caddie in Snead's 1949, 1952, and 1954 Masters victories. "Slammin' Sammy" wanted absolutely no input on club selection from his caddie and told him that bluntly beforehand one year. But one round they came to the par-3 sixth tee, and the wind was blowing in a different direction than normal. Sam was perplexed, so he asked O'Bryant if he remembered which way the wind was blowing the previous day, even reassuring him that there wouldn't be any ramifications for his advice.

"I ain't talking, I ain't talking," O'Bryant said over and over as he shook his head. "I know what you're trying to do and you ain't gonna give me hell."

O'Bryant never told Sam which way the wind was blowing, but his guidance was evident in keeping his player loose and being a part of a winning team. O'Bryant was living up to his word.

O'Bryant's enthusiasm was undaunted, however. In the classic eighteen-hole playoff with Ben Hogan in 1954, Snead trailed by one entering the par-5 thirteenth. Snead hit the green in two and had a makeable eagle putt. As the putt approached the hole, O'Bryant started screaming, "Get in! Get in!" and started waving his hand at the ball. The putt missed, Snead tapped in for birdie and was even with five holes to play on the way to a one-stroke victory, his final Masters title.

"O'Bryant, if you had hit that ball with your hand I would have buried you right in that there green," Snead told *Golf Digest* in 1983.

Snead's penchant for humor, even though often quite blue and condescending, was never lost on his association with his caddie. He was particularly humiliating when he wagered that O'Bryant couldn't recall all the names of his children, numbering as many as fourteen. Evidently, O'Bryant struggled to list them all at once, but the endgame was he recited their names and earned $20 for the put-down, which, in a caddie's world, made him the winner.

Loyalty is always evident among Augusta National caddies. When Lee Elder became the first Black man to play in the Masters in 1975, Billy "Baldy"

Ricks took the bus from his home in California to his native Augusta just to be there. Ricks, afraid of flying, said the bus stopped in Phoenix and on came a tiny, elderly Black lady, who happened to be Elder's godmother, and she rode all the way to Augusta beside him. It was the only time the former Augusta National caddie ever used a ticket to attend the tournament, one he acquired from an Augusta National member who was his age and a long-time friend.

When Ron Townsend became the first Black member of the club in 1991, the caddies made a point to search him out and give him a simple hand-shake. When Greg Puga, a Hispanic caddie at Bel Air Country Club in Los Angeles, made the 2001 Masters as the U.S. Public Links champion, he hired Joe Collins as his caddie. The veteran Augusta National caddie called it one of his proudest moments, despite Puga missing the cut, and said it was al-most as good as getting the bag of a potential Masters champion, especially when many of the clubhouse staff at Augusta National made time to watch Puga tee off.

In the time since writing *Men on the Bag* to today's era of heightened so-cial awareness, I have learned an additional lesson, not about golf but about getting along with others with different opinions or backgrounds and how the caddie could be an intermediary in more than just a sport. The attention brought to the story of the all-Black caddie corps at Augusta National has helped make amends for the forgotten efforts of a whole team of caddies, but especially two of notoriety. Nathaniel "Iron Man" Avery and Willie Pe-terson, caddies for nine Masters wins with Arnold Palmer and Jack Nick-laus, respectively, were buried in inner-city Augusta without markers on their graves, perchance because family members thought a brother, sister, cousin, or someone else would take care of the task, but the marker place-ment eventually was lost to time. Many families have experienced similar situations, only theirs were never remedied. Happily, in 2017 an anony-mous donor, in tandem with a documentary on caddies (*Loopers: The Cad-die's Long Walk*), provided a marker for Iron Man just one hundred yards from Willie Stokes's military-provided marker. In conjunction with a Golf Channel feature in November 2020, Nicklaus funded Peterson's marker at a nearby cemetery. Others who have made a name for themselves at Augusta National have also been remembered on elaborately worded tombstones at next-door Westover Cemetery, almost in clear view or at least within full hearing range of crowd roars from Augusta National: Fred "Hop" Harrison,

Raymond Floyd's caddie in 1976, and Joe Collins, whose marker was hand-picked by club member Brad Boss of A. T. Cross Co., whom he caddied for at Augusta National.

Additionally, a movement is afoot to recognize the entire group with a historic marker or artwork in the Sand Hills neighborhood as a small symbol of their long impact on the sport, and hopefully a revitalization of Sand Hills for those who have called it home for decades.

Much of the history and social ascension of caddying were brought further to light in 2019 when I was part of the *Loopers: The Caddies' Long Walk* documentary with Bill Murray, a former caddie himself, narrating. Visits were made to the United Kingdom and Ireland; to public, resort, and private golf courses; to the highly important Evans Scholarship program for caddies; and to the homes of those who have caddying in their blood. It was clear that caddying has come a long way since Old Tom Morris was assigned to manage an often drunk, poor, and unruly gang of caddies in 1860s St. Andrews, Scotland. They were townsmen who likely weren't given an opportunity to do much more than work in hard labor because of their caste in life, following a similar plight as the all-Black Augusta National caddie corps. They had to prove themselves worthy and became proud because they were important in this relatively new sport. As the game progressed to the United States and up to the present day, caddies have taken on a newly found respect as multitasking professionals instead of the long-standing stereotype as a disheveled and uneducated bunch of louts.

Teddy Julian of Ballybunion Golf Club in Ireland could very well be the Irish parallel of the Augusta caddie, a man totally dedicated to his craft. He is a third-generation caddie, with his son being the fourth, and fine with the simple life in his western Ireland home, which was quite evident as he opened *Loopers* in such an understated manner. Golf in the United Kingdom and Ireland is much more publicly accessible than in the United States and a part of the fabric of any small town's makeup, with caddies an essential element of many courses. Beside the road from Julian's home to Ballybunion where he walks to work daily is a cemetery where his family is buried and where he said he will one day rest eternally. When offered the opportunity to attend the international debut of *Loopers* in Edinburgh, Scotland, in the summer of 2019, Julian declined, saying he hadn't flown on an airplane yet in his middle-aged life and didn't plan to do so now.

American private clubs and resorts are about the only place in the States where you can now work with a caddie. But it's also a sign of caddies' escalated value when you visit a place such as Bandon Dunes in Oregon.

"The guest comes to play thirty-six holes per day over three days, and they spend all their time with the caddie and they're best friends for the moment," said Mike Keiser, the owner and founder of Bandon Dunes. "I want the caddies to be the happiest people on the grounds, influencing the happiness of our guests, and that's my pro-caddie philosophy."

There's even a location among the world's top golf courses that has a semblance of the Augusta National caddie experience. At the Teeth of the Dog course, a part of the sprawling Casa de Campo resort in the Dominican Republic, there's an all-Black, all-Dominican caddie group. The 170-person caddie contingent wears all-white jumpsuits, with short sleeves to fit the warm climate, and work as independent contractors for the resort. A caddie is required for those who play the Pete Dye–designed Teeth of the Dog and a couple other courses on property, most of which abut or have coffee-table-book views of the Caribbean Sea. A small group of these caddies, who live within walking distance of the resort, even follow the old-school caddie tradition of traveling to the United States to caddie during the summer when play slows at Casa de Campo. The handful of Dominican caddies take multiple buses from a summer residency with relatives in Washington Heights, New York, for an hour-plus commute to Ridgewood Country Club in New Jersey.

The true test of the acceptance of the *Loopers* film and the value of caddies came in late April 2019 when the film was shown to a cast of longtime Augusta National caddies and their families and friends at the Lucy Craft Laney Museum of Black History in downtown Augusta. Lucy Laney started the first school for Black children in Augusta in the late 1800s, and the high school across the street is named for her efforts. It's a safe bet that some of those in the communities surrounding the school during the following years became caddies.

This group in this setting would be the ultimate test for the project's thoroughness. Also, and more importantly, the film's reception was important because the country was struggling with a tug-of-war over racial and political issues that were polarizing the entire inner workings of American society—and still existed as 2024 approached. After a well-received viewing and a Q and A with former Augusta National caddies Jariah Beard, Robert Jones, and

Tommy Bennett, attendees including Augusta media and politicians were asked to stand and say their piece. One comment was particularly emotional and perhaps unexpected. From the back row one of Stokes's nieces stood to speak—in near tears: "The one thing this film did was give me hope," she said. "Hope that we can talk to each other, which we struggle with. Black to white. Rich to poor. Democrat to Republican. Northerner to southerner. I was motivated by that personal story of connecting—more than golf."

That was a solid shot that hopefully will carry forward.

1

Introduction

B egin with the crisp, bright white jumpsuit. Top it with a green base-ball cap inscribed with the cursive *Caddie*. Ground it with the white athletic shoes, sometimes trimmed in green. This is the uniform of the world's most famous caddie corps.

Add the mind of a scout, scanning the landscape to find any clues for how to tame the swirling winds of Amen Corner or the hidden breaks in the most deceptive greens on earth. Include the timing of a comedian, ready to break the tension of Sunday's back nine at the Masters Tournament with the sim-plest statement or gesture. And don't forget the heart of a daredevil, prepared to challenge his boss on a decision, anytime or anywhere, and particularly to compete against other players and caddies.

A caddie's checklist of duties is both physically and mentally taxing. One week of work at the Augusta National Golf Club during the Masters consists of at least eighty walking miles (estimated six-plus miles per eighteen-hole round) up and down the extremely rolling terrain to scout tee and pin place-ments before and during practice rounds and in tournament play. Practice rounds, with players hitting multiple golf balls and extensive notes-taking about the course, requires double the durability of a regular round. The hilly course is also challenging, with a climb of nearly 100 feet up the hill on the eighth hole and spilling down 111 feet on the ski slope–like descent on No. 10, equitable to ascending and descending a total of 100 flights of stairs.

"We had this caddie at Augusta National when I worked here who was six-foot-seven, and we nicknamed him 'Big Baby,'" said Carl Jackson. "He regu-larly caddied for this member, and it never failed when he got to No. 8, he would say, 'Excuse me sir, we need an escalator on this hole.'"

On most days of Masters week, the caddie may arrive at dawn and not leave the grounds until dusk more than twelve hours later after escorting his player to the practice range, the putting green, the course, and back to the practice areas again to close the day. That caddie trek mirrors and usually far exceeds the estimated average 11,000 to 17,000 steps and 1,200 calories burned on a typical eighteen-hole course by a player, according to a study by the Golf & Health Project, a coalition led by the World Golf Foundation.

Add in the unpredictable early April weather in Augusta, which could range from the chilly forties to wet conditions to high humidity with temperatures in the eighties. In 2023, temperatures ranged from ninety degrees with high humidity and profuse sweating during Wednesday's Par 3 Contest, countered by rain, high winds, and the wearing of multiple winter layers for a forty-eight-degree high during Saturday's third round. These factors add to the chore of carrying a fifty-pound golf bag packed with clubs, balls, rain gear, minor medical supplies, and light snacks. The caddie must also keep his player's clubs clean and dry, check that his fourteen-club limit is met just before tee-off, stay attentive to each player's scoring in his group and the overall standings on the scoreboards, and serve as a one-man gallery marshal when his player addresses the ball. Include the knowledge of standing in the proper place so as not to distract any players, keeping up with the pace of play, and expertly tending pins, replacing divots, and raking bunkers.

And most importantly, the caddie must serve as a psychologist, trying to figure the mood and level of play for his player on that day. When the time comes, what should he say and how forcefully? Will the player be able to hit the required shot under the gun to a dangerous hole location based on his warm-up session that morning and his play over the previous holes that day?

These are the characteristics that made up what has universally been acclaimed as the greatest band of men to ever carry a golf bag, the caddies at the Augusta National Golf Club. They were recognized as the most astute surveyors of the most difficult greens that the game had to offer. They were also the confidants to the game's greatest players. They were Tonto to the Lone Ranger, Robin to Batman, Keith Richards to Mick Jagger.

These caddies and their stories through the years have formed just as much a fixture of the Masters Tournament and Augusta National as any club founder, champion, azaleas, slick greens, green jackets, and pimento cheese sandwiches. This excellence has recently been remembered as the Western Golf Association, the organizing entity of the Caddie Hall of Fame, has made overtures to induct the entire Black Augusta National caddie corps in its Hall of Fame. Freddie Bennett, Jim Dent, Carl Jackson, Walter Pritchett, Willie Peterson, and Willie Stokes are individual members of this all-star group, but no other group of caddies from one place in the world has been so honored, leaving one final chance to lift them up in unison. A conversation between the Western Golf Association and Augusta National was being considered as of 2023.

The caddies who have toted golf bags at Augusta National over the years have become famous and colorful partners to those who played on golf's hallowed ground and won its most famous tournament:

- Stovepipe and Gene Sarazen, with Stovepipe's tall, silk hat
- Pappy and Ben Hogan, with Pappy born on the grounds before Augusta National was even a dream
- Cemetery and President Eisenhower
- The stoic Iron Man and Arnold Palmer
- Five-time caddie winner, the excitable Willie Peterson, with six-time winner Jack Nicklaus
- The quiet, perceptive Carl Jackson alongside Ben Crenshaw

Many a Masters participant or Augusta National member and their guests have been coached and humored by a caddie who could sleepwalk the four-hundred-plus acres at the corner of Washington and Berckmans Roads, particularly the tricky breaks on the famous greens. Who else can claim to know more about the inner workings as a player enters the psychological maze of the back nine at Augusta National on a Sunday afternoon in early April?

But things are different now. The spotlight long ago faded here. Pappy, Iron Man, Willie Peterson, and Jariah Beard are no longer with us, just like many of the famously named caddies of yesteryear. Pappy hung on until age eighty-six, but even just a few years before his death in 2006 he could harken back sixty years to recount untold Masters stories. Carl Jackson, age seventy-six in 2023, was the last vestige, hanging on with longtime friend Crenshaw until Ben retired from competition in 2015.

Forty years ago, the rule forcing participants to use only Augusta National caddies in the Masters was dissolved. Since 1983, the home club's publicly consumed contribution has continually dwindled to only rare instances when an amateur looks for an experienced looper. Most players have brought their regular PGA Tour or European Tour caddies, marquee names like Mike "Fluff" Cowan, Fanny Sunesson, Jim "Bones" Mackay, Stevie Williams, or Joey LaCava. The wide-eyed amateurs often bring friends, instructors, or relatives to share the once-in-a-lifetime experience of being the only "outsider"

Longtime Augusta National caddie Jariah Beard poses in 2020 at the Patch in Augusta, Georgia. *Still frame from the Golf Channel*

allowed with the contestant as Augusta National allows only players and caddies inside the ropes—in comparison to officials, scorekeepers, and media at other tournaments. Many a senior player whose Masters win is lost in the years, unable to compete for the title or even make the cut any longer, will grant a special wish to an associate to tote the bag in the sunset of his career.

So, the Augusta National caddies wait from their home base in the Tournament Services Building, as upscale a caddie shack as you will ever see. The building sits to the right of the teeing ground at the expansive Tournament Practice Facility. They just hope to grab a bone now and then, praying that a veteran player, hot-shot amateur, or emergency pickup of a decent player can lead to a big weekend paycheck. The weeks outside of the Masters—regular member play—are considered far more valuable now.

"It doesn't feel too good," said Joe Collins, a forty-year veteran who claimed a third-place finish with Jim Jamieson in 1973 as his best finish. "But I'm not bitter; it's just something that happens." Joe died at age fifty-six in 2009.

Others don't fade away quite as easily. Bennie Hatcher started caddying at Augusta National in 1963, worked for Arnold Palmer (post–Iron Man) from

1969 to 1977 and later for Lanny Wadkins. He died in 2006. He aimed his ire at the fact that the basic caddying code that made Augusta National caddies the game's benchmark was all but forgotten.

"As the years have progressed, a new generation of people has been coming on," Hatcher said. "We used to go out there and try to out-caddie each other, bet three dollars that your man could beat their man. And you worked it hard. You'd learn and try to feed off each other.

"Now, many people who caddie here come around just interested in making money. They don't give a damn whether they learn or not. They just say, 'How much does he pay? I want to go with him.'"

Freddie Bennett, the forty-five-year caddie master at Augusta National, retired in 2000 and on his way out the door swore he would never step foot back on the grounds, except for maybe an occasional tournament visit. Bennett was a former caddie who rose in rank to become responsible for creating many a winning Masters pair, a man with the sense to find matching personalities such as Beard for Masters rookie Fuzzy Zoeller, the winner in 1979. He is a member of the Professional Caddies Association Hall of Fame. Six years after leaving Augusta National, Bennett died in late 2006.

For his four years before retirement, Bennett was simply a figurehead, titled Director of Outside Operations, perched on a stool in the bag room that sits on the end of the clubhouse, just to the right of the first tee. Augusta National decided to "modernize" its caddie system, and Bennett got lost in the shuffle.

CaddieMaster Enterprises, a company that trains and provides caddies for some of the nation's most prestigious golf courses, including Pinehurst Resort, Blackwolf Run, and Sea Island, Georgia, was hired in October 1996 to oversee Augusta National's caddie corps. Today, CaddieMaster is owned by Troon Golf, the world's largest golf course management company. Tom Van Dorn, a white man, was the first man brought in from the outside to serve as the Augusta National caddie master and work with a stable of caddies, a mix of Augusta National veterans and newcomers from all reaches of the country, during the club's October–May season. Most of the current caddies are not Black and do not claim Augusta or Georgia as their roots. Caddies today at Augusta National fit a varied range. There are college-age kids looking for a once-in-a-lifetime opportunity to caddie at Augusta National. There are the promising young players looking for a few bucks to carry them on to minitours and the dream of one day playing the PGA Tour. There are the wise older heads devoted to the profession and coming from afar, such as Brian McKinley or Steve Kling, who world-ranked women's amateurs and Masters champions rely on to provide updated intelligence. Finally, there are the grizzled veterans of Augusta National from years ago who hang on mainly because they need the money and do not have another occupation.

No doubt, the new caddie system was good business, with better organization, more training up front, a refined method of picking caddies for everyday play, and more equal benefits, including unemployment during the offseason if necessary. But just like what occurred in 1983, much of the personality in being an Augusta National caddie has been diminished. The outgoing, individual caddies with distinct characteristics aren't evident anymore.

By 1997, not a single regular Augusta National caddie worked the tournament. Only Jackson with Crenshaw and Brian Poole, with amateur "Spider" Miller, made the Augusta National connection. Ironically, Poole, a white man who grew up in Augusta, would later become a CaddieMaster Enterprises caddie master during the 1999 U.S. Open at Pinehurst No. 2.

The number of Masters caddies with Augusta National ties has never reached double figures in succeeding years. In 2000, Tommie Smalley worked with 1967 champion Gay Brewer, Collins with 1973 winner Tommy Aaron, Jesse "Gray" Moore with amateur Sung Yoon Kim, and Jackson with Crenshaw. Hatcher was a second-round fill-in when marker John Harris, an Augusta National member, was asked to even out the field. In 2001, there was a sudden rush of National caddies, led by Jackson and including Robert Bass with amateur Jeff Quinney, Collins with amateur Greg Puga, Hatcher with amateur Milo Ilonen, Marion Herrington with amateur James Driscoll, Freddie Robertson with Aaron, and Ronald Whitfield with Seve Ballesteros. Bass did double duty that week, working as a dishwasher at the ultra-busy Outback Steakhouse on Washington Road until late at night and caddying during the day.

Still, the introduction of "outsiders" to the caddie equation, both the Tour caddies and the caddie management group, distanced Augusta National and the Masters even further from Augusta's Black community, which makes up more than 50 percent of home base Richmond County's population. When Augusta National had its all-Black caddie corps and an all-white competitors' field (prior to Lee Elder's participation in 1975), there was a perception of racial division nationally and internationally. The club was criticized for its closed-door policy and decidedly private way of dealing with issues.

There is even the repetitively used quote from Clifford Roberts, the Masters and Augusta National cofounder, about the everlasting racial makeup of players (white) and caddies (Black). While it's true that Roberts has been characterized to have racially toned actions, he was a huge supporter of the caddie corps, and they returned his admiration. The quote has never developed any attribution that would be suitable for journalistically ethical use.

However, most of the caddies did not consider their racial makeup a put down; they believed it was an opportunity.

They carried the bags at the National because they could unify to prove their worth as a group of accomplished men who plied a rare trade. They wanted to be known as the best their profession could offer, a creed very much consistent with Augusta National's motto across the board, whether it be an immaculate golf course and surrounding landscape or the precise way club members and employees carried themselves. The caddies learned the golf course as best as humanly possible and dressed impeccably in the bright white, wrinkle-free jumpsuits. Most of the caddies came from the Sand Hills section of Augusta, up on the hill above next-door neighbor Augusta Country Club and within easy walking distance of both courses. They learned the caddie game as youngsters at Augusta Country Club, went on to Augusta National, and, hopefully, to one day carry as the caddie of a winning Masters champion. Today, a chain-link fence separates the neighborhood from the sixteenth and seventeenth fairways at Augusta Country Club.

Nevertheless, the memories still exist as if it were yesterday despite Jackson, Herrington (Seve Ballesteros, 1980), and Ben Bussey (Craig Stadler, 1982) being the only remaining winning former Black Augusta National caddies. Beard and Johnnie Frank Moore (Gay Brewer, 1967) died in 2023.

"There ain't many of us left anymore," Beard said in 2022 (months before passing). "A lot of those guys who were coming along in the early 1980s found something else to do. Our stories get us by now."

1

The Caddies

1

Nicknames

FROM BALDY TO WAYNESBORO

Caddies developed their colorful nicknames by spending hours together in the caddie shack or on the course in addition to their off-course relationships. These nicknames catch on for life, and caddies live by their nicknames instead of their given names. Mike Cowan? No, it's "Fluff." Willie Perteet? That's got to be "Cemetery."

The famous Scottish links courses had the first caddies of renown, bearing nicknames such as Big, Fiery, Ol' Da, Skipper, Poot, and Pawkey. By the 1880s, when golf was first played in the United States, caddies started to work here also. World Golf Hall of Famers such as Francis Ouimet, Gene Sarazen, Byron Nelson, and Ben Hogan all got their starts in golf by serving as young caddies early in the twentieth century.

The Augusta National caddies have developed a wide assortment of caddie nicknames, most in relation to a physical characteristic or a particular incident that affected their lives. These colorful monikers offer a glimpse into who they really were.

For example, Nathaniel "Iron Man" Avery earned his nickname because he survived some sort of physically harmful experience, such as a knife fight or firecracker explosion, with little damage. Multiple legendary stories live on about his nickname, lending a mysterious angle to its origin.

Stovepipe, Sarazen's Masters caddie, earned his nickname simply because he wore a tall, silk, black hat that resembled a stovepipe.

Many of the Augusta National caddies are known by only these nicknames. There is not an official record of Stovepipe's given name, even though there are hints, and it may be lost to history since he caddied in the 1930s. Other caddies with unique nicknames at the outset of the club were "The Deacon" and "Old Moses."

Willie "Tassall" Mason and "Big Henry" Avery, who served as successive caddie masters at Augusta Country Club, labeled many of the caddies with nicknames when they were just starting to caddie. Augusta Country Club was the place where young, teenage caddies first went to work before "going across the creek" to Augusta National. Saturday mornings were reserved for caddie lessons for school-age caddies, with Mason showing the youngsters the ropes and even giving playing lessons and conducting informal tournaments on the practice facility at Augusta Country Club.

"Big Henry would yell from the caddie house over there to get some caddies to work," Carl Jackson remembered of his first experiences at the country club. "We'd be standing in a field across from the country club waiting for a bag. If [Henry] didn't know your name, he would call you by what you looked like or who you were related to. My big brother [Austin] was 'Tweety.' [Henry] didn't know my name, so he just called me 'Little Tweet.'"

John Henry Williams, nicknamed 'Leven, and his successor, Freddie Bennett, as caddie masters at Augusta National, handed down other nicknames when caddies "graduated" to Augusta National.

The caddies even gave nicknames to the golfers. Iron Man often referred to his longtime player Arnold Palmer as simply "Par." Gary Player earned the nickname "The Aferkin" around the caddie shack because of his South African heritage. Willie Peterson simply called Jack Nicklaus, "Mr. Jack."

Sidney Matthew, the Bobby Jones historian, caddied for PGA Tour pro Kenny Knox, a friend, in the 1991 Masters. Matthew was asked where he was from and his occupation during a pretournament visit to the caddie master. When he told the surrounding caddies that he was an attorney in Tallahassee, Florida, Matthew was labeled with the nickname, "The Judge."

"By the end of the week I was asked by every caddie there about how to handle a divorce, a ticket, any legal action," Matthew said. "They just said, 'Hey, Judge, I got this problem . . .'"

The golf course earned its own nicknames as well. The big hill on the par-5 eighth hole climbs nearly seventy feet from the tee shot landing area to just more than one hundred yards short on the green. The caddies have labeled it "Big Bertha," because of the difficult walk and the two noteworthy moguls that sit on the top of the hill, reminding the caddies of a woman's shapely figure.

Following are some of the more colorful Augusta National caddie nicknames, with a short explanation where available. Most of the nicknames are obvious:

PAPPY: Willie Stokes. The five-time winner as a Masters caddie was given the nickname by his family when he was small because of his slow, pensive movement and attitude, like an old man.

CEMETERY OR DEAD MAN: Willie Perteet. Ike's caddie survived a knife attack from a dumped girlfriend and her friends. He was left for dead in the hospital morgue before reviving. Thus the nickname, which President Eisenhower altered from Dead Man to Cemetery.

BURNT BISCUITS: Tommy Bennett. Tiger Woods's first Masters caddie burned his legs as a teenager when he turned over a pot of boiling water while trying to escape through a window after stealing some fresh biscuits that were cooling on his grandmother's woodburning stove.

PETE: Willie Peterson. Nicklaus's caddie simply had a shortened version of his last name. Also called Brother or Bro.

SKILLET: Carl Jackson. Ben Crenshaw's caddie was given the name when he was a young baseball player in Augusta "because I pitched and couldn't break an egg. I just threw junk." Also called Little Tweet (after his older brother).

DAYBREAK: Bennie Hatcher. No, Arnold Palmer's Masters caddie through most of the 1970s didn't stay up all night partying and show up at the course just in time to caddie as the nickname would infer. "I never showed up late. I was always at the course early in the morning. Before sunup. That's where that came from," said Hatcher, who succeeded Iron Man on Palmer's bag.

'LEVEN: John Henry Williams. The first caddie master at Augusta National, serving through 1959, was a former caddie. He earned his nickname either because eleven was the uniform number he wore while caddying in early Masters tournaments or because he was the eleventh of eleven children.

WAYNESBORO: Marion Herrington. The caddie for winner Seve Ballesteros in 1980 was born in Waynesboro, Georgia, about thirty minutes south of Augusta, but was raised in the Sand Hills neighborhood. Following his Augusta National career, he served as the caddie master at Sage Valley, an exclusive private club across the Savannah River in South Carolina, before moving to Charlotte, North Carolina.

EDGAR ALLEN POE: No nickname, but the given name of an old Augusta National caddie. "Poe?" an Augusta National guest once asked about his caddie's name when introduced. "Like the poet, Edgar Allan Poe?" "That's me," the caddie shot back. "How did you know?"

PO BABY: Ron Whitfield. Given to him because he was always complaining, possibly also because he lacked money. When Whitfield picked up Ballesteros's bag in 2000, he made sure to track down Seve at the end of the second round after the two-time champion missed the cut. "Got to go," Whitfield remarked to a group he was talking with as he sprinted away. "I hear he doesn't pay if you don't find him after the round."

SHORTY MAC: Matthew Palmer. Short in stature, but a great greens reader. A short-order cook who only caddied in and around the Masters, he guided Billy Casper to his 1970 victory. It took six years before Casper finally listened to Palmer's advice on the greens. In an eighteen-hole playoff with Gene Littler, Casper took only twenty-seven putts, twelve on the front nine, and had nine one-putt greens. "I'm just hardheaded, I guess," Casper said about why he didn't listen to Palmer earlier. In ninety holes, Casper didn't have any three-putt greens in 1970.

SKINNY: Frank Ware. Tall, thin man who led George Archer to his 1969 victory.

BIG BOY: Jim Dent. One of the first Black golfers to successfully compete on the PGA Tour and who made a bigger name for himself on the PGA Tour Champions after he turned fifty. Earned his nickname because of his size (6' 3", 225 pounds) and prodigious length off the tee. Dent once caddied for Bob Goalby in the Masters. He played high school football in the late 1950s at Augusta's all-Black Laney High School with future New York Jets 1969 Super Bowl fullback Emerson Boozer.

BEAVER: Wallace Ware. Earned the nickname because of bad dental work. Famous for once quitting on the twelfth hole while on the bag of a rude and demanding Englishman who was the guest of a member. The guest kept putting down Beaver and wouldn't take his advice. "Mister, they pay me to carry your bag, not kiss your ass," he said as he dropped the bag at Amen Corner and walked in. Also once told a member whom he regularly caddied for and worked for off the course that he needed a loan: "Boss, I got lots of dust in my wallet."

HARRISBURG: Johnny Garrett. Raised and lived in the Harrisburg section of Augusta, located between Augusta National and downtown Augusta. One of the oldest caddies to continue working at Augusta National into the early 2000s.

IRON MAN: Nathaniel Avery. Arnie's caddie earned his nickname as a youngster because of his durability, but folklore indicates that he survived an accident with a firecracker, injured himself trying to chop open a golf ball, or withstood an axe or knife attack. Usually, the firecracker and knife incidents are paired with alcohol consumption. The only documented background on the nickname was his propensity to work hard as a young caddie.

BALDY: James "Billy" Ricks. Lacked hair. In the late 1940s, he thought original Augusta National pro Ed Dudley was praising his ability to quickly pick up balls on the driving range, leaving the green grass clean of range balls or picked "bald," instead of talking about his receding hairline.

LITTLE EARL: Jariah Beard. Fuzzy Zoeller's caddie in the 1979 victory earned this nickname because Earl was his father's name. Also called Bubba because that was his father's nickname. He earned another nickname, 4-Iron, because he got into a confrontation with another caddie, and that caddie hit him in the head with a 4-iron.

MARBLE EYE: Frank Stokes. He had large eyes. Was on Goalby's bag in his controversial 1968 victory. Earned $2,500 from Goalby, whom he caddied for occasionally away from Augusta National. When Stokes, an Atlantan who was good friends with another Masters caddie, George "Fireball" Franklin, showed up for the next tournament after the Masters, he was sporting bright green alligator shoes and fancy new duds. "I'm not caddying this week, Bob," he said proudly.

WHEEZY: Fred Searles. Not his given nickname and no one referred to him by this nickname, but they should have based upon his winning characteristic and health issues. After winning with Byron Nelson in 1937 and 1942, Nelson had to find a new caddie soon after. Searles started wheezing on the practice tee before the round, and his breathing got so bad, he had to quit midway through the front nine. Turned out he had emphysema.

HOP: Fred Harrison. Raymond Floyd's caddie in his 1976 victory. Also called Hopalong because he walked with a limp since one leg was shorter than the other. He earned the nickname from an Athens, Georgia, attorney after Harrison was run over by a car as a child and walked with a limp. A full-time mill worker in Augusta, he took vacation around the Masters and began caddying at age twelve.

BULL: Charles Williams. The longtime driving range supervisor at Augusta National during the Masters because of his powerful physique. Also— in no disrespect to this Bull—a derogatory nickname for a caddie, according to Beard, that suggested that a caddie was ignorant.

STABBER: A flattering term for a caddie, Beard said, because it means "you could pull clubs that went right to the heart of the green." The name was carried by Ike "Stabber" Choice, who grew up in Sand Hills and began working at Augusta National in the late 1960s and was still occasionally caddying there in early 2023. "I caddied for some good players, and they always hit the ball close," Choice said. "That's why a bunch of kids I grew up with gave me that nickname." Among the people Choice caddied for in the Masters were J. C. Snead, Joe Inman, Doug Ford, and Mark Pfeil.

FIRST BASEMAN: Cleveland Holmes. Played first base in baseball as a youth.

SNIPES: Ernest Nipper, Gary Player's caddie for his first Masters victory. Also called Nip, but the Snipes moniker was more descriptive since he was labeled as a caddie who could read a golf course like a sniper with a rifle.

E. B.: Eddie McCoy, Gary Player's caddie for his last two Masters victories, who was referred to by his initials.

MUTT: Mutt Boyd. Ken Venturi's caddie. Had a brother that everyone called Dude Boyd.

FIREBALL: George Franklin. Doug Ford's temperamental caddie in their 1957 victory, who disagreed with Ford's strategy.

CRICKET: Walter Pritchett, who was known for his distinctive towel headdress in Charles Coody's 1971 victory. Earned his nickname because of his tall, lanky build.

HICKY: Wayne Hawes.

RED: Tim Reid. Red complexion and hair.

BANKS: Mark Eubanks. Johnny Miller's former caddie who was known as a profusive sweater on the course but also one of the authors of a manual on how to caddie at Augusta National in the 1970s. In the May 2002 issue of *Golf Digest*, Miller said he was saddened to hear that Eubanks had passed away. Come to find out, Eubanks was still alive and kicking, but he did die in 2016.

POOKIE: James Harrison.

CIGARETTE: Robert Jones. Calvin Peete's regular Tour and Masters caddie needed a nickname to differentiate him from Bobby Jones, the Augusta National cofounder. Jones earned the nickname when the Laney High football coach found him sneaking a smoke behind the gym during his high school football career.

ROUNDHEAD: Walter Newton. Known for having an extraordinarily round head.

GARDOOLIE: Guy Dooley. Two names were run together to form his nickname.

SHOO POON: George Brooks.

HAWK: Arthur Johnson. There is no indication of his nickname's origin or if it had any relation to Ben Hogan's moniker. At age seventeen, Johnson was put on the bag of Japan's Takaaki Kono for the 1970 Masters. Kono, who stood but five feet two, didn't speak English. Johnson received a tip from his cousin Elijah who carried for Kono in his 1969 Masters debut. "If I pull a boner, and he wants to chew me out, I can't understand what he says," Johnson said. "He may call me a dumb so-and-so, and as far as I know he is saying I am a great guy." Kono finished tied for thirteenth in 1969 and tied for a career-best twelfth place in 1970.

EIGHT-BALL: Clarence Harris. Earned the nickname because of his dark skin, like an eight ball in billiards. Pulled off a rare double in 1955 by carrying for winner Cary Middlecoff in the Masters and for Patty Berg in the Titleholders, the women's version of the Masters held at neighboring Augusta Country Club.

LONG DISTANCE: Given name unknown.

POKIE: Leepot Dent. Jim Dent's nephew.

RAT: James Gilbert. Earned his nickname because he had short, pointed teeth, like a rat.

CADILLAC: Given name unknown.

LAMB CHOP: Given name unknown.

BODIDDLY: Eugene Jones.

EGGY: Horace Avery, the brother of Iron Man. Horace earned his nickname because he had a bump on his head that resembled a fried egg.

CROSS-HANDED HENRY: Henry Brown. Played golf cross handed. He had two of the most noteworthy nonwinning bags in Masters history. He worked for Roberto De Vicenzo in the Argentinian's 1968 Masters loss to Bob Goalby where Roberto, tied after seventy-two holes, incorrectly signed his scorecard and failed to make a playoff with Goalby. In 1975, Brown worked for Lee Elder, the first Black man to play in the Masters. He impressed Elder with his playing ability, and Elder invited him to play in an Elder-sponsored tournament in Virginia after the 1975 tournament. However, Elder wanted to play by yardage instead of Brown's preferred method of estimating yardage and handing Elder a club. Eventually, Brown changed to walking off yardages and letting Elder determine his club.

Beard contends that Brown may have been the best golfer ever among Augusta National caddies. "I played him one day and he beat me five-up playing cross-handed right-handed," Beard recalled. "The next day he said he'd play me left-handed, and he dusted me that way, too."

To prove Beard's point, Brown had the unusual situation of trying to qualify for the U.S. Open, beginning in 1980. He wrote the USGA to try and qualify for the 1980 U.S. Open, asking to be released from an Augusta jail where he was serving time for not paying alimony. In 1982, listing a South Bend, Indiana, junkyard as his residence, he finished one stroke away from qualifying. He tried to make it on the Senior PGA Tour but died of cancer at age fifty-three in 1992.

"I'll never forget what he said when he just missed the Open," Larry Adamson, then the USGA's director of championship administration, told the *Chicago Tribune* in 1997. "He never was angry or upset. He said, 'Mr. Larry, all I ever told you was I wanted a chance.'"

LITTLE BUTCH: Samuel Littles Jr. Butch became known as possibly one of the best caddie golfers. In 1999, he qualified for the U.S. Senior Open in Des Moines, Iowa. A longtime friend of Beard, Littles became a big-money gambler at Forest Hills and the Patch, following in the footsteps of his father, Samuel Sr., who also caddied at Augusta National. Little Butch had Sidney Brown, another Augusta National caddie, on his bag in Iowa. Littles listed his biographical background as the lead singer in the Playback band and as a member of the "Chitlin' Circuit," an all-Black Southeastern United States minitour. Littles shot a first-round 81 and was disqualified during the second round for inadvertently changing golf ball brands.

1

The First Caddie

William Bowman frequently swam in Rae's Creek as a teenager. He wasn't hunting golf balls. There wasn't even a golf course on the grounds at the time. The land at the corner of Washington and Berckmans Roads was still called Fruitland Nurseries.

"We used to go swimming in that water," Bowman told the *Boston Globe* in 1990. "There were alligators in there. We'd sell the baby alligators to the hospital. They had an aquarium, and they'd put them in there and let the kids see them."

Bowman was resourceful enough to make a living in a couple of ways just before and after Augusta National was first built and the Masters Tournament debuted. For three years, he secretly ran a still in the woods where the course would be built. In the days of Prohibition, Bowman sold half-pints of moonshine for twenty-five cents.

"I made a good living at it," Bowman said. "This was before they took the woods down and then I couldn't hide anymore. They built the golf course, ran me off the property and out of a job."

Caddying was his main line of work anyway, and it became more of a calling when the still dried up. He began carrying bags at neighboring Augusta Country Club years before and served as a gardener at the nearby Bon Air Hotel, where most of the Masters field would take residence for the week. Once, he was asked to give a playing lesson to an Augusta Country Club visitor from New Jersey. The man insisted on paying a caddie fee, and eventually the two played for the money, at the visitor's insistence. Bowman pocketed $175 and was promptly sidelined by the Augusta Country Club caddie master for two weeks.

Luckily, Bowman was downtown shortly thereafter, and the manager of the new Augusta National Golf Club recognized him.

"Augusta National is opening tomorrow, what are you doing?" the manager asked.

"Nothing," Bowman replied.

"Be over there tomorrow morning and get all the good caddies you can find," the manager said.

Bright and early the next day, in December 1932, Bowman was the first caddie in line as the bags came out for the first rounds of an informal course opening. A more eventful club opening was scheduled for January 1933. Tommy Armour, the famed "Silver Scot," was the first bag grabbed by Bowman.

Bowman would never win on a bag in the Masters, but he did caddie for the famed Ben Hogan. And as all Augusta National caddies to follow over the years testified, with a gleam in their eyes, even players of Hogan's magnitude should have listened more intently to their caddies' input.

"[Hogan] always said, 'I didn't listen to you. I could have won the Masters. I made one mistake by not listening to you,'" Bowman said. "Hogan got in trouble one year on the fifteenth hole. I told him he couldn't reach the green with a 4-iron. He went in the pond in front of it."

Bowman moved to the Boston area after World War II. He gave up caddying to raise his eight children and worked at the American Barrel Company in Chelsea, Massachusetts, and on construction jobs. He rarely returned to Augusta—"When I pick up and leave a place, I don't want to go back too soon," he said—and he died in 1998 at age eighty-nine.

However, his caddying wisdom lives on every spring at Augusta National. Just listen to how he assessed the tournament in the 1990 interview: "Do your scoring on the first nine," Bowman said. "On the back side, you're getting into Disneyland."

1

Stovepipe

There is little doubt that Gene Sarazen's double eagle on the par-5 fifteenth hole in the 1935 Masters is the tournament's most famous shot and the one that spurred the tournament on to major championship fame years later. What adds even more intrigue is the role that Sarazen's caddie, the aptly named Stovepipe, played in the famous shot.

Sarazen was already a caddie supporter. Growing up in Harrison, New York, Sarazen started caddying at age ten to make some extra money for the Saraceni family, who had immigrated from Sicily. Gene would change his last name to Sarazen at age sixteen because he believed Sarazen sounded more like a golfer. For the 1932 Open Championship at Prince's Club in Sandwich, England, Sarazen retained an old, down-and-out English caddie, Skip Daniels, who guided them to Sarazen's only Open Championship victory with the key club being a Sarazen invention, the sand wedge. Daniels would pass away a few months after that victory.

Stovepipe was assigned to work with Sarazen for the second Augusta National Invitational (later changed to the Masters Tournament). Sarazen was making his first appearance at the Augusta National Golf Club in 1935, the year after skipping the inaugural event because of a conflict with a trip to South America with Australian Joe Kirkwood for a series of golf exhibitions to make money he couldn't earn playing in tournaments.

Stovepipe wore a tall, battered silk hat that resembled a top hat or "Stovepipe" hat while caddying, a lid that President Abraham Lincoln popularized in the mid-1850s and a style that was the "irrepressible symbol of prestige and authority," according to historian Debbie Henderson. Rarely has the caddie's given name been divulged, maybe because few of the competitors and caddies knew his real name or perhaps because the magnificent nickname simply stood out.

Stovepipe and Gene Sarazen together in 1935, the year Sarazen
won the Masters with his double eagle on No. 15. *Photo from*
Thirty Years of Championship Golf: The Life and Times of Gene
Sarazen (New York: Prentice-Hall, 1950)

There were indications twenty years ago that his name was Thor Nordwall,
an unusual, Swedish-sounding given name for a Black man in the South.
However, there was confusion, as Nordwall's 2020 obituary revealed that the
ninety-eight-year-old former Minnesota caddie had carried for Sarazen at
the 1939 St. Paul Open. Sarazen was still using the 4-wood he swung to make
the famous Masters double eagle four years before, but upon finishing the
St. Paul tournament poorly, he tipped the teenaged caddie and gave him the
4-wood, which Sarazen had angrily slammed into his bag upside down—or

headfirst. Wilson Sporting Goods had made duplicates after the double eagle, but Nordwall's story of being given the club drew people over the years to believe that he was the caddie for Sarazen at Augusta, which wasn't true.

More likely, Stovepipe's given name was John Henry Gordon, as revealed via two short news stories of the police blotter variety. Headlines included "Stovepipe" in a couple of late September 1950 editions of the *Augusta Chronicle*, and then research into Stovepipe's name and later life began from there. Unfortunately, due to segregated newspaper coverage, there is little recounting of Sarazen's caddie in the 1935 *Augusta Chronicle*, and most coverage of Black people in the newspaper was relegated to special coverage just one day of the week or to police reports of law breaking—seldomly good news. The September 25, 1950, edition of the *Chronicle* mistakenly indicated that "Stovepipe" was Fred Searles, most famously known as Byron Nelson's winning caddie in the 1937 and 1942 Masters, and police were searching for him in connection with "assault with intent to murder, unlawful possession of a deadly weapon and disorderly conduct" in relation to Eddie Scott being cut on his side by a knife. On September 26, correcting the previous day's reporting of a police error without noting the mistake, Searles was not mentioned in a follow-up story headlined, "Assault to murder charge facing 'Stovepipe' Gordon," which noted he had been arrested and released on bond for the same charges. Finally, on October 25, Gordon was paroled for three years and ordered to pay a $60 fine and an $81 doctor's bill. In other words, Stovepipe's given name may have been revealed in an unseemly way and without any mention of his caddying accomplishments.

A rare photograph, taken from a distance and out of focus, appears in Sarazen's 1950 autobiography, *Thirty Years of Championship Golf* (coauthored by Herbert Warren Wind) in which the duo share a big smile. Stovepipe is wearing his signature black hat and a white shirt underneath a jacket. Without the patented white jumpsuit, to be instituted over a decade later, there is no indication that this man was a caddie. Another posed image shows Stovepipe among his caddie brethren in 1936, smoking a cigar and showing off Sarazen's double-eagle club as a group of eight admires his notoriety, with the caption reading in part, "Gene Sarazen's favorite caddy Stovepipe (last name unknown)."

At well over six feet tall, a height increased by his unusual hat, he towered over the five-foot-five Sarazen. They gave the impression of a Mutt and Jeff tandem, one short and stout and the other tall and lean.

Stovepipe was described as very religious, spending much of his free time at an Augusta church.

"How are things going?" Sarazen once asked Stovepipe.

"Not so good, Mr. Gene, not so good," Stovepipe answered. "Collections were mighty poor today. We got to win."

Sarazen's week of preparation held championship promise with four unprecedented practice rounds. Having never seen Augusta National before, he scorched the course to total 17 under par and quickly became the tournament favorite.

Surely, Stovepipe was partially responsible for Sarazen's quick adjustment to the brand-new Augusta National course. In the 1934 tournament, the current nine-hole configuration was switched, leaving the now-famous Amen Corner near the start of the golf course. Because morning frost in the valleys of what was then the first and second fairways caused a delay in membership play, the nines were reversed to their current setup, making the back nine famous and positioning Sarazen for his great shot. Sarazen didn't take to Augusta National at first, thinking the layout was too simple. Stovepipe offered Sarazen the support to conquer this new course, as evidenced by the excellent practice play.

But as the tournament days arrived, the weather became cool and rainy. After three rounds, Craig Wood was 7 under par, 1 in front of Olin Dutra, 2 ahead of Henry Picard, and 3 in front of Sarazen.

Sarazen came to the fifteenth, then a 485-yard par-5, standing 1 over par for the final round and three strokes behind Craig Wood. In those days, the fifteenth was a very generic hole, with a wide-open driving area, only a stream guarding the green (not a pond), and no sand trap set on the right edge of the putting surface as is in place today. The pairings were also not arranged according to placement in the tournament standings. Wood teed off at 1:00 p.m., with Picard, approximately an hour and a half ahead of Sarazen. Wood sank a long birdie putt on the final green to complete his tournament at 6-under-par 282. The press and tournament officials were already congratulating him on winning the title.

Sarazen, paired with Walter Hagen in the next-to-last group of the day, was walking to his tee shot on No. 15 at approximately 5:30 p.m., as Wood finished. Hagen, on the way to a 79, was anxious to complete the round because he said he had a big date planned for the evening. The atmosphere was quite casual as the players talked about old times, the tricks they used to play on each other, and, of course, Hagen and his girlfriends. Joe Williams, the New York newspaper columnist, walked alongside the pairing before bolting to the clubhouse just as he got word that Wood had finished.

"Well, I've seen enough of you bums," Williams said as he strolled off. "I'm going up to see the winner."

Bobby Jones, the Augusta National Golf Club and Masters cofounder, had walked down from the clubhouse to watch his friends complete their round. Byron Nelson, in a group ahead, was coming up the seventeenth fairway.

Hagen, having nothing to lose, played first to the fifteenth green. His approach shot with a 3-wood flew left of the green and beaned one of the approximately twenty spectators who surrounded the green—a man who had apparently had too much to drink—leaving the gallery laughing.

As Hagen's shot stirred the gallery, Stovepipe became a central character in golf history. Sarazen was studying his approach shot. At first, he asked Stovepipe how the tournament standings stood.

"What do I need to win?" Sarazen asked.

"You mean to beat Craig Wood, boss?" Stovepipe said.

Sarazen nodded. Stovepipe groaned.

"You need four threes, Mister Gene. Three, three, three, three."

Stovepipe apparently suggested that Sarazen lay up as they assessed their strategy.

"He wanted me to play it safe," Sarazen said in 1995. "He was a minister in town. He told me the money bag was very short [at church], so I should play it safe."

Sarazen finally won out, and he and Stovepipe discussed club selection. Stovepipe wanted to pull a 3-wood to avoid the creek in front of the green at all costs. Sarazen was worried about his poor lie, so he chose the new Wilson Turf Rider 4-wood, his own invention that was in his bag, a club reminiscent of today's utility woods and one with which he could propel the ball higher in the air to fly over the hazard.

Sarazen also remembered an encounter the night before at the Bon Air Hotel, a massive structure on Walton Way in Augusta where most of the players stayed during Masters week. Bob Davis, another New York sportswriter who had traveled the world with Sarazen, had queried him about his chances the following day. As they parted, Davis gave Sarazen "a lucky ring" to wear the next day, which he purported to have been owned and worn by the great Mexican national hero Benito Juárez (even though he admitted weeks after the Masters it was merely a trinket). Sarazen couldn't wear the ring as it would interfere with his grip, so he carried it in his pocket. As the time to hit his second shot came, Sarazen felt the ring, "extracted it from my pocket and rubbed it over Stovepipe's head to give its reputed powers every chance to work," Sarazen wrote in his autobiography. The brief theatrics may not have been lucky, but they surely eased the tension a bit.

Sarazen's shot flew just short of the green, bounced up on the putting surface, and curled from right to left into the hole as the handful of people—though thousands over the years claimed to have seen it—howled in delight. Sarazen had achieved Stovepipe's "three-three-three-three" with one swing, then parred in to tie Wood and defeated him in the Masters' only thirty-six-hole playoff, 144–149, the following day.

When Sarazen completed his playoff victory over Wood, he wondered how Augusta National would commemorate his famous shot of the previous day. Probably jokingly, he asked Stovepipe sometime the week after the tournament if he had heard any rumors of plans for a marker to be placed at the spot of his 4-wood second shot.

"Mister Gene," Stovepipe began, "they went down there this morning, some of the greenskeepers, I mean, and they done sprinkled a little rye seed in the divot and covered it up."

A half century later, Sarazen said his decision-making may have changed had the finances been different.

"First-place money was $500 then [actually $1,500]," Sarazen told the *Augusta Chronicle* in 1995. "I remember after Chip Beck played it safe at Number 15 in 1993, people asked me what I thought about it. I said if they had prize money like they have now, I wouldn't have gone for it either. When [Beck] finished second, he won $183,600. Second-place money in 1935 was $300 [actually $800]."

Sarazen was a bit despondent about how much Augusta National chairman Clifford Roberts tried to take advantage of the miracle shot. Roberts asked Sarazen to pose for publicity photographs on the fifteenth hole, organized a contest in 1955 where pros tried to duplicate the double eagle (no one could), and had Sarazen appear on the Rudy Vallee radio show. In 1941, Sarazen estimated he had received approximately twenty thousand dollars in business opportunities because of the shot. By 1958, the Sarazen Bridge, located left of the waterway guarding the fifteenth green, was dedicated. All of this and only a $1,500 first-place prize. Sarazen even lamented the measly

fifty-dollar bonus he and Wood each received for playing the thirty-six extra holes on Monday.

"I had to give Stovepipe more than that," Sarazen said.

And so goes the story of the first prominent player-caddie relationship in
Masters history, unfortunately with just a smidgen of information available
on the famous Stovepipe.

There are no references in the *Chronicle* tying Gordon to Stovepipe and his
caddying work for Sarazen. Even at his death, on October 14, 1971, the *Chronicle* simply wrote the particulars of his death and services and burial in rural
Midville, Georgia, at a family cemetery at Clear Spring Missionary Baptist
Church in the Burke County town one hour's drive due south of Augusta National. A late 2022 visit to Clear Spring revealed a host of Gordon markers
and extended family, but there is no marker for John Henry Gordon, who
had moved to St. Petersburg, Florida, with his wife years before he passed
away there at age fifty-five, with an occupation listed as "municipal laborer."

Perhaps the mystery of his off-course life is best left to supposition since it
has been nearly a century since he became semifamous. At least his hat carries forward as an everlasting symbol.

1

Pappy

Pappy Stokes told Ben Hogan that "the Hawk" needed his caddie to win the Masters Tournament. Hogan agreed. Jackie Burke didn't rely much on a caddie to ply his trade, but the 1956 Masters champion was surely impressed with Stokes's demeanor and course knowledge. Jordan Spieth can attest that the intel handed down over nearly a century is truly impactful.

No surprises there, considering that no one was ever born to caddie more than Willie Lee "Pappy" Stokes, the true greens whisperer of Augusta. Pappy built a legacy as a caddie who was born and grew up on the grounds and watched the course spring up around the Stokes family as he went on to become the winningest caddie in Masters history. Noted historian and two-time Masters champion Ben Crenshaw calls Pappy the godfather of Augusta National caddies.

"I was the best caddie they ever had at the Masters," Pappy exclaimed, unsolicited, in 2003, then age eighty-three. "I was born on the golf course, born and raised on the golf course. Washington Road used to almost come right through my yard."

Pappy's prominence may have faded over time, evolving into a *Hidden Figures* storyline like the Black women revealed in the 2016 film who were essential to the NASA space program during the early 1960s. Even though Pappy and one of his pupils, Willie Peterson (who caddied for five of Jack Nicklaus's six wins), share the most caddie wins in Masters history, the names Peterson, Nathaniel "Iron Man" Avery (four wins with Arnold Palmer), Steve Williams (three wins with Tiger Woods, one with Adam Scott), and Carl Jackson (two wins with Crenshaw) are remembered much more often.

Pappy died at age eighty-six in the summer of 2006, his last residence being the Georgia War Veterans Nursing Home in downtown Augusta, approximately four miles from where he was born and became famous. Pappy came into this world in the spring of 1920, near where the Augusta National grounds are today, a couple years after the Fruitland Nurseries ceased operations and before Bobby Jones and Clifford Roberts even knew about the property. He worked for four different Masters champions in five separate title runs, including Hogan twice, over a fifteen-year span.

He is widely recognized in Augusta National caddie circles as the man who taught most of the home-grown Black caddies how to read the undulating greens at Augusta National, to figure the wind as it swept through the trees behind the twelfth green, and the ins and outs of keeping your golfer focused and loose. He clubbed players by feel and sight, not via a yardage book. Nearly every winning Masters caddie from the 1950s through the early 1980s learned from Pappy, and those who came after received advice from others who Pappy had tutored.

"He was the best green reader I've ever seen in my life," said Jariah Beard, Masters rookie Fuzzy Zoeller's winning caddie for the 1979 Masters and another Stokes disciple. "And if he liked you as a kid and you didn't get out of line with him, he would help you. And he wouldn't let the member know he's helping you because you made your tips by how well you read the greens. Just believe whatever Pappy told you. It was going to happen, in fact."

Pappy quickly figured out a secret that Augusta National caddies carried for decades. In the caddie facilities adjacent to the Tournament Practice Facility, simple framed maps of green complexes hang on the walls. On every drawing, there is a distinct red dot, showing the direction of Rae's Creek from that green—and the tendency for putts to break to the lowest point on the property when it's not evident to the naked eye. Many caddies over the years have denoted that red dot in their personal Augusta National yardage books.

Many a Masters winner has used that knowledge to win the tournament over the years. The most prominent example may have been Jack Nicklaus's sixth Masters victory in 1986. After winning his first five Masters with one of Pappy's students, Peterson, on the bag, Nicklaus had learned the greens from his own personal experience and Peterson's input as taught by Pappy. Same goes for 2015 Masters winner Spieth, whose caddie, Michael Greller, studied the course at the elbow of Carl Jackson, another Augusta National caddie who was in Pappy's outdoor classroom.

Possibly Nicklaus's most famous Masters moment in '86 had a touch of Pappy. On the par-4 seventeenth hole, Nicklaus and his oldest son and caddie, Jack Nicklaus II, discussed the break of an eighteen-foot birdie putt that

Pappy Stokes watches as Ben Hogan chips during the 1952 Masters. Stokes was on Hogan's bag in the 1951 and 1953 victories and shares the most Masters caddying victories (five) alongside Willie Peterson. *Masters Historic Imagery/Getty Images*

would give him the lead. Son read a right break on the putt, but Dad over-ruled him.

"No, Rae's Creek will pull it back to the left or straighten it out," Jack replied as the ball went on to fall to the left at the very end for the decisive stroke.

"Most people think 12 green is the lowest point," Crenshaw said in 2019. "That's not quite right. It goes to the left of 11 green. That's the place that's called 'the Pull.' On every green, Carl would point through the trees to that point. Many of the young golfers don't really understand that. It's just fascinating."

That intimate knowledge was necessary at the outset as there were no yardage books to call out landmarked yardage spots, no distances stamped on sprinkler heads or bushes to denote 150 yards to the green, and surely no greatly detailed green-reading books. Yardages were memorized by individual bushes, trees, or land features.

Beard recalled that in the 1960s and 1970s, Augusta National caddies would often hand drivers to members for their next tee shot and then putt on the previous green to better understand the subtleties, a practice often defended by Masters chairman Clifford Roberts. Jackson recalled caddies asking members to hit putts again on certain greens so that they could understand the tendencies.

"A member questioned us putting one day, and Mr. Roberts said, 'Well, how in the hell do you think he can learn to read them?'" Beard recalled.

"Pappy knew something that nobody else knew," Jackson said in the early 2000s. "Many people know 85 percent of the putts out here, but the other 15 percent they don't know. He told me, but I'm not telling. He taught me everything about this golf course."

In 2003, as a hard-of-hearing senior citizen living in the Your Home Sweet Home retirement home in inner-city Augusta, Pappy's usual post-breakfast routine included a nap, but when informed that the topic offered by a spring visitor was caddying in the Masters, his eyes brightened, his back straightened to attention, raising his height to more than six feet, and he had a sudden pep in his step and raised volume in his voice. When he was told that this day was the Saturday of the third round of the Masters, it's as if Pappy is transformed back to his twenties prepping for a round at Augusta National.

When Pappy was asked the secret to reading the greens, he paused and considered his answer, getting introspective and serious, softly rubbing the imaginary surface of the green as he explained his learning process.

"I could tell which way the greens break just by looking at the golf course," he said. "Just look at it. Feel it with my hands to tell which way the grain runs. Nobody told me how, I just learned it myself. When I watched the man putt, I just watched the ball and remembered."

"He could be in the middle of a fairway," Jackson recalled, "look up at the green and say a certain putt was going to break six inches to the right."

The Stokes family was born with familiarity with the rolling hills of the Augusta National property. Latimer Stokes Sr., Pappy's father, was originally an employee at the local dairy, but then he transitioned into work at Fruitland Nurseries with plants and in the various greenhouses on the property. Many of the assortment of plants that beautify the course today were the result of the handiwork of the Berckmans family, who owned the property, and workers such as Latimer Sr., who helped cultivate the exotic trees and plants that were imported from all over the world. Fruitland Nurseries was the predecessor to Augusta National.

Belgian Baron Louis Mathieu Edouard Berckmans, a horticulturist by hobby, purchased the land that was once an indigo plantation in 1857. He teamed up with his son, Prosper Julius Alphonse, an agronomist and horticulturist by profession, beginning in 1858. They developed one of the largest nurseries in the world, which became the purported first commercial nursery in the South. A great number of flowering plants and trees are still prominent at Augusta National today, including the long row of sixty-one magnolias, planted in the 1850s, that frames Magnolia Lane and a plant that Prosper Berckmans popularized: the azalea, which is the signature beauty symbol on the grounds and in much of the South. Louis, Prosper's son, helped rehabilitate the plants when the course was completed and later joined with Jones and Roberts to determine which plants would specifically be planted on each hole and thus have the hole named for that plant.

Latimer raised a family in a home on the edge of the property, probably somewhere in the vicinity of Washington Road, which was a dirt road in those days. The five children included Rupert, the oldest daughter who was born in 1915; Willie, born on May 22, 1920; Garrett, born in 1923; Gussie Mae, born in 1930; and Latimer Jr., the baby, born in 1936. Rupert recalled that they moved from nearby Lincolnton, Georgia, to just across the street from Augusta National in the late 1910s, just before Fruitland Nurseries became defunct when its charter expired in 1918. For a time, as a youngster, she served as a maid for the Berckmans family, who resided in the Old Manor House, now the central part of the Augusta National clubhouse. All the siblings except for Garrett, who passed away in 1977, lived long lives, a tradition in the Stokes family: Latimer Sr. died at age eighty-six in 1981.

"I'm just happy God spared me and all of us this long," said Rupert Jones in the early 2000s when she was in her late eighties and still enjoying volunteer work five days a week from 7:00–11:00 a.m. at Augusta's Veterans Administration hospital. She passed at age 104 in 2019. "And thank God for letting Pappy get as old as he's gotten."

Rupert remembered Pappy being a mischievous person with an old soul even as a little boy. He earned the nickname Pappy then because he was "always moving slow and unconcerned."

In the late 1920s, parts of the Fruitland Nurseries property were utilized as a farm, and Pappy helped plow for the planting of cotton and corn. When Jones and Roberts purchased the Fruitland Nurseries property to build their dream golf course in 1931, there was little twelve-year-old Pappy one year later among the workers who were clearing trees and planning the routing of the course. He provided water for the construction workers, toting the bucket around to give them some needed refreshment. He remembered workers cutting down trees to clear the routing of the current tenth and eleventh holes. This is probably where he learned the lay of the land for his future profession. He watched as the water from rainstorms drained toward the lowest part of the property where Rae's Creek flows. He studied how the mules pulling equipment to mold the land for the golf course created subtle angles in the earth.

When Augusta National opened in December 1932 and then held its formal opening in January 1933, twelve-year-old Pappy jumped into the mix as a caddie, much to the chagrin of his father.

"When we were growing up, Pappy would skip school and go caddie," Rupert remembered. "And Daddy sure would get a hold of him for that. You know what he got? A big whipping. Daddy talked to him about going to school and didn't want him mixing with some of those caddies. But Pappy had his mind made up what he was going to do. He wanted to be a caddie.

"Even when he got older, when he was working in construction on homes, putting on roofs, when it came time to caddie, he went right to the golf course. That's mostly all he did his whole life."

"My parents were both insistent that I not caddie, that I get an education and do something else," said Latimer Stokes Jr., the last surviving sibling at age eighty-seven, in 2023. "I wasn't even allowed to go out to the caddie yard. I was brought up in churches and became a bookkeeper and accountant at an Augusta hospital until I retired. But I respected and loved Pappy, and a lot of other people, both Black and white, had that same feeling."

By age seventeen, Pappy already had won a Masters title as a caddie. In 1938, the last tournament called the Augusta National Invitational before officially being changed to the Masters, Henry Picard never shot above par, finishing at 3-under-par 285 for his most prominent golf moment. Picard, who grew up caddying in Massachusetts and settled in Charleston, South Carolina, won $1,500 for his victory.

"When I won, I think they had to take up a collection from the members to pay me," Picard told *Sports Illustrated* in 1995 from Charleston, where he gave lessons into his late eighties. "Now it's the best tournament in the world."

World War II called next, and Pappy was inducted into the U.S. Army in early 1944, with the *Augusta Chronicle* of February 3 denoting draftees in separate stories. The prominent story was on white draftees, positioned above a story with a much smaller headline announcing "64 Negroes Called" with Stokes among the final listees in alphabetical order. Stokes fought in the European theater near white men, just as he worked beside them as an Augusta National caddie. By this time, he was also married, to Odella Avery, Iron Man's older sister.

When Pappy came back from World War II, the opportunity to caddie was still there. His next successful bag was that of Claude Harmon, a club professional who had never won a PGA Tour tournament. Harmon would later become famous as the father of Tiger Woods's coach, Butch Harmon, and three other professionals at some of the top clubs in the country.

In 1948, Harmon practiced with Hogan at his winter golf club job at Seminole Golf Club in Palm Beach, Florida, in preparation for the Masters. After regularly beating Hogan on his home course in the practice rounds, the Savannah, Georgia, native proceeded to equal the 9-under-par 279 Masters record for a five-stroke victory over Cary Middlecoff. He became the first native Georgian to win the tournament.

This caddie contact wasn't lost on Hogan. He had become the bridesmaid of the Masters, with eight consecutive top-ten finishes dating back to 1939, his second career start. That included back-to-back runner-up finishes where he should have won. Childhood friend and rival Byron Nelson, from Fort Worth, Texas, played the final thirteen holes 5-under par in an eighteen-hole playoff in 1942 to nip Hogan 69–70. After World War II, in the 1946 Masters, Hogan rallied from five back, entering the final round only to three-putt for bogey from twelve feet above the hole on the super-fast eighteenth green to lose by one to journeyman Herman Keiser.

"Congratulations, Herman," Picard told Keiser in the clubhouse after Hogan's three-putt. "The Little Man really took the choke. Those were the three worst putts I've ever seen him hit."

As Hogan prepared for the 1951 Masters, he searched for a new caddie and arrived ten days before the tournament to study the course and pound hundreds of balls from the right side of the old practice range, with Pappy shagging balls out of the air or on one bounce in the distance, moving only to avoid being beaned by other players' balls. Pappy quickly recognized Hogan's eagle-eye focus and recalled a conversation.

"Mr. Hogan, you play pretty good, and you could win the Masters if your caddie helped you any," Pappy said.

"Yep, we'll see. I want you to work for me during the tournament," Hogan replied.

That hiring immediately evoked a response from Harmon when he arrived in Augusta.

"Hey Ben, you've got my caddie!" Harmon yelled.

"Yeah, I'm gonna keep him," Hogan blurted back as he turned to Pappy offering, at the time, a hefty twenty-dollar tip.

"I still might have been caddying for Claude Harmon if it wouldn't have been for that twenty dollars," Pappy said. "I took that money and went to get a drink of liquor and something to eat right after Hogan gave it to me."

Hogan began a great four-year run with a win in the 1951 Masters, shooting a final-round four-birdie, no-bogey 68 to beat Skee Riegel by two strokes. Two years later, once again with Pappy on the bag, Hogan set the tournament record of 14-under-par 274 to take home the first of three major championship titles that year. A wind-blown final-round 79 in 1952, complete with five three-putts after he was tied with Sam Snead for the third-round lead, and a 70–71 playoff loss to Snead in 1954 kept Hogan from winning four consecutive Masters.

"Ben Hogan made fun of your course, didn't he, Cliff?" President Dwight D. Eisenhower joked with Roberts two days after the 1953 tournament when Hogan joined them for a casual round.

It was during this time that Hogan perfected much of his strategy on how to attack a golf course, particularly Augusta National. There is no account that Hogan and Pappy consulted on how to work around the course, especially seeing that Hogan was a lone wolf on the golf course in determining his blueprint for a round. "Hogan always talked to his caddie, but it was always about anything but golf," recalled Burke, the 1956 Masters champion and a compatriot of Hogan's in the 1950s. But consider that Pappy and Hogan have long been anointed as the ultimate tacticians of their professions. Also remember that Hogan was nicknamed "the Hawk" by fellow competitors for his intense breakdown of course management and was introduced to golf as a caddie at Glen Garden Country Club in Fort Worth, Texas, overcoming poverty and a nasty hook during the 1920s through hard work to become a golf icon.

Similarly, Pappy passed along much knowledge to his Augusta National caddying brethren not only on the course but also through occasional Saturday morning clinics, held both at Augusta Country Club and Augusta National, where the basics of where to stand, proper etiquette, and intelligence on reading the golf course, both the greens and various hole location characteristics, were passed down to younger caddie candidates.

"No yardage man, he was the best at pulling a club by eye," longtime Augusta National caddie master Freddie Bennett said of Pappy in the early 2000s.

"I don't know the yardage. I didn't want to know the yardage," Hogan once said. "There are too many variables—the wind, the air density, how you're playing that day. I would remember if I had been beside a certain tree or trap or something like that and what I hit and how I played that shot. I don't think I could play by yardage."

Therefore, here is how Hogan learned to play the devilish par-3 twelfth hole at Augusta National, famous for its swirling winds that have blown many a tee shot into Rae's Creek: It was the only place where Hogan's pre-shot routine varied. Instead of his standard couple of waggles with the club before beginning his takeaway, he would waggle until "I felt the wind on my cheek and, therefore, the flag [on No. 12] would be up, the wind would be consistent, it would be normal—instead of coming up or dropping down."

Who else but Hogan, partnered with Pappy's inherent knowledge of the course, could figure out such a complex strategy?

Hogan also tested unusual ways to play Augusta National's key holes during this era. In 1951, he regularly began playing his approach shot directly to the right of the par-4 eleventh green to avoid the newly built pond, added in 1950, that tightly guards the left side of the green. "If I hit that green, you know it's a mistake," he said. He also practiced a knockdown shot for the par-3 sixteenth hole and developed guidelines for when to go for greens in two on the par-5 thirteenth and fifteenth holes.

In the years following this unprecedented Masters run, Hogan was reaching his early forties, and his putting was becoming a severe problem. "I'm not afraid of missing the putt. I'm afraid I can't draw the putter back. When I look at the cup, it's filled with my blood," Hogan lamented. That was something that not even Pappy could help cure even though his assistance had developed a Masters legend who has a bridge (Hogan Bridge is left of the twelfth green) and a dinner (Hogan developed the idea of the Masters Champions Dinner in 1952) on property to his credit.

Pappy's last hurrah came in 1956 when Burke rallied from a record eight strokes back in the final round to beat Ken Venturi by one stroke. Burke's winning score of 1-over-par 289 is still the highest winning score in Masters history (tied with the 289 of Hogan and Snead in 1954 and Zach Johnson in 2007) causing Jones to call 1956 "the hardest playing conditions we've ever had in this tournament."

High winds rushed through the course during most of the week, resulting in a record eighty-seven rounds of 80 or higher. That was culminated by twenty-nine scores of 80 or higher on Sunday, including amateur Charles Kunkle's high-water mark of 95, still the highest single recorded score in Masters history.

The wind was such a factor that in the second round Bob Rosburg, a future longtime ABC-TV golf broadcaster, suffered an embarrassing occurrence. With a stiff, forty-mile-per-hour wind in his face on the par-3 twelfth hole, Rosburg chose a 4-iron on the 155-yard hole. Just as he slammed his ball into the wind, the gale force ceased completely and the ball flew over the fronting of Rae's Creek, the green, the bunkers, and the woods behind and into neighboring Augusta Country Club—out of bounds and nearly twenty-five yards over the green. Rosburg shook his head in disbelief, re-teed, and with the consistent wind, played to within ten feet.

Burke and Venturi also experienced the wind tunnel on the long par-3 fourth hole. Venturi used a driver into the wind on the then 220-yard hole and ended up ten yards over the green. Burke also used a driver and finished sixty yards short of the green.

It may have been Pappy's finest hour as a caddie. Burke had failed to win a major championship to that point. He had learned under the tutelage of his father, Jack Burke Sr., a renowned teaching pro, and another star Texan, three-time Masters winner Jimmy Demaret. Later in his career he even served as assistant pro to Claude Harmon at the Thunderbird Country Club in Palm Springs, California. Jackie had shot 69 at age twelve, qualified for the U.S. Open at age sixteen, and turned pro at age nineteen. His career highlights had occurred in assembling an unbeaten record in three previous Ryder Cup appearances and a stellar 1952 season, where he totaled five victories and four in a row at the Texas Open, Houston Open, Baton Rouge

Open, and St. Petersburg Open in consecutive weeks. But the thirty-three-year-old Burke hadn't won since 1953, mainly because his trusty putting was letting him down, some of that attributable to the fact that his favorite putter had been stolen a few years before and he couldn't get comfortable with a replacement. In 1955, Burke held the first-round lead in the Masters but floundered with a final-round 80 and finished thirteenth. Some also thought his serious attitude on the course needed to be softened. That, plus he had priorities at home.

"I choose to spend a good proportion of my time with my wife and our kids because twenty years from now I'd like to have a few other things in my life than just the joy of being recognized when I walk into a restaurant," Burke said in the mid-1950s.

Burke was interested in having a caddie who would simply join him for a walk around the course, but he needed an infusion of confidence to resurrect his career. Augusta National member Phil Harison—the official first-tee starter beginning in 1948 and on that job into the early 2000s and the originator of, "Fore, Please [insert player name] now driving"—helped pair Burke and Pappy, with the consent of Roberts, of course.

"I didn't want a caddie on the green or on top of my golf ball," Burke, who died at age one hundred in January 2024, said in the early 2000s. "I needed some air out there. I didn't need a Stanford graduate to tell me how to play like the guys on tour do today. Sometimes the players and caddies today look like they're preparing for an economic meeting the way they study every shot. Anybody would know that everything at Augusta National breaks toward Rae's Creek, so I didn't think I needed much help.

"Pappy was very good. He never got upset. He had an even keel. That's why a lot of players liked Pappy. Things were never as bad as they seemed or as good as they seemed with him."

As the final round began, amateur Ken Venturi led by four over Middlecoff, seven over Doug Ford, and eight over Burke and Lloyd Mangrum. Burke's goal was to finish second and win the six-thousand-dollar first-place prize money given to the low professional since Venturi wasn't eligible for a payday. However, the day dawned cool and very windy for CBS's first televised final round of the Masters.

"When I got up that morning, I thought, there's no way anybody's going to break one hundred around here," Burke said. "You just had to be ready for five or six hours of torture."

Burke and Pappy glided around the course for a final-round 71, joining Snead's 71 as the only subpar rounds on the final day. Burke used his patented popping putting stroke to record only twenty-nine putts that day and had just one three-putt the entire tournament. Venturi skied to an 80 and Middlecoff to a 77, clearing the way for an improbable victor.

The key moment occurred on the par-4 seventeenth. Burke trailed Venturi, playing behind him, and Middlecoff, just in front of him, by one stroke entering the straightaway par 4. Middlecoff made double bogey after duffing a chip from the front edge and three-putting. Burke played an 8-iron to within fifteen feet of a tricky hole position just behind the front bunker. The path to the hole was strewn with sand that had been blown out of the greenside bunker by the thirty-mile-per-hour winds. Using his boyhood experience of putting on sand greens in Texas—a recollection probably repeated to him by Pappy—Burke recollected that sand makes a green putt much faster. At first glance, he thought the putt was going to stop halfway to the hole, but it kept moving and finally skidded in for a birdie. "It was one of the few balls that even stayed on that green all day," Burke said.

Playing partner Mike Souchak, the stocky former Duke University football player, embraced Burke as they walked off the seventeenth green toward the eighteenth hole. "C'mon, man," Souchak shouted. "They're still making bogeys out here. Let's go."

Surely enough, Venturi's approach to seventeen was long, and he made bogey to put Burke one stroke up. When Venturi parred eighteen, Burke had won his first major title and rode the momentum to capture the 1956 PGA Championship and earn PGA Player of the Year honors. That season also enabled Burke to join Demaret in 1958 to build their dream course in Houston: Champions Golf Club, one of the nation's most-respected courses. By 2000, Burke had been elected to the World Golf Hall of Fame.

The caddie accounts of Burke's surprise victory give more credit to their input. "Mr. Roberts told [Burke] whatever Pappy tells you, you do it," said longtime Augusta National caddie "Pee Wee" Reid.

"I just told him all he's got to do is hit the ball," Pappy remembered. "Shut your eyes when you walk up to the ball. I'll tell you what to hit. I picked the club. If I gave him the right club, it gave him confidence that he could play the course. He could go on and play his game then and not worry about misclubbing long or short.

"On Sunday on eighteen, we were walking up the fairway, and Jack Burke Jr. just said, 'How much money do you want?' He picked me up, and he was much littler than I was. He asked me again how much money I wanted. I just told him a sack full."

Pappy was so assured that Burke would make a great comeback that he made a quick wager the morning of the final round.

"I bet a man at the package shop in downtown Augusta that we were gonna win that tournament against Ken Venturi," Pappy said. "The man just laughed at me. He finally said, 'Pappy, you're eight strokes behind. If you win that tournament, I'll give you a gallon of liquor.'

"After Jack Burke Jr. came back to win, I went downtown late that afternoon, walked into the package shop, and saw the man. All I said was, 'Here I am.'"

Burke was impressed, but not enough to call Pappy's name: "I don't know what my caddie's last name is. Just call him Willie Burke," Burke told the press after winning, indicating a reluctance in those days to know much about the caddie beyond the knowledge bestowed on the golf course.

Nearly fifty years later, Burke's recollection focused solely on the confidence that Pappy instilled in players. He didn't know until years later that Pappy had caddied for a succession of champions even though Pappy worked with Burke for much of the late 1950s.

"On eighteen, I hit my second shot in a bunker and blasted out to about five feet," Burke said. "I was as nervous as a cat on a hot tin roof, so I needed to talk to somebody. I read the putt and finally asked Pappy, 'Is it inside the left edge?' That's the only time I asked him the line. I just wanted to be sure. He just nodded his head and said, 'Just cruise it in there for us, just cruise it in.'

"Pappy was very alert all the time. Nothing got by him. He had great timing and a sense of balance. You could always tell a guy who had a great sense of feel by the way he walked. Like Snead. They both had a great stride as if they would never stumble no matter where they were walking. Pappy was very easy to work with. The ball was clean, the clubs were clean, and he never bitched about anything. He never needed any money or bugged me about getting paid. I would do anything for my caddie. It was just sometimes I didn't want them to do anything for me."

Pappy's influence, however, is significant in relation to multiple players, not just one legendary figure. Picard, Harmon, Hogan, and Burke never won a Masters before or after Pappy was their caddie.

By the 1960s, Pappy had fully established his reputation. He caddied regularly for various members and tutored many of the young caddies. If he saw caddies in his group or those nearby clowning around, Pappy was quick with a harsh word about straightening up.

"If you were lackadaisical, Pappy would say, 'God's got his eyes on you,'" Reid said.

"He would walk up behind you and say this putt goes two inches to the left and say it quietly," Beard said. "And you could believe it. It was going to happen. Just believe whatever Pappy told you. It was going to happen."

"I didn't go out there on the golf course to play," Pappy said. "I went out there to try to make a living. Some of them couldn't caddie; they were just bag toters. They never did nothing but tote a bag."

But he could also add some levity to the situation.

"You couldn't help but like him," longtime Augusta National caddie "Buck" Moore said. "He was comical off the course. He'd always say something funny if you had a bad day to pep you up."

When he was finally getting his due, Pappy was well into his fifties and unable to carry a bag throughout the Masters. Many at Augusta National lost track of his whereabouts. He had a fondness for alcohol, which probably took him down the wrong road, getting arrested and serving a stint in jail for a DUI in 1985, being homeless for a spell, and moving from home to home. It was evident that he couldn't lean on his caddying gig to fulfill his days. He became a mystical figure with all the secretive talk among golfers and fans about every putt breaking to Rae's Creek and the fascination with Hogan's unique strategies for playing various Augusta National holes.

"The last time I caddied, I went out there and couldn't even get up the hill on eighteen," Pappy said. "I'd had enough when that happened."

Finally, in the late 1990s, as he approached eighty years old, Pappy found a home at "Your Home Sweet Home," a small assisted living home located on Martin Luther King Jr. Boulevard near downtown Augusta. The worn, wood-framed house blended in with the residential neighborhood, and no signs indicated this was a retirement facility. Pappy shared the home with a handful of other elderly Black people, but none as old or peppy as Pappy. His vision and hearing were not as good as they used to be, and he had arthritis.

Pappy Stokes is buried at Southview Cemetery in downtown Augusta, Georgia, memorialized with a military marker. *Photo by Ward Clayton*

Still, Kathleen Beasley, the owner of the home, enjoyed hearing stories about how this old man with a checkered recent history had transformed into a docile character with a glorious early life.

"I quit smoking and I quit drinking a few years ago," Pappy said. "I just threw my glass away, broke it."

Pappy's baby brother, Latimer Jr., came by weekly to give him a haircut and was a key cog in getting Pappy into the Veterans Administration hospital during his last few years of life. Rupert, his older sister, visited to chat and cut his fingernails and toenails. Jack Stephens, the former chairman of the Augusta National Golf Club, would send one-hundred-dollar Christmas gifts. Some old-time caddies would stop by periodically just to say hello. Tom Van Dorn, the Augusta National caddie master at the time, had voiced an interest in getting him back out to Augusta National as part of a reunion of the old caddies.

1

Cemetery

Mention the name Willie Frank Perteet and you get little response, a blank stare. But invoke the name of U.S. President Dwight D. Eisenhower and the nickname "Cemetery" and you discover an instant celebrity.

Perteet was Eisenhower's regular caddie at Augusta National from the time Ike became a member of the club in 1948 until 1957, a period when the thirty-fifth president of the United States led the game's national popularization. Coupled with the emergence of Arnold Palmer late in the 1950s, they caused an even greater wave in the sport. In 1948, the National Golf Foundation listed 2.8 million golfers who played at least fifteen times annually. By 1969, when Eisenhower died, there were well over 10 million golfers in the country. The sport was making a transition from a recreational activity for the wealthy into a more accessible pastime.

Eisenhower's history in Augusta is quite extensive. The Eisenhower Pine, more commonly called Ike's Tree, was the tall loblolly pine that guarded the left side of the fairway on the par-4 seventeenth hole until it succumbed to an ice storm in early 2014. Eisenhower, who fought a slice in his golf game, all too often saw his tee shot rattle around in that tree and drop to the ground. He once requested that Augusta National chairman Clifford Roberts have the tree chopped down. Roberts avoided addressing the issue during a club meeting by quickly adjourning the gathering. Ike's Pond, which occupies three acres at the eighth and ninth holes on the Par 3 Course, was named for the president in the late 1940s after he suggested to Roberts that it would making a nice fishing hole. The Eisenhower Cabin, also called "Mamie's Cabin" after Eisenhower's first lady, was the first of ten cabins built for members. The structure, which stands left of the tenth tee area, was built in 1953 for $150,000 and funded by the Augusta National membership to house the president on his visits to Augusta. Reid Memorial Presbyterian Church, located on Walton Way in Augusta, was the regular Sunday worship site for the Eisenhowers when they visited. Their usual up-front church pew is adorned with a gold plaque. A stained-glass window with the president's likeness memorializes his visits. In late October 2023, army installation Fort Gordon—named after Confederate General John Brown Gordon—was redesignated as Fort Eisenhower as part of a nationwide process by the Naming Commission.

And there was Perteet right in the middle of it all, being interviewed for national magazine and newspaper articles and radio broadcasts. His celebrity was groundbreaking in the circle of Black Augusta National caddies, particularly as widespread as his name and story were shared in traditional (i.e., predominantly white) media outlets. In the late 1970s, Perteet said being a caddie "should be the same to golf that a mechanic is to a car."

Perteet was a slight man—5'6", 135 pounds—and got his start caddying in the Masters at the relatively old age of thirty-two in 1936. He was in his mid-forties when he began caddying for Ike. His nickname was originally "Dead Man," until Ike decided to change it to be less gruesome. "All dead men belong in cemeteries," Ike said, "so from now on I'll call you Cemetery."

Perteet came by his macabre nickname in a frightening yet humorous manner. Various accounts over the years stated that he was caught in bed with a woman when her boyfriend came home and took a knife to him, with Cemetery suffering only minor wounds. However, in a 1953 *Life* magazine story, Perteet gave a more detailed story.

In the early 1920s, when Perteet was in his late teens, he broke off a long-time relationship with a young girl because he said he loved another.

"I explained honestly why I couldn't marry her," Perteet said. "And I thought that was the end of it. But not with that girl. She got two friends, and them three waited for me with knives outside a place where I was drinking beer. It was dark when I came out, and I didn't see them. And they laid aboard me. They didn't miss. Cut me up real bad. I started running, them after me, yelling like she-devils. I didn't yell, man. I was saving my breath. I run to a taxi stand, and a cabbie took me to the hospital. That was on a Monday night.

"They must have given me too much ether when they wanted to operate. Leastways, that's my opinion. And I went off into a trance, like, for four days, and they finally thought I was dead. They took me to a room in the morgue for an inquest on Thursday. Few minutes before the inquest I sud-

Willie "Cemetery" Perteet (left) rides in a golf cart alongside President Dwight D. Eisenhower in 1953 at Augusta National. *Masters Historic Imagery/Getty Images*

denly rose up, and that orderly ain't been seen 'round town since. Everybody say I cheated the cemetery so that's how come they all call me 'Cemetery' or 'Dead Man' 'round here."

Perteet was also noted as the leader of a local jazz band that entertained around the area. Perteet played the drums, usually sporting a dress coat, white shirt, and black bow tie, as the band played tunes such as "Chattanooga Choo Choo." Perteet publicly lauded his lead singer, a tenor named Teddy Adams: "Man, he's solid!" Perteet said. Perteet occasionally played with Clarence Pinckney, a famous name among 1950s musicians because of the formation of the Drifters. Perteet also was famous for his singing, particularly a comic rendition of "Who Stole the Lock off the Henhouse Door?"

"I've been playing music for some kind of money almost as long as I was a head high to a drum," Perteet said. "That's breath of life to me."

Mostly, the band played for predominately white crowds—many times until 1:00 a.m.—that grew larger when Perteet began caddying for Eisenhower. Once, in 1953, the president flew in late from Washington to play golf at Augusta National. He changed clothes immediately and quickly played seven holes until darkness fell, retiring to a bridge game with fellow Augusta National members. As a result, Perteet was late for his gig at Rich's Club on Sand Bar Ferry Road in south Augusta.

"I apologize to you folks for being late 'cause I know you-all been waiting for me to play," Perteet announced to the crowd upon arriving after the band had played a few tunes. "But, ladies and gentlemen, I been unavoidably detained by the president of the United States."

Aside from his brush with death and late hours as a musician, Perteet was deemed reliable by none other than John Henry "'Leven" Williams, the caddie master at Augusta National until the late 1950s.

"For somebody as important as General Eisenhower, I knew I had to get him a reliable caddie," Williams said. "None of the no-count boys we got so frequently applyin' for caddie jobs 'round here, some of them smelling just like they come out of a whiskey barrel. Cemetery now—he's mature. He's got sense. And he plays golf. Does right well in the caddie matches in the evenings after the members get off the fairways. Knows the course and he knows his clubs.

"So I give the General Cemetery. 'Cemetery,' I say, 'you do right well out here, you hear?' When the General come back, I say, 'General, how do you like that boy I give you?' An' the general say, 'Eleven, he was fine.' So him and Cemetery been together ever since."

Perteet became quite a celebrity for his relationship with the president. In 1953, *Life* featured him in its May 11 issue, where he was pictured both caddying and behind his drum set. He was withheld from the normal Masters caddie rotation for a few years so that he would be fresh for Ike's usual arrival after the tournament. On many occasions, Ike would play on consecutive days, including a tee time with the just-jacketed Masters champion. Perteet was okay with this as caddying for a president was as high a position as any caddie could ask for, even Masters-winning caddies.

"I wouldn't say he was no pillar of the community," one person in the Augusta Black community said of Perteet, "but he's well known, no doubt about that, and especially since he and the president been connected."

Eisenhower wasn't the greatest golfer, just the most famous. Cemetery recounted years later that the best score Ike ever shot was a 78, playing the forward tees during a round with Palmer. According to Roberts, Eisenhower broke 80 four times during forty-five trips to Augusta National over a 17-year span that included 29 visits and 210 rounds while he was in office. Eisenhower was bothered by a knee injury suffered during his days as a football player at the U.S. Military Academy at West Point. He swung mostly with his upper body, didn't generate much power, and sliced the ball. He was also a poor putter, often stroking putts before his caddie could consult with him on the break. Playing partners would occasionally concede difficult putts to Ike because they felt sorry for his poor putting ability.

Perteet did reveal details on Ike's golf game after Ike passed away in 1969: "Mr. Ike was a pretty good golfer," Cemetery said in 1970. "He wasn't no Nicklaus, no blockbuster. When the pros use an iron, he'd use a 3- or 4-wood. But he kept the ball in play pretty good.

"One of the promises I made Mr. Ike was, I'd never tell anybody what he paid me. Don't guess it makes much difference now. He used to give me $10 plus an extra dollar on Sunday for church. I remember one time he's down here for 10 days and we're setting up and he said, 'My word, Cemetery, if this keeps up I'll be working for you.'"

Eisenhower's penchant for slipping out of the White House for numerous rounds of golf drew criticism from political rivals. His first trip after winning the 1952 presidential election was a flight to Augusta National for a ten-day victory celebration with political aides and future cabinet members. He had a putting green built in 1954—funded by private donations and designed by the United States Golf Association—just outside his White House office door on the South Lawn, much to the dismay of many executive office traditionalists. When squirrels damaged the green, the president wanted them shot, but some were eventually trapped and relocated. He often dictated letters in the Oval Office while swinging his favorite 8-iron. Many times, he would complete his hectic day by slipping on his golf shoes and then leave small cleat marks in the historic wooden floor as he walked, putter or wedge in hand, to view the South Lawn. On average, he played approximately thirty-six holes per week when at home in Washington. Many opponents questioned his dedication to the office because of his love of golf. When that didn't faze the former general, they began to take potshots at his questionable golf ability.

As the 1956 presidential election approached, a campaign began—obviously from the rival Democratic Party—with a prominent bumper sticker, "Ben Hogan For President. If we're going to have a golfer, let's have a good one." That effort to demean Eisenhower didn't work either. Later that year, *Golf Digest* began a campaign, with Ike's participation, where buttons saying, "Don't Ask What I Shot," were circulated, endearing him to hackers nationwide who were taking up the game.

If he didn't play well, at least Ike didn't draw out the agony. Much like the golf-playing Bush family, a round of golf with Ike was more of a sprint than a marathon. He often played "ready golf," taking the tee out of turn before the rest of his group arrived. Political pundits in Washington, D.C., lamented that midweek greens fees at Burning Tree Golf Club, the course of choice for government officials in the nation's capital, were made higher by Eisenhower to discourage play so that he could zoom around the course. Keeping up with the president may have been the most difficult task for Cemetery.

Ike was also very talkative, particularly with his caddie, and showed respect for any advice the caddie dispensed. He also tipped more than normal, handing out five-dollar bills and two of his Dunlop Dot golf balls engraved with "Mr. President." Cemetery recalled the day that Eisenhower pulled his drive into the left woods on No. 10. The ball was behind a log, prohibiting the president from swinging.

"Cemetery, do you think you are a man?" Ike asked loudly. "Well, come over here and help me move this log."

Cemetery put down the golf bag and sped over.

"The Secret Servicemen rushed over to help, but Mr. Ike told them to get out of there and he got on one end of the log and me the other and he said, 'Lift!' and we picked it up and toted it ten feet away.

"He was a nice man. A very nice man. A very, very nice gentleman."

Perteet caddied under unusual circumstances. The Secret Service would often station a man carrying a Thompson submachine gun in a golf bag in the same foursome. A United Press International report in 1952 indicated that "Secret Service agents looking somewhat out of place in their conservative business suits, ring the cottage [then the Jones Cabin], standing about 50 feet from it at intervals of 75 to 100 feet." Once, a paparazzi hiding in the woods at Augusta National was nearly shot by the Secret Service because his photo equipment looked like a sniper's gun. Walkie-talkies were always available in case of a national crisis. Pinkerton security guards, utilized for Masters play, were also hired to scout the grounds when the president was on site. When Eisenhower was in Augusta, Augusta National members could enter the club grounds freely but could not bring guests. By 1953, Augusta

National built a chain-link fence around its periphery to keep out trespassers, an addition that was a Secret Service suggestion, later to become a necessity as the club became a national landmark. Perteet had to rise early after his late-night band gigs to get to Augusta National by 8:00 a.m., in time to shag balls on the driving range as Eisenhower warmed up and took lessons from head professional Ed Dudley.

Perteet may have been privy to classified information during Eisenhower's visits to Augusta National. He said the president rarely discussed policy with his playing partners, but the Korean War was in progress and it was the start of the Cold War. You could sense Eisenhower's political temperature by his golf game: If a call came from Washington, Ike was often surly and played poorly. If the coast was clear, he was noticeably jovial and competitive. Perteet not only kept that information secret, if he knew anything, but he also didn't share anything about Ike's private life.

"You heard all the secrets of the H-bomb. And how that is classified information—unfit for public information," Perteet said in the early '50s. "Well, as far as I am concerned, the general's golf score lately is just the same—classified information."

As the late 1950s came, Perteet had reached his early fifties. Dudley opted to make a change on Eisenhower's bag because "Cemetery is getting a little decrepit," and "it is advisable to give the president a younger and more alert man." In Cemetery's place was "Slim" Jenkins, a man in his mid-thirties.

"The president plays like a whirlwind," Dudley said. "He hits the ball and—swoosh—he's gone. It takes a young man to keep up with him. So I had to make a change."

Perteet was admittedly disappointed at the move.

"I'm not ready for the grave yet, even if they do call me Cemetery," Perteet said. "If anybody thinks so, they should see me at the night club where I play drums at night. I can stand on my hands and walk to that first tee there. How many of these young squirts can do that?"

By 1964, Perteet was left out of the caddie roster for the Masters. He tried to get a bag but was late arriving and didn't make the cut. At a mere 112 pounds, he was only a shadow of his former bubbly self, described as "looking like a scrawny bantam rooster," in an Associated Press account. Even his drumming work had fallen by the wayside.

Perteet did capture a regular Masters bag through the mid-1970s, working with esteemed amateur Bill Campbell for nine tournaments. Campbell, who was a former United States Golf Association president and captain of the Royal & Ancient, played his final Masters in 1976 and recounted his experience with Cemetery for *Sports Illustrated* in 2008: "My caddie was a smallish man, not young even when we started together, named Willie Perteet," Campbell wrote. "Willie had to be near his end too. He was very likable, and what he knew, he knew. He didn't use a yardage book and didn't need one. If I wanted a yardage, and I seldom did, I'd say, 'Cemetery, what do you think it is?' He'd eyeball it."

The only thing left was the memory of being the right-hand man to the president, a title that few men in any profession could claim.

1

A Caddie's Letter

James L. "Baldy" Ricks was a caddie at the Augusta National Golf Club off and on from the mid-1940s until the late 1980s. During that time, Ricks served as the caddie for future president Dwight D. Eisenhower in the fall of 1950 when Eisenhower was president of Columbia University and for players Bobby Jones, Chick Harbert, Dick Chapman, and Vic Ghezzi through the years. Ricks attended high school at Haines Institute in Augusta before his family moved to Oklahoma. After graduating from high school there, Ricks went to Wilberforce University in Ohio, becoming a rare college graduate among the Augusta National caddie ranks. He returned to Augusta in the mid-1950s to serve at Fort Gordon in the U.S. Army and continued his caddying. Even though he spent much of his career as a mail carrier for the U.S. Postal Service in Detroit and Beverly Hills, California, Ricks would trek back to Augusta every spring to caddie in the Masters. Scared of flying, he always rode a bus back for his spring homecomings.

Ricks retired from the U.S. Postal Service in 1999. Even at age seventy-nine and living in San Bernardino, California, he still returned to Augusta annually to visit old friends, including former Augusta National caddie master Freddie Bennett. He wrote the following letter about his caddying experience to the *Augusta Chronicle* in the late 1990s. Most noteworthy is the brief encounter with Bobby Jones, one year after Jones played his last eighteen-hole round because of the early effects of syringomyelia, the condition he eventually died with twenty-two years later:

> The year was 1949. It was about midweek, 5 o'clock in the afternoon.
> I was sitting in the Old Caddy House waiting for a ride downtown.
> "Shorty," the driver, as well as a lot of the caddies, were engaged in
> card games called Koon Kang and Tonk, trying to increase their daily
> earnings before heading downtown to the watering hole on Broad

Street called "Doc Norval's." While waiting, the Caddy Master came into the Caddy House and asked me if I would like to go a few holes. Naturally, I accepted because my chances of adding to my earnings were much better than playing cards with my quick-handed buddies.

As we walked back up to the clubhouse, waiting was Mr. Jones. I had seen him on several different occasions talking with Mr. [Clifford] Roberts but never up close. He asked me if I could drive a car. Immediately, I replied yes sir, so he put the clubs in the trunk and said drive me out to 15 tee. At that time he had a green 1949 Cadillac. I got behind the wheel and drove down the service road parallel to the No. 1 hole. As I drove down behind the No. 1 green, to go down the hill on No. 2 toward the No. 15 tee, I turned the contour of the road, but I didn't turn wide enough to prevent the rear wheels from going into the dirt in the middle of this narrow road. Mr. Jones smiled and said you had to allow for the break, turn your front wheels a little wider so your rear wheels will stay on the road. "Yes sir," I replied. We finally made it to 15 tee. He told me he was going to play 15, 16, and 17, which would bring us back to the car.

So he teed off on 15 with a fluid swing, not very far but accurate. He hit his second shot somewhat short of the creek that approached the green. He hit his third shot on the green. In the customary fashion of caddies, you always stay in front of the player. But when I got to the wooden bridge crossing the creek he yelled, "Wait up." He jokingly said if he fell in the water he was going to take me with him. There was a slight climb from the end of the bridge and up the embankment to the green, but needless to say we didn't go in. Sixteen was a "piece of cake," mostly level. Seventeen was a test, almost all uphill until passing the Eisenhower Tree on the left of the fairway. He completed the 17th hole, we got back into the car, and I didn't drive into the middle isle on my return. He paid me and said "thanks." Naturally, I thanked him back for allowing me to drive him.

As I looked back to my caddie's days at Augusta, which covered about 20 years, I am in awe of how caddying has changed. First, outside [Tour] caddies were not allowed, which gave the local caddies exclusive rights to the tournament. Most of the caddies and Caddy Master ["Eleven"] had names we never knew. Pappy caddied for Hogan, Banny caddied for Demaret, Shorty caddied for Mangrum, Iron

Man caddied for Palmer, and there were often names like Cigarette, Roundhead, Nipper, Gardoolie, Cemetery, and Shoo Poon. I caddied for Chick Harbert. My nickname ["Baldy"] was given to me by Mr. [Ed] Dudley [the head professional]. I, of course, thought he gave me this nickname because I ran very hard shagging balls when he would give golf lessons. Apparently, he saw something then that would become a part of my headdress in later years.

Caddies today are mathematicians, accountants, professional golfers, globetrotters and investors. Today, caddies don't linger nor memorize the cards, they chart the yards. It's big business, 10% of the golfer's earnings plus bonuses. Caddies earn more today in one year than the leading money winners from 1945 to 1965.

"Eleven" passed away and it was then that I found out his real name [John Williams]. I owe him great thanks for allowing me to outdrive the only grand slammer in golf.

Billy "Baldy" Ricks

1

Fireball

George "Fireball" Franklin earned his nickname because of a quick temper. On the fifteenth hole of the 1957 Masters is where another hotheaded individual, Doug Ford, scored the decisive shot, whether Fireball liked it or not.

Ford stood on the hill overlooking one of golf's most historic, demanding second shots—down into the valley, over a narrow stream that fronts a slick green which steeply slopes from back to front. It was here, in the shadow of Ford's ball, where Gene Sarazen made a name for the Masters, the sport of golf, and himself by launching his famous double eagle in 1935. This is also where Seve Ballesteros would smother-hook a 4-iron approach shot into the enlarged hazard, now a pond, clearing the way for Jack Nicklaus to don a sixth green jacket in 1986.

That's enough perspective to wreck the nerves, but here stood thirty-four-year-old Douglas Michael Ford, native New Yorker, former pool shark, 1955 PGA Championship winner, remembering yesterday with just three and a half holes remaining in the 1957 Masters. He grew up in New York City, not far from the Polo Grounds, the New York Giants' home baseball field in Upper Manhattan, and developed an affection for pool-hall billiards as a youngster, racking up as many as twenty-five to thirty-five consecutive shots in "straight" pool. His grandfather was an Italian immigrant railroad man with the name Fortunato, which Doug's father, Mike, a golf pro, changed to Ford. During the Depression, Doug Ford recalled that his father lost his golf business and that the family ate potatoes as a main course four or five times weekly.

Also understand that Ford was considered somewhat of a hothead in those days. Ford was known to openly criticize the slower-paced players and once berated the Professional Golfers Association of America authorities to penalize a player who held back the New Yorker's brisk pace of play.

George "Fireball" Franklin watches as Doug Ford chips to a green during a 1950s Masters. Fireball and Ford teamed up to win the 1957 Masters. *Masters Historic Imagery/Getty Images*

In 1955, Ford once even questioned whether women in the gallery should be allowed to wear shorts to tournaments because he found them "distracting."

So you would have to believe that any negative thoughts from either the previous day or about the fifteenth hole in general could erode Doug Ford's confidence.

It was in this exact spot on Saturday that Ford had watched in horror as his 3-wood second shot flew to the bank on the other side, stopped in its pitch mark, and slowly rolled back into the hazard. Ford gallantly took off his shoes and socks, rolled up his pants legs, trudged in to blast out his ball in a shower of muddy creek water, and salvaged a bogey. Good-bye Yankee, most thought. Ford trailed the third-round leader, West Virginia's Sam Snead, by three strokes.

"When I got to the clubhouse after that round, a couple of old-time pros said if I got a chance at fifteen tomorrow, lay up," Ford said. Adding another negative thought, it was on this back nine the year before where Ford was tied with Jackie Burke and "blew up" to finish five strokes behind Burke, the eventual champion.

Twenty-four hours after his wet fifteenth on Saturday, Ford reached the exact same position, staring some 230 yards into the distance on the 500-yard par-5. He had played brilliantly—4-under par through fourteen holes—to catch and pass Slammin' Sammy, who was one stroke back after consecutive bogeys early on the back nine.

Enter Franklin, an Atlantan who was first assigned to caddie for Ford in his 1952 Masters debut. Franklin was pals with a couple other Atlantans, future caddie winners Frank "Marble Eye" Stokes (Bob Goalby, 1968) and Walter "Cricket" Pritchett (Charles Coody, 1971). Their process was to drive two and a half hours over from Atlanta approximately one month before the tournament and caddie for members and players making scouting trips to Augusta, either full-time or on the weekends. Often, the out-of-town caddies were left with players who hadn't already been assigned to full-season Augusta National caddies or those who caddie master Freddie Bennett was having difficulty with because of the player's hot temperament or his history of firing caddies during the tournament.

"I like to carry sticks for a fast golfer," Fireball said. "When you go fast you got no time to think of anything but the next shot. But when you play with a slow one ... well, my mind wanders. First thing you know I'm thinking about my gal uptown, or bad whiskey, or something like that."

As Ford tried to forget about Saturday, Fireball wouldn't let him. Ford was noted for his rapid-fire pace of play and a quick, flat golf swing that he depicted as that of a "gorilla golfer." His self-confidence was legendary as well. In the weeks leading up to the 1957 Masters, *Golf World* magazine polled 150 golfers to predict the Masters winners; Ford was the only one who picked himself. Ford was reaching to select the 3-wood when Fireball spoke up.

"Use your 4-iron," Fireball shot out. "Gonna cost me $100 if you go in the water."

Ford went ahead with his attempt to unsheathe his 3-wood. Fireball, acting the part of a good banker, stood firm. Ford grasped again. Fireball moved the bag a bit, away from Ford's reach. The gallery noticed the goings-on and a murmur of nervous laughter came up.

Finally, Ford took charge.

"Snead is right behind us, and he'll easily be able to reach this green in two," Ford said forcefully. "I'm no good at playing safe. Besides, they don't remember you here unless you go for it and win."

With that, Fireball let his guard down. Ford drew a 3-wood and ripped at his second shot. The ball took a low trajectory, barely cleared the hazard and, instead of retreating as it had done on Saturday, hopped up on the green. Ford, a deft putter, easily two-putted for birdie.

Ford punctuated his victory with a hole-out birdie from a bunker on the eighteenth hole, a shot that completed a 6-under-par 66, the best final-round Masters score to date. It was also one of only three Masters bogey-free final rounds to date. Ford tossed his sand wedge skyward and rejoiced at what would be a three-stroke victory over Snead. As luck would have it, the CBS cameras didn't catch the finale, coming on the air just after Ford completed his round.

But as Ford signed his scorecard and awaited the final pairings, Fireball was still fuming at the give-and-take on fifteen.

"It worked this year," Fireball said. "But it ain't gonna work next, I'm telling ya. Man 4-under par shoulda played it safe."

Fireball would continue to tote for Ford through the mid-1960s. Ford described him as a "steady caddie."

"We got along real well," Ford said in 2000. "He knew the course."

True to Fireball's steadfastness, Ford was the Masters' man of one mind, a champion of the past with a gruff exterior and eternal pride in his accomplishments. Until he and other veteran Masters winners received a letter from Augusta National chairman Hootie Johnson in 2001 asking them not to play any longer, Ford had played in a record forty-nine Masters (third behind Gary Player's fifty-two and Arnold Palmer's fifty). Critics chirped up every year, questioning his place among golf's elite. Here was a man in his late seventies who hadn't played the Champions Tour in nearly a decade, hadn't broken 80 in the Masters since 1990, hadn't made the cut in a Masters since 1971, and often called it a tournament after eighteen holes or even just nine or fewer.

Many an inquisitive media member would monotonously ask: Why play?

"Because I won the damn tournament," Ford said with a scowl on his face.

Somewhere, finally, Fireball was smiling.

1

Iron Man

For Arnold Palmer, it was all about being a flamboyant player and wearing his heart on his sleeve. Go for broke, show emotion, capture the crowd with good looks and a quick smile. He did that to display self-confidence and bring out the best in his game. If anyone could take the game of golf on his shoulders and rocket the sport to a higher echelon in the early days of televised golf of the late 1950s, it was the man everyone simply called Arnie.

Arnie did not require someone to dramatically share the stage or direct his playing path. He simply needed an understanding compatriot, a caddie who knew how to press Arnie's buttons, a man who could walk quietly by his side and offer a few words of encouragement or, better yet, instill discipline when the time came.

That man was Nathaniel Avery, an Augustan who was born to golf and claimed the most endearing nickname in the caddie yard, "Iron Man." It was a nickname that fit the bill as the second to a man with steel-town roots and the hard-working, go-for-broke persona of Arnold Palmer from Latrobe, Pennsylvania. It became a partnership shared in four Masters titles, with Avery displaying his extensive family heritage in the caddie business and his expert player's knowledge of the game.

Described by Will Grimsley of the Associated Press as "a lean rope of a man, with just a trace of a mustache and a goatee, standing about 6-foot, 155 pounds," Avery was the perfect balance for Palmer. He had a loping stride, was quiet and usually expressionless on the golf course (called "sad-faced" in one early 1960s newspaper account), and could be found oftentimes resting his haunches on Palmer's bag or sprawled casually on his side, head propped up by a hand, as Palmer putted. "He was rather quiet and laid-back," Palmer said in the early 2000s. When Palmer birdied the last two holes in 1960 to capture his second Masters title, there was Avery sitting on the bag on the

Nathaniel "Iron Man" Avery and Arnold Palmer study the tee shot on the par-3 twelfth hole during the 1964 Masters, the last of Palmer's four Masters victories, all with Iron Man on the bag. *Masters Historic Imagery/Getty Images*

right side of the eighteenth green as Palmer jumped up and down, and the entire gallery responded. The emotion was usually left to Palmer, whom Avery simply called "Par."

Born in 1939, Avery was the youngest of eight children, four boys and four girls. His oldest brother, "Big Henry," was the longtime caddie master at Augusta Country Club and the man largely responsible for training young caddies and giving many of them their nicknames when they "graduated" to work north of Rae's Creek at Augusta National. Big Henry earned his nickname because of his 6'4", three-hundred-pound build and booming voice, quite a contrast to the smaller, thinner Nathaniel.

Another brother, Horace, was the assistant caddie master at Augusta National. A third brother, Willie, also became an Augusta National caddie. Nathaniel's future brother-in-law, Willie "Pappy" Stokes, married Nathaniel's sister Odella. Pappy was a five-time Masters winner as a caddie, mentor to the caddies from the 1950s to 1970s, and claimed by many as the best to ever step foot on Augusta National.

Decades later, a great-nephew, William, would become a star guard in basketball at Duke University. He was a first-round draft pick of the NBA's Minnesota Timberwolves, where he played for three years as a backup guard before playing in Europe for a few years in the early to mid-2000s. William had become a famous person in another sport, making headlines in a similar but different time than his great-uncle. A public, outdoor basketball court located approximately one mile from Augusta National, around the corner off Berckmans Road, on Wheeler Road at Big Oak Park, bears the names of William and Ricky Moore, former Augusta National caddie Buck Moore's son. William and Ricky formed a deadly backcourt duo to lead nearby Westside High School to the 1995 Georgia Class AAA state basketball title, losing only one game all season. William's number-one-ranked Duke team and Moore's Connecticut Huskies faced off in the 1999 NCAA championship game in St. Petersburg, Florida, with the Huskies prevailing.

It was before the family's widespread fame that Nathaniel Avery naturally hung out in the caddie yard in the early 1950s. As a 115-pound kid, he boasted about carrying the heaviest bag of the day's rounds at either Augusta Country Club or Augusta National and then would come back for more. That was the first time, he said in a mid-1960s interview, that someone jokingly called him Iron Man.

Another tale claims that Avery was missing a couple of fingertips after some sort of accident. One theory, told by veteran Augusta National caddie Joe Collins, claims that Avery, evidently under the influence of alcohol, once tried to cut open a golf ball with an ax and lopped some fingertips off in the process. Another states that he suffered the injury by holding an exploding firecracker. Yet another account relates that wounds suffered in a knife fight didn't bleed. All the stories build a character who is mysterious and formidable.

This nickname came before the more widely known Iron Man of Marvel Comics and Stan Lee fame, which debuted in March 1963, approximately one year before Palmer's fourth and final Masters win.

Whatever the origin of the nickname, the question was inevitably asked: "What do you think, you're an Iron Man or something?"

Caddying would be Avery's future, for sure, but playing was his first love. By the mid-1950s, a teenaged Avery was able to shoot sub-par golf. In those days, caddies could occasionally play both Augusta National and Augusta Country Club at specified times, and Avery's best scores were an even-par 72 at Augusta National and a 68 at Augusta Country Club. In 1961, he shot a final-round 70 at an open tournament in New York and then made his way back to lug Palmer's bag in the Masters. He won the Augusta National caddie tournament, held in late spring before the course closed for the summer, at least four times.

"With the right opportunity, he could have played the [PGA] Tour," said Freddie Bennett, the former Augusta National caddie master.

Unfortunately, the world of the 1950s would not accept a Black man making his way on golf's top circuit as a player. That, and Arnold Palmer came on the scene.

It was 1955 when Palmer first came to the Masters, invited as the reigning U.S. Amateur champion. Palmer and his wife, Winnie, towed their twenty-six-foot trailer into Augusta and steered it into a trailer park off Gordon Highway for tournament week. Hotshot young players like Ken Venturi, Mike Souchak, and Gene Littler drew most of the attention from the press and the caddies. Caddie assignments were made either by request of the players, reference from the caddie master (then "'Leven" Williams), or simply by assignment.

"The caddie master came down to the lot and said, 'If you take this bag, you got to keep it.' I said, 'I'll keep it,'" Avery said. "Even though Ken Venturi was the heat, I'll keep it."

For fourteen years, Avery was Palmer's right-hand man at Augusta National. He was the rare caddie who was interviewed by the press, calling the partnership "a corporation, a team." Avery often responded with down-home insight about golf's new superstar. He even painted the long-lasting image of Palmer and his patented charging style.

"He just hitch his trousers, jerk on his glove, starts walking fast, and said, 'The game is on,'" Avery said in the 1960s. "When Mr. Arnold do that, everybody better watch out. He's gonna stampede anything in his way."

On the player-caddie relationship: "Anybody who can't get along with Mr. Arnold can't get along with anybody. I should know. I been almost in his pocket on every hole.

"Sometime he go with my advice—and it better be right. If I mis-club him, he don't chastise me. He just look a little mean, and I feel like going through the ground. But he is a great man."

On Palmer playing his best golf when the tournament began: "'Par' hittin' the ball just as good as ever, but he's puttin' worse than I've ever seen him putt in a long time. . . . He ain't too worried, though, and I ain't either. When they ring the bell, he'll be there. He lays one up for birdie, he'll make it."

On Palmer's ability to overcome adversity, rallying from a double bogey in the final round in 1962 to force a Monday playoff where he beat Dow Finsterwald and Gary Player: "He just look up in the sky like he is wishing for some miracle to come down. And the miracle come down—like somebody was answering him."

Palmer's first Masters win in 1958 evoked humor. Entering the final round tied for the lead with Sam Snead at 5-under par, word was passed down to all players near the lead by Augusta National chairman and cofounder Clifford Roberts that a Sunday victory could possibly mean an invitation for a Monday tee time with the most famous American golfer, Dwight D. Eisenhower, the president of the United States and a member of Augusta National. Eisenhower's passion for golf, paired beginning in the late 1950s with Palmer's rise to fame, would bring great new exposure to the game.

"If you couple the pressure of contending at the Masters with the thought that you might play golf with the president of the United States the next day, you can imagine what I went through the final eighteen holes that day," Palmer said.

The tension was heightened early in the back nine when Palmer and an ornery rules official, England's Arthur Lacey, butted heads on the twelfth hole. Palmer's tee shot on the par-3 hole embedded in rain-soaked, soft turf behind the green, just a few feet below a bunker. Palmer studied his lie and upcoming second shot and asked for relief from the wet area. The rules official denied his request. According to legendary golf writer Herbert Warren Wind's account, there was "an animated and protracted discussion" between Palmer and the rules official. With his dander up, Palmer still had enough patience to think through the process. He slopped the ball out and made a double bogey. However, he then played a provisional ball and got up and down for par. It was in question whether Palmer retained a one-stroke lead over playing partner Venturi or fell one behind the San Francisco amateur. The final verdict was yet to come.

Palmer took care of some of that indecision on the next shots at the dogleg left, par-5 thirteenth. He slashed a 250-yard drive around the corner, then a choked-down 3-wood onto the green eighteen feet to the left and above the hole, and rolled in the eagle putt. Two holes later, Bobby Jones came out to officially inform them that Palmer's par on the twelfth hole stood. A photograph of Jones and Clifford Roberts conferring on the fifteenth tee with Palmer is revealing as just to the right, listening closely to the conversation, is Avery. Palmer beat Doug Ford and Fred Hawkins by one stroke to capture his first major championship.

The hysteria that resulted from the victory among tournament attendees and officials caused nearly as much confusion among the Palmer family.

"I told Winnie right away that I was going to play golf with the president the next day," Palmer recalled. "And in the same sentence, I asked Winnie to write Iron Man a check. It was normal to give a sizable check to the caddie of the player who wins the Masters."

Palmer asked Winnie, who doubled as his traveling secretary and bookkeeper in those early days, to pay Avery $1,400. An overjoyed gallery and friends gathered to give their congratulations. Avery and Palmer evidently were also engrossed in a debate that had something to do with a set of clubs as Winnie wrote out the check. Finally, the Palmers were able to break away from Augusta National as a group of friends and club representatives from Wilson Sporting Goods treated the winning couple to dinner and drinks in downtown Augusta at the Town Tavern, the traditional restaurant and watering hole for Masters participants. But before they could complete the meal, an urgent call came from Augusta National officials.

Winnie had written a check for $14,000, more than the $11,250 first prize, and Avery was attempting to cash it at the clubhouse. Augusta National officials immediately contacted the Town Tavern to question the exorbitant fee. The matter was resolved, with an extra zero being eliminated from the check. Avery was told to pick up the new check at the Richmond Hotel, the Broad Street hotel where many of the players stayed during the tournament.

The date with Eisenhower was delayed until after Palmer's 1960 win at the Masters, but by then Avery had become a fixture. In June 1960, *SPORT* magazine chronicled a first-person account by Avery on what it was like to carry Palmer's clubs. He was one of the first Masters caddies to be interviewed by the press, indeed a rarity in those days when caddies were often perceived as nothing more than a hired hand, much less a good subject for an interview, and their all-Black makeup didn't help the matter when just about all golfers and golf fans at the time were white.

Most importantly, Avery may have issued the most important message of Palmer's career in 1960 on the way to winning his second Masters title. Chain-smoking L&M cigarettes and swigging Coca-Colas on the back nine to fight nervousness, Palmer was throwing away shots left and right. He trailed by one stroke entering the back nine, failed to birdie the short par-5 thirteenth, and saw the tournament slipping away. By the time Palmer reached No. 14, Venturi had already posted a 5-under-par 283 total. Palmer needed a birdie coming home to tie. A poor pitch from beside the par-5 fifteenth green blew another birdie chance and infuriated Palmer. He tossed his wedge at Avery, who was standing nearby at Palmer's bag.

The stare he got back was startling.

"Mr. Palmer," Avery said in his usual, low-pitched growl. "Are we chokin'?"

The query perked Palmer up. He might not win, but nobody accuses him of being gutless. On the par-3 sixteenth, a bold long birdie putt rattled the flag, and he was left with a tap-in for par. Faced with a birdie-birdie finish to win, Palmer drilled a 35-footer on the seventeenth to tie Venturi, and then sank a five-footer on the closing hole to win his second Masters. Avery's message was delivered emphatically.

"His scowl [on the fifteenth hole] was eerily reminiscent of the disapproving glare Pap [Palmer's father, Deacon] used to give me as a kid whenever I threw a club or failed to keep my mind on the job," Palmer wrote in his 1999 biography, *A Golfer's Life.*

"Iron Man wasn't the greatest caddie. I'd be less than honest if I said he was. His distances were often inaccurate, and I relied, instead, on my own calculations and the knowledge of the course to get around Augusta. But his understanding of what made me tick was perhaps instinctive and definitely profound. I stared back at him and realized he was right—I was foolishly beating on myself instead of taking care of the business of playing the golf course."

Years later, Palmer recounted that Iron Man "was a good Augusta caddie—he was solid and did his job."

If Avery was the steadying influence on the golf course, he struggled with the fame away from Augusta National. In the Black community, he was a celebrity who wasn't shy about public displays of exultation in the late 1950s and 1960s. With every one of Palmer's four victories, Avery went out and purchased a new, shiny Cadillac or Pontiac to transport him and his current girlfriend to the nearest gathering or nightclub.

"In my mind, he was the black sheep of the family," said Carl Jackson. "He was a real gambler, a ladies' man type of guy, not a family man. On weekends, you'd see him all over the area, gambling and shooting dice. He also visited the jailhouse a few times."

Henry Avery Jr., the son of Big Henry, remembered his uncle as "a free-wheeler, but a nice guy."

"I looked up to him as a kid," Henry Jr. said. "That's the way we were led to believe. Every time he'd buy a new car, he'd come by and pick me up and take me for a ride. He'd let me think I was driving that car.

"He was just loving life. He loved the nightlife. It wasn't anything out of the ordinary; he just loved to party."

The partying took a toll on Avery and his prized cars. Late on the Friday following Palmer's third victory in 1962, it didn't take long to dispose of the caddie's share of the check, which was approximately two thousand dollars from Palmer's first-place prize of twenty thousand dollars. Avery was cruising down Mt. Auburn Street of his Sand Hills neighborhood in a new Pontiac purchased just that afternoon, with a female acquaintance close by his side and an alcoholic beverage in hand. The car veered off the side of the road and struck a tree near the Rock of Ages church. No serious injuries were reported, just a few cuts, a totaled vehicle, and an Avery visit to University Hospital, where the medical staff soon discovered his identity and took pity on his quickly lost wages.

"Too bad you don't have anything left from caddying for the new Masters champion," one doctor remarked.

"Oh yes, I have, I got these thirty-dollar shoes," Avery said as he grinned and proudly stuck one foot in the air from the hospital bed.

"The bark peeled off that tree where the car hit it and stayed off for years and years," Henry Jr. said. "People used to say that's where Iron Man left his mark. That mark stayed there till that tree died."

By the late 1960s, Palmer's reign as the King of the Masters was at its end. With a second-round 79 in the 1968 Masters, Palmer totaled 151 to miss the cut for the first time. He trudged through the round as Arnie's Army sat on its hands at the horror of the occasion. Palmer was invited by Roberts to stay around for lunch and a quick tour of the course in a golf cart for Saturday's third round, which he obliged, then took off in his jet, bound for home in Latrobe.

It was also to be the last time that Avery and Palmer shared the bag in the Masters. The previous year, Palmer had used Charlie Reynolds as his caddie early in the week because he said Avery "was sick and in the hospital." The talk was that Palmer had enough of Avery taking too much credit for some of the successful run at Augusta National. "He was getting too big for his britches," was the word around the Augusta National caddie shack. Another report stated that a national magazine wished to do a story on Palmer and asked for Avery's input. His response: "How much you gonna pay me?" Winnie was standing nearby, overheard the pay request, and grew disgusted with Avery's attitude.

Palmer was also famous for changing caddies on a whim. An Associated Press account in 1964 said that in the U.S. Open that year at Congressional Country Club in Washington, D.C., Palmer changed caddies three times before the tournament even started. But, most likely, Avery's caddying skills had been eroded by his off-course antics and failing health. Palmer simply said in 2003 that "[Avery] didn't show up the next year [1969]." Bennie Hatcher, a longtime regular caddie at Augusta National, was hired to take Avery's place and carried the bag through 1977.

"Players didn't really rely on the local knowledge of the caddies very much," Palmer said in the 1990s. "It was just a rule that we had to use them. The rule was changed when Tour players gained more influence."

By the mid-1970s, Avery was a sad figure, hanging around the fringes of the tournament, trying to catch any odd job that came his way. Caddying was out of the question for a man who was still only in his mid-30s. His life was centered around Augusta National, where for decades he caddied during the October–May Augusta National season, played in the caddie tournament before the summer heat hit, and worked with the maintenance crew during the summer and into fall.

"I ain't got nothing now," Avery said in 1974. "I've had no action since 1971. I got a job this year carrying a photographer's equipment. Then they fired me. Said I was too slow."

Still, there was the confident attitude that said this man believed he could still tote with the best of them.

"But no man knows this course like me," Avery said. "I know every tree, every blade of grass, every break of the greens. Arnie will be lucky to make the cut. He's having his problems. He'll never make a comeback until he gets me back. You just wait and see."

True to Iron Man's prediction, Palmer never contended again after the breakup. His best finish was a tie for eleventh in 1974.

Avery's name was fading from the headlines, but by the mid-1970s, the Avery family became involved in a dispute against Augusta National.

On the afternoon of Tuesday, October 18, 1976, three young Black males were shot at Augusta National after they entered the grounds to fish in Rae's Creek near the twelfth green. Charles Avery, age nineteen, suffered the worst damage, listed by the hospital as serious wounds to the upper right side and chest area. Charles's brother, Robert, age twelve, was wounded in the upper right arm and right thigh. A third injured person, Justin Jackson, age nineteen, was wounded in the right leg. All three were admitted to University Hospital. Charles and Robert were the sons of "Big Henry" Avery, the Augusta Country Club caddie master, and the nephews to Horace and Iron Man.

Phil Wahl, Augusta National's general manager, said that the shooting was an accident. A group of boys was spotted on the grounds in midafternoon by nurseryman Rogers Bennett, who said one of the boys was carrying a small shotgun, probably used to ward off snakes, which can be found in Rae's Creek, most often in the tributary that flows left of the thirteenth fairway. The boys left when Bennett asked them to. They returned to the Rae's Creek area a short time later, apparently without the gun, and Bennett summoned security guard Charles Young when he spotted them on the property. The club had just opened for the season, and interlopers weren't allowed. Armed with a 12-gauge pump-action shotgun, Young accompanied Bennett down to Amen Corner. When the boys saw the men approaching, they ran.

"The guard was in the act of loading his shotgun with the thought of firing over the heads of the boys as a means of causing them to stop and identify themselves," Wahl said in the October 19, 1976, *Augusta Chronicle*. "Unfortunately, the gun was discharged [from about fifty yards away], quite by accident, according to the club guard."

The Richmond County Sheriff's Department began an investigation. All the boys were released from the hospital shortly thereafter, but the community was stunned. Just eighteen months before, Lee Elder had become the first Black man to play in the Masters. Then this occurred, oddly enough to a well-known, longtime Augusta National/Augusta Country Club golf community family and just six years after horrendous race riots in downtown Augusta.

By May 1977, the three wounded boys began a series of legal proceedings. Robert Avery, through his father "Big Henry," filed an eleven-million-dollar damage complaint in Richmond County Superior Court against Augusta National, stating that Robert suffered "permanent disfigurement and disability." More alarming was the conclusion of the filing, which stated that

"Augusta National Inc. deliberately pursues a policy of racism in membership, employment, ticket sales and other matters, and that Young's actions occurred because the plaintiff and his companions are black." Charles Avery and Justin Jackson followed soon after with similar charges of damages for their injuries.

By June, Augusta National attorney William C. Calhoun argued that the shooting was an accident and asked the court to delete the portion of the suit referring to racism. The boys returned a suit also charging the maker of Young's shotgun, which was claimed to be faulty. Their three final suits, filed in 1978, eventually totaled six million dollars in damage requests.

The cases dragged on until the week after the 1979 Masters when the U.S. District Court in Augusta was scheduled to hold a jury trial. Juries were selected for two of the cases. Three days after Fuzzy Zoeller won the Masters on his first attempt and two and a half years after the shooting incident, Augusta National and the firearms manufacturer settled for an undisclosed sum with the three victims.

Nevertheless, a bitter taste was left in the mouths of the Avery family.

Iron Man's name was not mentioned in connection with the legal tug of war. That was probably for the best since his caddying life was nearly at its end. He worked for Calvin Peete in the early 1980s but was only a shadow of his former self. The hard life had caught up with him.

"He really regressed," Jackson said. "He didn't take care of himself at all. He got senile, in my opinion. I caddied in the same group with him one time about then at Augusta National, and he had the bag of a guest of one of the members for the weekend.

"The man studied a shot on one hole and asked, 'How far have we got?' Iron Man just sort of stared at him and then blurted out, 'About a mile.' The man's face turned red; he was really offended. When the round was over, he let Iron Man go, fired him right there. Iron Man was a sick man."

Henry Jr. said Iron Man's cause of death at age forty-seven on May 6, 1985, was liver disease caused by alcohol abuse. He had also developed tuberculosis a few years before, according to Beard, thereby accelerating his ailment by drinking too much.

The *Augusta Chronicle* carried a simple sixty-one-word obituary on May 7, 1985. It gave his nickname, "Iron Man," and stated that he was a member of Elim Baptist Church in Sand Hills but listed no occupation or tie-in to the Masters or Palmer. He never married or had children. There would be no

Nathaniel "Iron Man" Avery was buried in an unmarked grave for thirty-two years before an anonymous donor paid for this marker in 2017 at Southview Cemetery in downtown Augusta, Georgia. *Photo by Ward Clayton*

other stories or reminiscence about his glory days as a caddie. Nathaniel E. Avery died a broken man with what some deemed a glorious past.

A simple funeral was held at Dent's Undertaking Establishment. Avery is buried in the expansive Southview Cemetery in downtown Augusta near the intersection of Martin Luther King Jr. Boulevard and 15th Street. There was no headstone or marker on his final resting place for thirty-two years, just a map and listing in the cemetery office that points out the location as "Grave No. 3, Lot No. 12, Section G."

By 2017, the lead-up to filming the caddie documentary film *Loopers: The Caddie's Long Walk* helped fund a marker for Avery's grave, with a price tag of $796.60 given by an anonymous donor and approved by the Avery family and Palmer's office for a ground-level granite marker. Southview Cemetery owner Julius Clark helped assure that Avery was indeed buried in this plot. Clark, a former grave digger at the cemetery, used a vault probe, a T-shaped

Augusta's Will Avery, the great-nephew of Nathaniel "Iron Man" Avery, was a key player in Duke basketball's drive to the 1999 NCAA Final Four. Avery became an assistant coach for the Blue Devils in 2023. *Courtesy of Duke University Athletics*

rod contraption, to strike the buried casket six feet below the ground's surface, clearing the way for a marker to be purchased.

The film and publicity for the marker were particularly enlightening for Will Avery. He had been at the heights of the basketball world and returned to Duke in the fall of 2019 to resume the pursuit of his college degree, helping the Duke program unofficially in coach Mike Krzyzewski's last couple of years at the helm, talking with various players and observing how the coaches strategized and interacted with today's athletes—not unlike what his great-uncle Iron Man used to do in devising tactics for navigating Augusta National. Avery earned his Duke degree, a bachelor of arts in African and African American studies, in May 2023, twenty-four years after departing the university for the NBA.

"I don't think I knew much about who Iron Man was until I was twenty-three or so," Will Avery, who turned forty-four in August 2023, said in 2017. "So, more than half my lifetime. I was just five when he died, so it was a process to learn about him. . . . I don't care what I did in my playing career. It doesn't compare to what he did. That was historic."

Will Avery's knowledge of his uncle's past heroics may have been influential in his later life, particularly in earning the college degree, with retired coach Krzyzewski by his side. It was the transformation from a high school student who didn't exert himself academically in Augusta, left college early for the NBA to Krzyzewski's disapproval, and now possesses a degree from one of the nation's top universities. That led to his July 1, 2023, hiring as an assistant basketball coach by second-year Blue Devils head coach John Scheyer. The degree is a requirement for all coaches at the collegiate level.

"My children, without a doubt, were my motivation," Avery said in June 2023. "No matter how hard this seems or how crazy it may look to them, this proves you can do anything you put your mind to. Age doesn't matter. Nothing matters.

"It was definitely challenging, being in school and classes with younger students. But I was mentally prepared for it."

Henry Jr., who died in early 2021, had a more pointed perspective: "[Iron Man] didn't die with any celebrity status," said Henry Jr., who served as a pallbearer at his uncle's funeral. "He was just a caddie. I mean, I'm proud of him, doing what he did. He was famous. But just remember, he was just a caddie."

Still, Nathaniel "Iron Man" Avery had become the first Black caddie in the Masters to break through and be mentioned for his expertise and influence on possibly the most popular Masters champion ever, Arnold Palmer. Before his rise as a caddie with a superhero's nickname and lore, caddies were seldom mentioned in Masters recaps, no matter their contributions. That was a position of great prominence to the Black caddies at Augusta National and to the minority neighborhood where Iron Man grew up.

One of the great keepsakes that Henry Jr. possessed was the caddie identification card that Augusta National issued for his uncle in 1981–82. It may

Nathaniel "Iron Man" Avery's 1981–82 caddie card at Augusta National, a keepsake that his nephew Henry Avery Jr. held for years after his uncle's death in 1985.
Photo by Ward Clayton

have been one of the last meaningful items that was passed along from him to a family member. During a marker-placing ceremony in 2017, Henry Jr. smiled as he shared a view of the laminated card similar in size to a driver's license, which included a color photo of his uncle. Other attendees viewed it and rattled off stories of Avery kin and the fact that Iron Man would now be remembered forever with the marker. The caddie card was a piece of memorabilia to be cherished.

"I keep it in a safe place," Henry Jr. said proudly.

1

Snipes and E. B.

Gary Player arrived at the 1978 Masters Tournament with two green jackets in his closet and the career Grand Slam on his résumé. He had earned a spot in the World Golf Hall of Fame and was already revered as one of the game's foremost international ambassadors.

Still, his caddie felt comfortable enough with their relationship to confide in the forty-two-year-old dynamo. Eddie McCoy wanted to inspire his boss and make a big payday in the process.

"You gotta win this tournament, man," McCoy lamented as the tournament began. "I'm in trouble, and I need a new house. We gotta win."

The house was on order when Player stormed through the final round. He birdied seven of the final ten holes, including a downhill fifteen-footer on the eighteenth hole, to come from seven strokes back and win the Masters, at that time becoming the oldest champion in tournament history. Player and McCoy walked onto and off the eighteenth green arm in arm with huge smiles on their faces following Player's record-tying, final-round 64.

"I don't know what kind of trouble Eddie was in, but when I came from seven strokes back on Sunday, you've never seen a man as happy as Eddie was," Player said, finding out later that McCoy needed a new roof on his house and that his caddie was also a master carpenter. "There's a picture taken just after I holed the putt on eighteen. In it, you see Eddie flying toward me like Batman, from the left of the green, with an expression on his face as though he'd just won the lottery."

The pressure of a tight Sunday at the Masters was enough for anyone. But Player's Masters performances are full of stress, both on and off the course. He won three titles with two different caddies, Ernest Nipper (1961) and McCoy (1974 and 1978), and almost a third time with another famous caddie, Carl Jackson. Player made a record fifty-two starts in the tournament, from 1957 to 2009.

Begin with 1961. Player was far from the fan favorite, not only because he wasn't an American but also because Arnold Palmer was charging toward a third green jacket. That's when the green-side bunkers on the eighteenth hole made the difference. Palmer, holding a one-stroke lead in the final pairing, made double bogey from the right greenside bunker. Player got up and down for par from the same place just a few minutes earlier to get a chance to make a game of it.

Perhaps what kept Player in the race that week was his caddie, Ernest Nipper. Nipper was known as a great player who stalked the course as if he were trying to win the tournament himself. He earned the nickname "Snipes" because of his thorough examination of the entire round, much like a sniper who has an accurate shot with a rifle. Right away, he established some credibility with Player.

"We were playing the fourth hole, a par-3, in the first round," Player said. "I had a putt of about fifteen feet left of the hole, going up to the hole. I thought I had to hit it to the left edge. Most of the time, I read all my putts. But this putt confused me. So I asked Nipper. He said, 'Right edge,' so emphatically. I wasn't so sure of that.

"All he said was, 'Gary, if it doesn't break to the left, you don't have to pay me this week.' Sure enough, the putt broke left into the hole. That made the difference in my confidence all week. I had somebody with me who could really help."

Player's relationship with Nipper continued through the 1960s, but it ended in bizarre fashion at the 1970 Masters.

Protesters of apartheid, South Africa's racially exclusive policy, were focusing on Player as a high-profile representative of South Africa. Even though Player was opposed to this type of government, he was duly associated with the movement. His usual all-black garb drew the attention of fans and political activists. Player wouldn't criticize the South African government for fear of endangering friends and relatives back home.

The protests got ugly during the 1969 PGA Championship at NCR Country Club just outside of Dayton, Ohio. During the third round, protesters from the Dayton Organization, a coalition representing such groups as the Students for a Democratic Society and the Southern Christian Leadership Conference, broke through the gallery ropes and charged onto the tenth green. A bearded, young white man exchanged words with Player. A few other protesters approached Jack Nicklaus, Player's playing partner, as the

Ernest "Snipes" Nipper (left) caddied for Gary Player in Player's first Masters victory in 1961. Player, from South Africa, became the tournament's first international winner.
Masters Historic Imagery/Getty Images

Golden Bear was lining up a putt, but Jack pulled back his putter in defense just as one of the protesters picked up his ball. Player was jostled as security forces arrested the demonstrators. Later in the round, a 278-page PGA Championship program, water, and a golf ball were tossed at Player in separate incidents, with security rushing to apprehend the demonstrators. Through it all, Player somehow focused and finished second to Raymond Floyd on Sunday.

Two years later, during the 1971 U.S. Open at Merion near Philadelphia, Player would be heckled by a couple of Black spectators in the first round and had to be accompanied by a uniformed police officer for the remainder of the tournament.

So, you could picture the tension around Gary Player during these trying times. Here was a small, unbelievably physically fit man who could be billed the Jack LaLanne of golf. Player stayed in the condition of a lightweight boxer by doing push-ups and sit-ups and even tried weight lifting, long considered a no-no for golfers, long before the current craze of hitting the gym before and after a round of golf. Player also traditionally wore black to bring attention to his golf game, differing distinctly in dress from the usually placid grays and whites of 1960s golf fashion. He wore black because his father told him to differentiate himself from the norm. Player's favorite cowboy, Richard Boone as Paladin in the 1950s Western TV series *Have Gun—Will Travel*, wore an all-black getup. Player also silently figured that by wearing the dark color in the heat he could draw power from the sun. There was no symbolic gesture toward his home country, whatsoever.

But it was also ironic that Player regularly had a Black caddie, both at the Masters, which made its all-Black caddie corps mandatory, and during regular play elsewhere in the world. Alfred "Rabbit" Dyer, a tall, gangly Black man, was Player's right-hand man just about everywhere but the Masters. Rabbit wore colorful clothing, outlandish hats, and dark glasses and was an intimidating presence beside the much-shorter Player.

By the middle of 1971, Player was breaking new ground for his stance on racial efforts. In June, Player offered Lee Elder, the top Black American golfer of the day, an invitation to visit South Africa and play in the South African PGA Championship. After some deliberation about the specifics of the visit, Elder accepted and played in the December event, opening the doors for many South African Black golfers to participate in their national tournaments. The participation would lead Player to lobby former Masters champions in early 1972 to issue an invitation to Elder as the first Black Masters invitee. Player found out from 1959 Masters champion Art Wall that the former champions' invite was canceled a few years prior. Player pulled for Elder to win a PGA Tour event and earn a Masters spot (he did three years later in 1975) and told the Associated Press in March 1972 that "Charlie Sifford would have been in the Masters years ago had qualifications been as they are today."

Still, Player's ties to his homeland were placed in the spotlight as the 1970s began.

Security for Player was tightened for the 1970 season. A trench-coated security guard was scheduled to hover around Player during his season debut at the PGA Tour stop in Miami at Doral Resort and Spa the first week in March, less than two months before the Masters. But Player withdrew just before the start of the tournament, leaving Nipper without a job for the week.

Nipper hung around Doral, waiting for the trip to Orlando for the next week's Tour event. One day while sitting around the putting green with a few other caddies, a large Black man with a beard approached.

"You caddie for Gary Player?" the man asked quietly.

"Yes. That's me," Nipper responded with his head down as he gazed at the putting green.

"You're Ernest Nipper. Well, you don't want to caddie for that man," the stranger shot back.

"Aw, man, the hell with you," Nipper said as he looked up with an angry glance.

The man paused, then reached into his pocket and quickly showed Nipper a silver handgun. He knew the name of Nipper's wife and son, his home address in Augusta, and many of his family and friends.

Nipper didn't want any trouble. Normally a nervous man while caddying, he became fearful off the course for the first time.

"Let me caddie for him one more time," Nipper said. "I can't just drop his bag now."

The man nodded slowly and said, "I'll see you again," as he walked off.

Nipper kept the confrontation a secret at first. He worked for Elder the next week in the Citrus Open Invitational in Orlando since Player didn't enter. Then Nipper was back on Player's bag March 12–15 at the Monsanto Open Invitational in Pensacola, Florida. Walking down the second fairway in the first round, he broke the news to Player about the Doral incident and that he wanted to change jobs.

"What will we tell the press?" Player asked.

"Just tell 'em we couldn't get along," Nipper said.

Player did more than that. He mentioned the incident to a few other people, and word of Nipper's concerns made it into *Life* magazine. Nipper became more nervous than ever and jumped to Chi Chi Rodriguez's bag despite urges by Player to stay with him.

Player won the Greater Greensboro Open three weeks later on April 5, the week before the Masters, as Rodriguez and Nipper placed in a tie for eighth. Player's game was in gear, and he wanted Nipper back with him for a run at a second green jacket. Nipper considered it.

"When I got to Augusta, the people at the tournament called me up and brought me to Ike's Cottage," Nipper recalled. "These FBI guys were there in this room. They said, 'Look at these pictures.' The first picture was of the guy who pulled the gun on me. They said these were some militants, some Black

Panthers, who they were keeping an eye on. 'Are any of these faces familiar?' they asked. There was no way I was going to say anything. I wasn't worried about me. I was worried about my wife and baby. All I said when I got done looking at those pictures was, 'I don't see him.'"

There were stronger talks of protesting Player at Augusta National that spring. Player met with Masters officials behind closed doors a couple times, once after shooting a 67 in Monday's practice round.

"I have no comment," Player said when he emerged from the meeting in the clubhouse. "I think it would be better if this whole thing were dropped. I am not mad at anybody. I love everybody regardless of race or religion."

Nipper opted to caddie for Rodriguez that week after viewing the photos. For years, Nipper had met Player in Florida during the weeks preceding the Masters to prepare for the first major championship of the year. Without his crutch, Player leaned on a young, inexperienced Carl Jackson.

"The club officials didn't tell me too much about what was going on," Jackson said. "I was twenty-one or twenty-two, and I wasn't paying too much attention to the newspaper accounts. Rumor was that Nipper got some death threats and that really scared him. Pretty soon, I started to pick up on things. We had our own Secret Service–like guy walking by my side, especially during the practice rounds. He told me that even when I didn't see him, he would be there. We went through the whole tournament like that."

But it was a successful relationship, particularly when Jackson gained Player's trust. Despite the presence of five plainclothes officers and three uniformed Pinkerton guards at one time, Player was a strong contender. At first, Player told Jackson that he would club himself and read his own putts. After Jackson volunteered some suggestions in the practice round, Player gave in and utilized Jackson's input during the tournament. A bogey on the seventy-second hole kept Player out of the Billy Casper–Gene Littler playoff.

Nipper would never caddie in the Masters again. He worked for Rodriguez on Tour until later in 1970 but didn't find it "very profitable." He chose to move to New York, where he had family, and enter private business, the details of which he would not disclose, never to caddie again. He retired in the Bronx in his late sixties and married for a second time, with six adopted children and thirteen total. Nipper died in 2018.

With Nipper departed and Jackson assigned to work for Charlie Coe in 1971, on came McCoy. The relationship with McCoy lasted for more than

Caddie Eddie "E. B." McCoy (left) and Gary Player, pictured in 1981, teamed up to win two Masters titles, in 1974 and 1978. *Masters Historic Imagery/Getty Images*

twenty years, until 1992, with McCoy toting some for Player on the Senior PGA Tour.

"The caddie I have working for me this week was with me at Augusta when I won the Masters in 1978," Player told the Associated Press in 1992 at the Digital Seniors Classic in Massachusetts. "I looked at him and I thought to myself, 'What was I doing when he caddied for me then?' And it all started to click in my head."

When Dyer made his only two trips to work for Player at Augusta National in the early 1990s, Player made sure that McCoy had a bag, working for David Frost, a young South African star. McCoy worked for Frost through 1994 and passed away at age seventy-one in 2013.

The Player-McCoy duo took their first title in 1974, thanks to one of Player's greatest shots ever. Leading by one stroke as they walked to Player's tee shot on the par-4 seventeenth, the pre-shot thoughts weren't good. The straightaway par-4 hole with the difficult green had always been a thorn in Player's side.

"Eddie, in all the years I've played here, I don't think I've hit this green six times," Player remarked as they started at the approach shot from just under 150 yards.

Faced with a 9-iron approach shot to the usual right-side pin placement, Player hit his shot and almost immediately put the club back in the bag and began to walk toward the green.

"No, I didn't look," Player said. "I asked Eddie, 'Do you think we're going to putt this one?'"

He almost didn't have to, as the ball stopped within inches of the cup on the way to his second Masters title.

Player's reliance on his caddies in his Masters victories stood in contrast to the controversial issues he confronted during the socially active 1960s and 1970s.

"The caddies in the U.S. Open don't mean much," Player said in 1974. "They usually give you a young boy, so you won't ask him for information. The British Open is about the same thing. In the PGA, you also get young caddies.

"But in this tournament, the majority of the caddies live here. Eddie lives here and knows the greens well. Caddies in the Masters play a more important role than any major tournament."

Gary Player can attest to that.

1

Cricket

In every Masters Tournament victory, there is a key swing thought, a lucky charm or a moment that puts the player at ease, a simple antidote to get rid of the jitters or convince the player that this is his week.

For Charles Coody, the 1971 Masters brought the usual assortment of superstitions: his favorite sweet potato biscuits, a pair of lucky old green trousers, and an English halfpenny that his eight-year-old daughter had given him to mark his ball. But more than anything, the path to the green jacket was paved by one Walter Pritchett, better known in caddie circles as "Cricket."

Cricket worked occasionally for Coody at other events on the PGA Tour and was his caddie for the 1969 Masters when they almost won. But Coody, one stroke ahead with three holes to play that year, bogeyed in to allow George Archer to sneak in. Coody placed in a tie for fifth, two strokes back.

Cricket didn't come back to Augusta National in 1970. He deferred for a steady job as a bus driver in his hometown of Atlanta. Coody started out with another caddie in 1971, but that caddie and Coody didn't mesh.

"After a practice round on Sunday, I was walking through the parking lot, and there was Cricket," Coody remembered. "He had gotten off from his bus-driving job in Atlanta and was just looking for a bag. So, since they assigned caddies, I had to go down to the tournament office and really discuss the situation. I eventually convinced them to let Cricket work for me."

The everyday Augusta National caddies didn't care too much for an "outsider," albeit a former Augusta National regular, moving in on their turf for this one week. But Coody wanted his lucky charm.

Coody surprised many by taking the first-round lead with a 6-under-par 66. Nobody was more shocked than Cricket come the third round.

As the duo walked up the par-5 eighth fairway on Saturday, the possibility of a tense weekend loomed. Coody was in contention, vying with Jack

Nicklaus and Johnny Miller for the lead. But Cricket had other things on his mind.

"What time does the TV coverage start, Mr. Coody?" Cricket asked.

It seemed that Coody didn't hear.

"What hole does the TV start on?" Cricket came back again.

"Huh? I don't know," Coody muttered in his slow Texas drawl, then paused and looked at Cricket. "Why do you need to know that?"

There was another moment of silence as Cricket pondered Coody's question.

"Well, I told my boss in Atlanta that I needed time off to go visit my sick grandmother in Houston," Cricket said rather sheepishly.

"To be honest . . . I didn't expect that you would play this well."

That broke the ice. Coody laughed all the way to the green and couldn't escape the thoughts of his caddie ducking his regular payday. As the back nine came during each weekend round, Coody was reminded again and again of Cricket's secret identity. As the players teed off the eleventh hole, the caddies got ahead of the players and waited for them to walk from the tee set back in the woods. Cricket would appear from the right of the fairway in "his disguise," a small green-and-white Masters golf towel that he had acquired on the range before the Saturday round began. He had taken the towel off Coody's bag and draped it over his head under his Masters caddie cap to hide from the CBS-TV cameras. All you could see were his wire-rimmed glasses and his nose poking out. Coody laughed out loud as the team viewed the second shot on the long par-4 eleventh, one of the course's most difficult holes.

"It looked like I had some kind of Arabian caddying for me," Coody said. "It kept me from worrying about Nicklaus and Miller all the time."

Coody, tied with Nicklaus to begin the final round, fashioned a closing 2-under-par 70 to beat Nicklaus and Miller by two strokes for his only major championship. This time, with Cricket urging him on by reminding him that three final pars would win the tournament, Coody birdied the par-3 sixteenth, the place where his trouble began two years before.

After the win, where Coody pocketed twenty-five thousand dollars, Cricket was ready to get back behind the wheel of his bus on Monday morning in Atlanta. As he innocently strolled into the bus office, his supervisor peered over the counter with a big smile.

Caddie Walter "Cricket" Pritchett (right) and Charles Coody teamed up to win the 1971 Masters. Cricket kept Coody loose by wearing a towel over his head on the back nine to hide from the TV cameras and his Atlanta bus company boss.
Masters Historic Imagery/Getty Images

"You had a nice week, didn't you Cricket?" the supervisor said with a laugh. "Hope your grandmother didn't miss you."

Cricket died in December 2018 at age seventy-five while playing golf in Huntsville, Alabama. Coody, eighty-five, attended his fifty-second consecutive Masters Champions dinner in 2023, never missing one since his 1971 win when his caddie all but stole the show.

1

Pete

Here are the words used to describe Willie Peterson, Jack Nicklaus's right-hand man in five of his six Masters victories: character, luck, hustle. These descriptions come from his peers in the Augusta National caddie ranks, his former boss, other players, his ex-wife, and his daughter.

Study these words carefully and you can quickly figure there could be a double meaning here. Did Peterson have character or was he simply a character? Was he a good-luck charm or just purely lucky to fall into a position of prominence among the famed Augusta National caddies? Did he prepare intensely to caddie, thereby earning a reputation as someone who hustled and worked extremely hard, or was he an out-and-out hustler, a man looking to make an extra buck in any way possible?

Peterson was truly a man of two faces, someone who could frustrate you with his penchant for being mischievous, yet also more often make you smile because of his bodacious attitude and good heart.

To a person, when you ask those associated with Peterson to assess his life and standing as a caddie, a smile creeps over their faces. Many shake their heads in memory of the tall tales about the man many simply called "Pete" or "Bro," the man who won more Masters titles (five, tied with Pappy Stokes) on one bag than anyone.

But rest assured, Peterson was the man who made Nicklaus tick at the Masters. He didn't pull many clubs or read putts, but he was a vital cog in Jack's first five Masters titles.

"Willie was always a character, a good guy, I enjoyed having him work for me," Nicklaus said. "Outside of that, every time I came here, he always said we [Nicklaus and company] had garnished his wages. Man, he was always in trouble, too, always in trouble. But he was fine. He was a great part of five of my six Masters titles."

Right away, you could see what made Peterson the most demonstrative caddie to ever loop in the Masters. Before play even started, there was Willie, full of himself, talking it up, pushing "Mr. Jack" as the out-and-out favorite, patting his man on the back to get him stoked for the round. To draw a parallel in another sport, Peterson was cornerman Drew "Bundini" Brown, in the entourage of the great heavyweight boxer Muhammad Ali, loudmouthed, noticeable, and supremely confident.

Peterson's calling card on the course was flamboyance. There were the celebratory leaps, kicks, and fist pumps when Nicklaus was charging. He carried a towel over his shoulder on most occasions and would whip it off to sweep toward the ground matador-like when a promising putt was approaching the cup. From time to time, Willie would sprawl on the ground to read a putt. He chattered from shot to shot like an infielder goading the batter in baseball. He would occasionally salute the gallery when Nicklaus made a long putt.

Just about any picture you see of Nicklaus on the way to victory in 1963, 1965, 1966, 1972, or 1975, there is Peterson nearby punching the air after a made putt, usually with the towel in hand. See the cover of the April 21, 1972, issue of *Sports Illustrated*, with Peterson confidently sticking his right arm straight up with the index finger extended and a cigarette tightly clinched between his pursed lips, just as Nicklaus sinks another birdie putt. Peterson is in the foreground, Nicklaus in the background. Of the more than fifty *Sports Illustrated* covers through 2022 featuring the Masters, Peterson is the only Masters caddie to ever appear in such a prominent position on the cover. Jimmy Dickinson, Nicklaus's longtime caddie in the British Open; Bruce Edwards, Tom Watson's longtime sideman; and Steve Williams, Tiger Woods's caddie, are the only other caddies ever to appear on any *SI* cover involving golf. But they were secondary figures in the cover images.

That he was the sidekick to the slow-paced, stoic, tunnel-visioned Nicklaus made for a diverse tandem. In contrast, Nicklaus's big rival of the 1960s, Arnold Palmer, was more like Peterson, outgoing and emotional on the course, and his caddie, Nathaniel "Iron Man" Avery, played the quiet, pensive role.

Nicklaus shared possibly his single most famous moment with Peterson.

It was Sunday, April 13, 1975, and the duel was on late in the back nine. Tom Weiskopf and Johnny Miller were on Jack's heels in what has been billed as the greatest Masters battle ever. They came to the par-3 sixteenth hole with Weiskopf holding a one-stroke lead over Nicklaus after the tall sweet-swinger birdied the par-5 fifteenth. Nicklaus chose to wait on the sixteenth green so that the upcoming roar from Weiskopf's putt on No. 15 wouldn't distract him.

"That is going to be evil music ringing in Nicklaus's ears,'" said CBS announcer Ben Wright from his tower position on the fifteenth hole after Weiskopf's successful birdie putt.

Weiskopf and Miller walked to the sixteenth tee, focusing across the pond as Nicklaus prepared for a long birdie putt. Play had been delayed when Nicklaus's playing partner, Tom Watson, hit two tee shots in the pond on the course's final par-3 hole. Wright and his British broadcasting partner, Henry Longhurst, were in the middle of one of the most historic calls in golf history.

Nicklaus faced a forty-foot birdie putt from the front left of the green, on the bottom tier, up through the long shadows of the tall pines late on Sunday afternoon, to a hole set on the top right shelf. It was a difficult two-putt at best. If the ball took the least bit of a turn to the left, it could filter down the bottom left portion of the green, still forty or so feet away. Willie tended the pin as Nicklaus hunched down over his putt and studied the line. Finally, he gave the ball a hard smack with his George Low–brand putter. As the ball rolled up the slope to the second tier, Willie began motioning the ball home, then started hopping up and down behind the hole as he pulled the flag and the ball fell in. Nicklaus, putter held high, charged around the lower tier of the green. The scene stirred legendary golf writer Dan Jenkins to write "it made Nicklaus and his caddie, Willie Peterson, resemble Fred Astaire and Ginger Rogers."

"I think that's one of the greatest putts I've ever seen in my life," Longhurst remarked on CBS from his tower behind the sixteenth green. Then there was a pause as the camera focused on the tee box. "Weiskopf has to take it this time having dished it out on the hole before."

Weiskopf, on the tee with the honor, looked as if he had seen a ghost and yanked his tee shot left, took three to get down, and fell one stroke behind Nicklaus, who steered the victory home.

"I was always afraid sometime that Willie was gonna hit the ball with that towel because he got so excited," Nicklaus said. "He would be sitting there waving the ball in the hole, and all I could think about was, 'Watch out!'

"Willie was a little more animated than me. You never knew what Willie was gonna do. He was a piece of work."

Another routine depicts the sheer cockiness that made Peterson the perfect fit for Nicklaus, the winningest major championship (eighteen professional, twenty including two U.S. Amateurs) and Masters golfer of all time.

Nicklaus would warm up on the driving range at Augusta National and then depart for the putting green to get his short game in gear before teeing off. Willie, with a sense that Nicklaus's game was primed, would leave the range and sprint down the hill toward the caddie shack, which was then stationed in the vicinity of where the main entrance corridor to the course is now located.

Willie would poke his head into where the caddies were lounging around, some shooting pool or playing cards, waiting for their respective tee times, and strike up a bold wager.

"Bet ya my man Mr. Jack doesn't make a bogey today," Willie would rattle off. "Anybody want some of that?"

Like a wildfire had hit the caddie house, Peterson recorded bets all over the place. He'd chime in with wagers for 69 or lower, nine-hole scores or high/low on how many birdies Jack would make that day.

Then he would continue his route to the other side of the clubhouse and catch up with Nicklaus at the putting green behind the first tee.

"Pappy, I hope you have a 68 and we have a red-hot 67," he told legendary caddie Willie "Pappy" Stokes in 1965 with the press corps listening. "If we get that 67, y'all can come back to talk to me, and I'll tell you what's gonna happen the rest of the week."

"He was the only guy who made those types of bets," said Bennie Hatcher, a veteran caddie who began working at Augusta National in the early 1960s. "That was a foolish bet there to say his man would shoot in the 60s. He'd bet four or five people and bet them fifty dollars apiece. Naw, he never won. You don't make those kinds of bets."

Willie may have lost a slew of wagers in the caddie house, but he loved every minute of being the center of attention. Maybe it's best to explain Willie Peterson by simply recalling how he developed this attitude.

Born in 1932, Willie was the second of five children in the Peterson household. The Petersons weren't poor—the reason some Black kids in those days

Caddie Willie Peterson (right) with Jack Nicklaus in 1961 during
one of the first years they worked together. Peterson won a
record-tying five times with Nicklaus, appeared on the cover of
Sports Illustrated, and was one of the more flamboyant caddies in
Masters history. *Masters Historic Imagery/Getty Images*

turned to caddying to earn a wage. Willie's parents, Willie Peterson Sr. and
his wife, Josephine, were in the funeral home business. Haynes and Peterson Funeral Home was one of Augusta's first Black-owned funeral homes, of
which Willie's grandfather was cofounder.

A young Willie just found it interesting to hang out with the personalities
at the caddie shack, first at Augusta Country Club, then at Augusta National.
He enjoyed the card games and the competition of caddying against others.
Stokes took him under his wing. Peterson was seventeen years old and a stu-

dent at Haines Normal Industrial Institute when he started caddying in the Masters in 1949, for a different player every year.

By the early 1950s, Peterson was serving a stint in the United States Air Force. After a four-year term, it was back to Augusta and seemingly to a career in the funeral home business. An aunt, Annie Peterson, wanted Willie to succeed her in the family business, but Willie had other things in mind than dealing with dead bodies. While in the air force, he had developed a love of cooking, a talent he would take to a job in the kitchen at Augusta's University Hospital, later as a short-order cook at a restaurant in New York and during Masters week in Augusta for various clients. Caddying was his main source of income, but it didn't hurt to have alternatives.

Willie also had his eyes on fifteen-year-old Rosemary Allen, eight years his junior.

"He just started coming around, and he was one of the top eligible bachelors in the area," Rosemary said. "He was a very real, open person. Very freehearted. Always smiling. A very, very, very aggressive person. Very positive. He could win you over like that."

The Petersons were married in 1955 and worked side by side in the kitchen at University Hospital. They went on to have six children over the next eleven years. Willie caddied and worked at the hospital.

Then, in 1960, Peterson struck second-hand gold.

Nicklaus was a hotshot amateur that year in his second Masters start, coming to Augusta as the U.S. Amateur champion. The chubby Ohio State University student hit the ball a mile, but the short game was an issue in 1959 when Nicklaus hit thirty-one greens in regulation during the first two rounds but was confounded by the fast greens as he totaled eight three-putts and missed the cut by one stroke in his Masters debut. He already had a reputation as an intense worker, both on the range and the course. Caddies would have to spend their day shagging balls on the range, walking eighteen holes, working on the putting green, and then back to the range to end the day. The caddies weren't lined up to work for him. Pappy Stokes was scheduled to give Nicklaus a try in 1959 but declined, leaving the bag in the hands of a caddie from Atlanta nicknamed Pon, according to Nicklaus.

"Jack Nicklaus was too slow for me," Pappy recalled. "I wanted somebody who would hit the ball and walk. I said, 'Pete, I'm going to give him to you.' Jack was paying good money, but he'd go out there at seven in the morning and come back at night. He'd stay out there all day on the practice field. I said, 'Man, you walked my legs off.'"

With input from his father, Charlie, and caddie master Freddie Bennett, Nicklaus was paired with Peterson, resulting in a share of the 1960 Masters' Low Amateur honors with Billy Joe Patton. This was the first indication that good luck followed the caddie who experienced success with Nicklaus.

"Freddie [Bennett] looked at the room of caddies and asked, 'Is there anybody here who would like to caddie for Jack Nicklaus?'" Nicklaus recalled. "And Willie Peterson raised his hand, and he said, 'I'm not afraid of working.'"

Nicklaus wasn't looking for a caddie who could continuously club him or read his putts, just an assistant to be there in a time of need. Angelo Argea, Nicklaus's regular caddie on the PGA Tour for years, offered that characteristic, as did Dickinson, the Scotsman who loyally carried for Jack in the British Open during the 1960s and into the 1970s.

Argea—full name Angelo George Argeropoulos—was a cab driver and caddie in Las Vegas in 1963 when he was picked by the tournament caddie master to work for Nicklaus, without Jack's approval, at the Bob Hope Desert Classic in Palm Springs, California. Angelo's long, wiry, and wild crop of silver hair, thick mustache, dark complexion, and talkative nature drew comparisons to a Greek playboy, in stark contrast to the all-American image of Nicklaus's blond hair, fair complexion, and chunky build. But Jack won that Hope Desert Classic in a playoff with Gary Player, came to Vegas a few months later for the Tournament of Champions, and again in the fall for the Sahara Invitational. He captured the Desert Triple, each time with Angelo on the bag. So began a nearly twenty-year week-to-week relationship on Tour, except, of course, for the Masters, which Angelo never worked because of the ban on outside caddies.

But Jack had Willie at Augusta before he even met Angelo.

"All that I ask is a caddie be dependable," Nicklaus said in 1973. "As long as he's there on time to carry the bag, that's all I'm asking. That's absolutely the truth. Never has he hit any shots nor has he picked a club.

"I'm not saying a thing against Willie as a caddie. He gives me tremendous moral support....I wouldn't trade him for a million dollars."

Peterson was the self-assured partner who could help with the little things. For instance, the twenty-three-year-old Nicklaus was on the way to the eighteenth green in the third round of his first Masters title in 1963, but Nicklaus couldn't figure out his standing with a quick glance at the big scoreboard to the right of the final green. Nicklaus is partly red-green color blind and couldn't make out the scoring designations from more than one hundred yards. He squinted to make out the green numerals that reflected over-par scores or the red ones that showed under-par scoring, two innovations that the Masters debuted to the golf world in the early '60s. Nicklaus was 2-under par as he finished the round and a passel of players were at 1-over at the time, but Nicklaus didn't know his leading margin.

"Willie, there's a lot of ones up there," Nicklaus said. "How many of them are red?"

"Just you, boss," Peterson answered. "Those others are all green numbers."

In 1965, Nicklaus came to the seventeenth hole in the final round with a humongous lead. He was on the way to a record 17-under-par total and a nine-stroke victory margin. But the approach shot on the short par-4 had the tandem baffled. Nicklaus wanted to hit 9-iron, and Peterson suggested a wedge.

"I'll hit it soft," Nicklaus said as Willie frowned.

Nicklaus proceeded to land his second shot within a foot for a tap-in birdie. Then he laughed, reached over, and pulled the bill of Willie's green baseball cap down over his caddie's eyes.

It was during this period that Jack was charting the golf courses he played by yardage, a novel idea. By the 1963 Masters, Nicklaus carried a small notebook for reference on various course landmarks that indicated distances to driving areas or greens. He was believed to be the first player to use such a system in a major championship. The course management Nicklaus became so famous for was already in process.

"This man don't miss a trick," Peterson said in 1970. "He walks off the course several times and puts down notes. When he pulls a club out, I don't question him. I know he is right."

In the early 1960s, Nicklaus was paired with Don January as they played the par-5 thirteenth hole. January had outdriven Nicklaus by 40 yards, leaving the thin Texan 190 yards to the green. Nicklaus, needing 230 yards to clear the creek that guards the green, debated with Peterson about strategy.

"I heard Willie tell Jack he didn't think he could get there [in two shots]," said Beard, January's caddie for that day before becoming famous by carrying Fuzzy Zoeller's winning bag in his 1979 triumph. "Jack said, 'Gimme my 3-wood, I can hit it as far as I want to,' and he blistered it. It landed on the green. January turned around to me and said, 'He's going to run us all off the Tour,' which is basically what he did."

Peterson was not the great green reader like Carl Jackson or the expert course analyst like Pappy Stokes. Testimony to this comes in the fact that Bobby Mitchell used Peterson on his bag regularly on the PGA Tour in the early 1970s, and David Graham hired Peterson for the 1979 PGA Championship, both solely because they were steadfast in their desire to play the course without input, just like Jack. Both won with Peterson on their bags. He was the ultimate motivator and comedic sidekick.

"Willie Peterson was just right for Jack Nicklaus," said Carl Jackson. "Nicklaus can do his own caddying. But Peterson was a good pep man. He was a good 'pat you on the back and let's go' man. He was good for Jack Nicklaus."

"Willie Peterson was a bag toter, but Jack Nicklaus liked him," Pappy said.

Hatcher said that "Peterson was just pure lucky" to get Nicklaus. But that luck transformed into a twenty-four-year relationship that carried Peterson all over the world.

"I remember when I first got Mr. Jack, I knew I had a winner," Peterson said in the early 1970s. "I figured he'd win ten Masters before he was through. I considered myself lucky—I had sort of an annuity."

Peterson gave Nicklaus the touch of humor that occasionally broke the intense four hours of work during a Masters round. He once told Nicklaus, "Mr. Jack, I need to have more than anyone's ever been paid."

When Nicklaus arrived at the practice range at midday Sunday before the final round of the 1975 Masters, Peterson was waiting there with Jack's big, green MacGregor golf bag. But he wasn't his usual chatty self. He just stared at Nicklaus's feet.

"I still had my street shoes on," Nicklaus said. "Willie just cracked, 'Did you forget something boss?'"

He also served as a buffer for some of the negative feedback from Arnie's Army, which resented the fact that this "fat" kid from Ohio had stolen the spotlight from their hero. They labeled the Nicklaus of the 1960s with unfavorable nicknames such as "Blobbo," "Ohio Fats," "Baby Beef," and the more familiar "Fat Jack." Willie's position when a gallery member or two would voice some displeasure was to "just smile and keep on fighting."

Unlike his caddie comrades, Willie also kept up with Jack. He arrived on time and stayed until the day was done. He would backpedal until he hit the bushes at the far end of the Augusta National practice range while shagging balls and watch as Nicklaus rocketed drives over his head into Washington Road, with the gallery *ooh*ing and *aah*ing and other Masters participants stopping their warm-up sessions to watch the display. Willie would play up the scene some 275 yards into the distance by whirling his towel over his head, like an umpire signaling to circle the bases for a home run.

Like Iron Man just a few years before him, Peterson became a celebrity in Augusta's Black community. That spilled over to the white areas, too, particularly the restaurants and bars that were building up along Washington Road in the late 1960s and 1970s. Most establishments prominently displayed Masters memorabilia, and Jack was always there, more times than not with Willie right by his side in the photographs.

But his big-man-about-town persona didn't always translate into a happy home life.

In April 1966, Nicklaus was the defending champion in the Masters. As was his normal practice, Willie would take a bag lunch packed by Rosemary and then pick up his brother Godfrey, who also caddied at Augusta National, on the way to the course.

It was the Monday of Masters week and the children were out of school for spring break. By the time Willie's car disappeared down the street bound for Augusta National, Rosemary was packing up the family, and they bolted out of town for New York. She was tired of Willie's extreme jealousy and his penchant for staying out too late, usually gambling or hustling, and wasting the money he had earned while caddying for Nicklaus over the early part of the 1960s. He provided clothes and food for the children and moved them away from the questionable surroundings of Dogwood Terrace, a low-income housing development in inner-city Augusta, but she thought they could do much better. Rosemary figured that with Willie working for Nicklaus in the Masters that week, it would be the opportune time to leave. Willie wouldn't follow them.

"I got married so young, and he was good to me," Rosemary said. "I just felt like we were missing out on a lot of things. I wanted something different. So, I decided we should move on. He eventually accepted that. And we both moved on."

In tow were the six children, who would see their father off and on over the next two decades. Rosemary remarried to Arthur Marshall Sr., a military man, and eventually came back to Augusta. Willie moved to Savannah for a period, where he started a relationship with another woman. At one point, the children didn't see their father for five or six years when they moved to Germany in the 1970s. They once stumbled on a *Newsweek* magazine on the newsstands in Europe that had a story on the Masters. Prominently pictured was Nicklaus with Willie right by his side.

Along the way, tragedy struck two of the older children. Tyrone, the oldest boy, was stationed in the army at Fort Bragg, North Carolina. While playing in a basketball game on base in 1974, he passed out and died from a heart defect. Pondra, the oldest daughter, died at age forty in 1997 of an aneurism.

Most prominently, daughter Vanessa's relationship with her father speaks volumes about the feelings in the young Black community of the 1970s toward the Masters. By the time she had returned to Augusta at age sixteen in the mid-1970s, Vanessa had seen the world through her stepfather's frequent moves as a military man. A few years later, she was prepared to go off to college at Georgia Southern University in nearby Statesboro, Georgia. The Black Power movement and race riots of the 1960s in the South had hit home hard for her generation.

"Being an educated woman and having traveled the world, I have a very, very strong sense of worth," Vanessa said. "It took me some time to understand that my parents came from a different time. I just didn't think being a caddie was such a thing I'd want to brag about. My dad participated and worked for a club where initially Blacks couldn't even play golf there. I think now about all the attention Augusta National is getting about not having a woman member. It took such a long time for a Black man to play there and become a member there. Daddy worked there since the 1950s. I got a sense he was in a situation where, 'You can work for us, but you can't work beside us.'

"Daddy was all hot and heavy about how great golf and caddying was. I didn't think caddies were really that important, that they didn't contribute much. I thought, 'How can you be proud of carrying a real big bag of golf clubs around for a guy?' I didn't realize they really contribute to the player. I just said I'm moving on to better things."

Willie encouraged his daughter to learn how to play the game. He even tried to introduce her to Nicklaus and get her a job with his vastly expanding company. But she went her own way. She married young also, in college, and began a life of her own as Vanessa Peterson-Fox.

About this same time, Willie's relationship on the course with Nicklaus was near its end. Willie closed in on age fifty in the early 1980s, had put on a lot of weight, and smoked too many cigarettes. While Jack had transformed from "Blobbo" to a sleek, stylish golfer in the 1970s, Willie morphed from a sturdy, athletic man into a heavyset, nearsighted, middle-aged caddie. When outside caddies were allowed to work the 1983 Masters, most players opted to bring their own guys. Nicklaus didn't, keeping Willie on his bag. Nicklaus even opted to have Willie work the 1982 PGA Championship at Southern Hills in Tulsa, Oklahoma, where Nicklaus finished in a tie for sixteenth. But, unfortunately, the 1983 Masters was cut short when Nicklaus suffered a back injury and had to withdraw before the second round. He tried to tee it up but couldn't make a full swing.

When Nicklaus officially withdrew from that Masters, Willie was sitting on the front porch of Augusta National's clubhouse, virtually hugging Jack's golf bag. He was near tears.

"Playing bad doesn't make me sad," Willie said. "I'm more sad when anything happens to him. Anything happens to him, happens to me. I've been around him for twenty-five years. I feel like part of me left, too. Fact, it is."

It was the last Masters for the team of Jack and Willie. Michael Downey was on Nicklaus's bag in 1984. Nicklaus tried to keep Willie in the fold by bringing him to Florida to work in various Nicklaus golf holdings, first as the caddie master at the new Loxahatchee Golf Club in Jupiter, Florida, in 1985 and 1986. But Willie was his old self, getting into trouble with what one person said was "taking bribes." Things didn't work out well at a couple other stops within the Nicklaus empire either. Willie even tried to caddie there some but suffered a severely pinched nerve in his back in the process, an injury that forced him to sleep on the floor or sitting up for much of the rest of his life.

Willie came back to Augusta briefly after the failure in Florida. His last real connection with Nicklaus occurred in 1986. He was watching the final round of the Masters on television with Vanessa, since divorced and living in Augusta, when Nicklaus began to charge. Willie went to Augusta National and watched some of the back nine.

"If he shoots 30 [on the back nine], they can hang it up," Peterson said to no one as he watched Jack play Amen Corner that Sunday. Sure enough, Jack shot that number and won by one stroke, at age forty-six. Willie Peterson, age fifty-three, had seemingly touched the sixth Masters title after guiding the first five.

From there, the rest of Willie Peterson's life is somewhat of a mystery. Augusta wasn't big enough to hold him. He got into financial trouble there and opted in the early 1990s to move to New York, where numerous relatives

Vanessa Peterson-Fox, the daughter of caddie Willie Peterson, experienced her father's caddying career from a distance, stayed in constant contact with him before his 1999 death, and interacted with Jack Nicklaus to place a marker on Willie's grave. *Courtesy of the Golf Channel*

resided. He moved into a building with mostly senior citizens. In search of work, he basically became a runner for a loan shark, an older white man who took a liking to Peterson. In a tight situation, this man probably could have put some serious pressure on his "clients," Peterson included, but Peterson's outgoing personality carried him through. Peterson ran the numbers, delivered money—whatever was necessary to make a living. New York's fast pace made his heartbeat faster but also probably got the best of him.

"My dad was a hustler," Vanessa said. "When I say a hustler, I mean he did whatever it took to make money, to survive. On the flip side, he was as sweethearted as he could be. He always said that if you had money in your hand and just hold it tight, nothing can go out, but guess what, nothing can come in either. He just lived. During his life, he never worried about savings. If my father had a thousand dollars and you were sitting in here and needed some of that badly, he would give it to you. I didn't understand, but that's the way he was. He was an ol' kook."

Willie's health deteriorated quickly in the mid-1990s. He was diagnosed with throat cancer, which prohibited him from speaking clearly. Vanessa had difficulty communicating with him via long-distance phone calls from Augusta, eventually learning his groans and squeaks as a form of language. By 1998, the cancer had spread to his lungs. Vanessa didn't realize the severity of the situation.

"I knew he was sick, but not that sick," Vanessa said. "It was a shock when he died."

Peterson died on March 20, 1999, in a New York apartment, at age sixty-six. He had discovered something that would defeat him—cancer. Vanessa got word from New York by phone.

What followed over the next few months was, in many ways, a catharsis for Vanessa. The girl who had scorned her father's profession realized what kind of pleasure and notoriety he had developed by simply toting a golf bag. She was the child with the closest relationship to her father and took the responsibility to give him a fitting burial.

Her first chore was to find her father's body. Over the phone, she called various New York City hospitals. Finally, she found him, two days after his death. At first, she thought about going to New York but then realized it was best to fly his body home. She asked her cousins not to touch anything in Willie's apartment in case there were old belongings or Masters memorabilia, but anything of value was gone.

The only problem was that Vanessa could not afford to pay the nearly one-thousand-dollar tab to get her father's body flown back to Augusta. Combine that with a myriad of other problems. Her son, born with a congenital heart defect, had recently undergone a fourth heart operation at age nine. Her job at a local department store, J. B. White, was an on-again, off-again proposition because of a recent buyout by Dillard's. Her stepfather had passed away from cancer eight months prior, and older sister Pondra and a grandmother died eighteen months before. To complicate matters, Peterson's life insurance policy had not been paid up.

What to do? Close friends suggested that she call Nicklaus, a man she had only met once years ago and just briefly. Unknown to Vanessa, when her older brother Tyrone died suddenly in 1974, Nicklaus sent a check for one thousand dollars. When Peterson became very ill in the late 1990s, Nicklaus sent a wheelchair to assist his former caddie. Those were just two of the known generous offerings. Twenty years later, Nicklaus stepped in again to help pay for a headstone on Peterson's grave in downtown Augusta in late 2020, a story documented by the Golf Channel.

"I was desperate, so I got on the phone and called this number," Vanessa

Caddie Willie Peterson is buried in Cedar Grove Cemetery in downtown Augusta, Georgia. *Photo by Ward Clayton*

recalled of her first call to Nicklaus upon Peterson's death. "I talked to Mr. Nicklaus's secretary, explained who I was and what had happened. They overnighted me a check for a thousand dollars. That just blew me away. This man didn't even know me, and Daddy worked for him years ago, yet he cared enough to send this money. We got him home."

With the recent burden of multiple deaths in the family, Vanessa wanted to celebrate her father's life instead of mourning again. "I was tired of death and dying. I wanted to remember my father with a smile on my face," Vanessa said. At the wake, held on March 27, 1999, at C. A. Reid Memorial Funeral Home, many of the old Augusta National caddies came to reminisce about Willie and their caddying days. Nicklaus sent a huge flower arrangement. They played a highlight tape, provided by the Golf Channel, of the 1975 Masters. Photos of Willie as a caddie were on display.

"I always had reservations about what Dad did because I didn't live here," Vanessa said. "But these people came to that wake, people who had worked with him, and went on and on about him. I haven't run into one person who didn't like him. He had a great personality."

The effect of those last rites made a big impact on Vanessa and Russell, the youngest Peterson.

Just two years old when Rosemary left town with the children in 1966,

Russell's only impression of his father's trade was once seeing a huge bag of money after a Nicklaus Masters victory. "That must be some kind of job," he thought. He takes after Willie in that he likes to cook and bears a strong physical resemblance to his late father. Russell worked as a booking agent who aimed to bring musical acts to the Augusta area. He was previously a real estate agent in Augusta and made attempts to organize a fundraising golf tournament for the old caddies at Augusta National. He met with a group of them a few times and wanted to unveil the program only when it was ready to be a big deal, not just a piecemeal arrangement.

"Those guys deserve something like this," Russell said. "They gave their lives to caddie at Augusta National."

Nearly one year after her father's death, Vanessa was driving down Washington Road and saw some Masters memorabilia for sale at a roadside stand. For some reason, she stopped to look. There was a huge painting of the 1975 Masters, with (as usual) Willie Peterson smack dab in the middle of the action. The cost: $1,500.

"I felt like crying right then," she said. "I couldn't afford that. I never knew his worth and never gave him credit for what he did. On some level, Daddy used to brag, just like my ex-husband used to brag, about catching a big fish. I used to just say, 'Yeah right.' It just dawned on me when I saw that picture that my dad was really a part of something great."

Yes, Willie Peterson was a character. And he had character, too.

Willie Beats Jack

About the only person who could beat Nicklaus in 1972 was somebody with Peterson on the bag.

Jack was thirty-two, considerably slimmed down from his previous weight, and in his prime, winning seven times and placing second four times in twenty starts in 1972 and nearly capturing the Grand Slam after winning the Masters and U.S. Open and then finishing second to Lee Trevino at the British Open. It was Nicklaus's second of four consecutive years as the leading money winner on the PGA Tour and the second of five years that he earned PGA of America Player of the Year honors. Nicklaus ruled golf.

So it was no surprise that Jack won the '72 Masters—the one that put Willie on the cover of *Sports Illustrated*. He coasted to the wire-to-wire victory, finishing at 2-under-par 286, the only man under par on an Augusta National course, which had extremely bumpy and unpredictable Bermuda grass greens that year because of infestation by Poa annua. It was Nicklaus's fourth Masters title, tying Arnold Palmer for the most in tournament history, and all came with Peterson by his side.

One player three back in a three-way tie for second was Bobby Mitchell, a journeyman pro from Danville, Virginia, who would be a blip on Nicklaus's radar screen a couple weeks later. Mitchell, playing in just his second Masters, might have finished a bit closer to Jack except that he played the testy par-3 twelfth hole in 5-over par during the tournament.

The twenty-nine-year-old Mitchell had quite an interesting story. He quit school in the tenth grade at age fifteen in 1958 because "I wasn't getting good grades and anyway I spent more time on the golf course than in the classroom." He immediately became an assistant pro at Danville Country Club, began playing in PGA Sectional events at age twenty-two, and then tried his wares on the PGA Tour in the late 1960s. He won the 1971 Cleveland Open Invitational, shooting 26-under-par 262 to win by seven strokes.

So Mitchell had game, even if he called himself golf's "Invisible Man."

"[CBS broadcaster] Ken Venturi said I'm the most underrated player on the Tour," Mitchell said in 1972. "Maybe I'm too plain. I don't throw my clubs. I don't wear colorful clothes."

As a gag late in 1971, he purchased a toupee to cover his balding head when he wasn't wearing his golf hat.

"I got to liking it, and it felt good, so I just leave it on all the time now," Mitchell said then. "I think it looks good."

But most importantly he had Nicklaus's caddie. Peterson worked solely for Jack in the Masters but was employed by an assortment of pros during the rest of the Tour schedule over the years. Jack's regular caddie, Argea, worked virtually everywhere else where outside caddies were allowed.

"I can't remember exactly when and where, but Willie just walked up to me on Tour one day late in 1971, and we started working together," Mitchell said. "I didn't have a regular caddie when I won at Cleveland. Then Willie and I worked together for the next two years.

"Willie was a good caddie, a real character. Let me just say he wasn't a quiet person. He was talking all the time. That was his way of doing things.

"I was the type of player who did his own work, I guess sort of like Jack did. All [Peterson] had to do was back up the yardage. I read my own putts. Basically, what he did was carry the bag and keep me loose. He didn't have a hard job."

The irony was that two weeks after finishing second to Nicklaus at the 1972 Masters, Mitchell had Peterson on his bag in the Tournament of Champions at La Costa Resort and Spa in Carlsbad, California. The tournament, for winners of Tour events for the previous calendar year, drew the elite of the sport to the ritzy Southern California resort.

As the final round came on April 23, Mitchell trailed Nicklaus by two strokes. Mitchell fired a 2-under-par 70 in the final round to catch Nicklaus at 8-under-par 280, forcing a sudden-death playoff.

"I didn't think anything about Willie working for Jack all that time," Mitchell said. "I had enough other stuff to think about playing against Jack."

On the first playoff hole, the par-3 seventeenth, Nicklaus pulled his tee shot into the left rough, and his second shot wouldn't hold the quick green. Mitchell ended the match quickly, sinking a twenty-foot birdie putt for the biggest win of his career and the biggest upset on Tour in years.

"Don't ever do that again," Barbara Nicklaus, Jack's wife, jokingly told Peterson after Mitchell's win. "If you need some money, come to me."

By 1973, Mitchell had lost his Tour exemption and the association with Peterson was no more.

"When you had a regular caddie then, you had to pay them a regular salary," Mitchell said. "When I wasn't playing regularly, that was too expensive. So he had to go find another regular job."

Willie and David at the PGA

Peterson's penchant for being an outwardly proud man was never more evident than in the 1979 PGA Championship at Oakland Hills Country Club in Birmingham, Michigan. Peterson becoming the only Augusta National–affiliated caddie to win in a major tournament other than the Masters is only a small part of the story that took place late that summer.

Australian David Graham chose the forty-seven-year-old Peterson, a five-time Masters winner on Nicklaus's bag, to caddie for him that week because, in large part, he wanted to closely emulate Nicklaus's self-guidance. Jack had become famous for calculating yardages, reading putts, and choosing clubs without relying on input from a caddie.

"It became a status thing to play like Jack did," Graham recalled in a March 2001 *Golf Digest* interview.

So here was Graham, age thirty-three, in the final round of his life at Oakland Hills, a course billed as "the Monster" by Ben Hogan during his 1951 U.S. Open victory there because of its extreme difficulty. Graham was near the end of a furious rally to come from four strokes behind third-round leader Rex Caldwell as he stood on the tee of the 459-yard, dogleg right par-4 eighteenth hole with a two-stroke lead over Ben Crenshaw. Graham was 7-under par for the day, cruising toward a major championship record-tying round of 63. To boot, a magazine offer of fifty thousand dollars for breaking the course record and another fifty thousand dollars for breaking the seventy-two-hole tournament record hung in the balance if Graham could just make a final par. The additional one hundred thousand dollars would exceed the sixty-thousand-dollar first-place prize.

With visions of the game's largest trophy, the Wannamaker Trophy, dancing in his head, Graham's drive sailed wildly to the right. Being like Jack had worked like a charm all week, so as Graham found his errant tee shot, he began to figure how many yards he had remaining from the unusual position in the right rough. Playing partners Jerry Pate and Caldwell were patient as Graham attempted to get his bearings. The converted par-5 usually required a driver and long iron to reach the green, but this was a completely different angle. As he walked toward the fairway, Graham couldn't clear the large gallery enough to locate a sprinkler head with a yardage remaining to the green stamped on the side that would indicate the distance for his second shot.

He walked back to his ball. Finally, he asked for Peterson's input.

"How far is it?" Graham blurted out as he studied the second shot.

Peterson quickly spouted off: "You haven't asked me one question all the way around. I don't know. Figure it out yourself."

"Excuse me?" was all that Graham could muster in response as he stared incredulously at his caddie.

Obviously shaken, he eventually pulled a 6-iron and blew the second shot over the green, then badly mishit a chip from the thick rough onto the fringe, chipped on in four, and missed a four-foot bogey putt to record a double bogey. Forget the record final round and bonus money, Graham settled for a 65 and was headed for a sudden-death playoff with Crenshaw, tied at 8-under-par 272.

Up charged Peterson as they left the final green.

"Don't worry, Boss, we'll get 'em in the playoff," a suddenly supportive Peterson offered.

"Don't even speak to me," a furious Graham said as he prepared to enter the scorer's tent. "The farther you stay away from me, the happier I'll be. Just carry the clubs."

Graham apparently was headed toward the biggest choke job in PGA Championship history. The gallery around the first tee for the playoff was soundly in Ben's corner. Crenshaw split the first fairway in the playoff, and Graham duck-hooked his drive. Graham was blocked from going for the green, had to lay up, then hit a poor chip to within twenty-five feet. Crenshaw made a standard two-putt par. But Graham miraculously holed the twenty-five-footer for par to extend the playoff.

On the par-5 second hole, Graham canned a ten-footer for birdie to stay alive as Crenshaw two-putted for birdie. Then, on the third extra hole, a par-3, after Crenshaw's approach found a bunker, Graham holed a four-foot birdie putt to win his first major title. A huge sigh of relief came to both player and caddie, although separately.

"If you watch the tape—you know how the caddies usually run and hug the player and do all of that kind of stuff?—you'll see a lot of apprehension before I put my arms around Willie," Graham said.

1

Jariah

I t's your first Masters Tournament, and you can get just one practice round
in at Augusta National. Only one month prior, at San Diego, you won for
the first time on the PGA Tour to earn a trip to Augusta.

What lies ahead for twenty-seven-year-old Frank Urban Zoeller Jr., better known as "Fuzzy"? Should he go ahead and reserve a Friday night flight
out of town from the 1979 Masters? Or just cherish how beautiful the flow-
ers are for a couple days?

Zoeller opted to put all his rookie trust in a caddie, Jariah Beard, a longtime caddie at Augusta National. He didn't have another choice.

"This is your course. Tell me what to hit and I'll hit it," Zoeller told Beard.

Beard grew up in the Sand Hills neighborhood and started caddying at age
eleven in the early 1950s, earning three dollars a day, a reward he hid in a coffee can under his front porch so that his parents wouldn't question him about
whether he was gambling or stealing. Prior to working for Zoeller, Beard
had caddied for veteran Don January since 1967. But Mike Shannon, one of
Augusta National's assistant professionals at the time and a future renowned
golf putting instructor, was a regular in Beard's foursome every Monday at
Forest Hills Golf Club. Shannon also was a roommate of Zoeller's at the University of Houston. He set them up before the tournament, in hopes that
Beard could give his friend some pointers.

When Beard reported to work on the Monday before Masters week, caddie master Freddie Bennett told Beard, "You don't have January anymore.
Your buddy Shannon got you a bag."

Bennett wouldn't reveal who it was until later in the day.

"What in the heck is a Fuzzy Zoeller? I don't know anything about him,"
Beard said.

Fuzzy, who earned his nickname from his initials (Frank Urban Zoeller),
was a laid-back pro from New Albany, Indiana, who loved to joke with the

gallery and whistle while he worked on the golf course. He had played most of his career with a painful back injury suffered as a high school sophomore on the basketball team in the mid-1960s in hoops-crazy Indiana. When he drove to the basket in a game, Zoeller jumped, had his legs cut out from under him, and came down smack dab on the back of his neck, suffering damage that would later require surgery. Since joining the PGA Tour in 1974, Zoeller had increasingly inched up the money list, topped by his five-stroke victory in the Andy Williams–San Diego Open Invitational in late January 1979, less than three months before the Masters.

He came to Augusta without his wife, Diane, who was at home expecting their first child within the next three weeks.

"I just like to play golf, and I think finishing fourth is better than fifth, and finishing fifteenth is better than sixteenth," Zoeller said early in the week.

Things worked out perfectly. Zoeller was never in the news and only within shouting distance of pacesetter Ed Sneed until the very end. The reason he was still in contention was Beard's input.

"He led me around like I was a blind man," Zoeller said years later. "That seeing-eye dog was great. He told me where to hit it and where not to hit it. He told me on the par-5s when to go for it in two shots and when to lay up. Those guys know.

"I was fortunate I was playing well at the time, and I was able to hit it where he told me to. I'm still trying to hit those damn areas, but the ball doesn't want to cooperate. It's the ball's fault, I'm convinced of that."

Zoeller started the final round at 6-under par, in a tie for fourth, six strokes behind Sneed. He was paired with Tom Watson in the next-to-last group of the day. "I was just trying to stay close to Watson, who's not a bad guy to stay close to," Zoeller said.

Fuzzy cruised around the course, seemingly nonchalant about the revered back nine at Augusta National on a Sunday. The biggest shot may have come on the 500-yard, par-5 fifteenth. Faced with a 235-yard 3-wood second shot into the wind, Zoeller wanted to lay up in front of the pond that guards the front of the green.

First off, know that Beard wasn't afraid of giving his opinion. In his Masters caddying debut as a sixteen-year-old in 1957, Beard worked for Bob Toski. On the twelfth hole in the second round, Toski asked Beard for his club selection on the tricky par-3, and the caddie offered a 6-iron. When playing partner Doug Sanders chose a 7-iron, Beard wavered. Toski pulled a 7-iron, hit his tee shot short into Rae's Creek, and missed the cut, first instituted that year, by one stroke.

"Don't ever let anyone influence you on what to do," Beard remembered Toski lecturing him after the round. "[Toski] just said to make up your mind and stick to your own opinion. That's the way I've always been. Do what you want, but this is what I think."

The moment of truth with Zoeller had come down to this moment at fifteen.

"If you're gonna have any chance to win, you've got to go for it," Beard said.

"The old saying back then was, 'If you see water, you go,'" Zoeller said. "Well, hell, I was on [Beard's] shoulders, trying to see water down in that left corner down there by the Sarazen Bridge. I couldn't see any water."

From the nearby gallery came the voice of authority. Fuzzy's father, Frank Sr., was listening in on the conversation.

"Son, he hasn't been wrong all week," Zoeller Sr. said. "Go ahead and do what he tells you."

Zoeller drilled the 3-wood and blindly asked Beard to tell him the result, half expecting a watery answer. Instead, the ball found the green, and Zoeller two-putted for birdie. "How far can I hit a 3-wood? 235 yards without any wind. I don't know how it got there," Zoeller said. He needed to gamble because he was four behind Sneed. Another Zoeller birdie on the par-4 seventeenth put him 2-under over the last four holes and seemingly in position for a great finish.

Zoeller waited behind the eighteenth green after signing his scorecard for an 8-under-par 280 total, tied with Watson for the clubhouse lead. Zoeller and Beard watched as Sneed three-putted the par-3 sixteenth and failed to get up and down from behind the green on the par-4 seventeenth. Then they saw Sneed miss the green short on the par-4 eighteenth and chip to within six feet.

"Get ready to go to ten. He doesn't know this putt," Beard told Zoeller quietly as Sneed lined up his par putt. Sneed's caddie was Bill Jackson, a brother to Carl Jackson. Perhaps because Sneed, a former Ohio State golfer, held Nicklaus in high esteem—and Jack's reliance on himself instead of his caddie—there was little input asked of Bill.

Sneed's miss forced the first sudden-death playoff in Masters history, going down the tenth hole between Sneed, Zoeller, and Watson. All three players made simple two-putt pars there, sending the match to the par-4 eleventh.

Normally, the caddies hand the players their drivers and then take a short-cut down the right side of the fairway to await the drives, but Zoeller asked Beard to accompany him to the tee box, set back and to the left of the tenth green.

"Give me a new nugget, Jariah," Zoeller said. "I want to beat high-ball-hitting Tom Watson here. I don't want to play him on twelve."

Zoeller cranked his longest drive of the week, leaving 136 yards to the pin, two fewer clubs into the green than Watson or Sneed. Sneed's 5-iron found the back bunker, Watson played a 6-iron to within eighteen feet, and Zoeller zeroed in on the flag, hitting a knockdown 8-iron to within six feet. Sneed nearly holed his bunker shot, and Watson missed. That set up Zoeller's short birdie putt.

"Two balls right and don't leave it short," was Beard's last direction for Zoeller's winning effort.

When Fuzzy's ball disappeared into the hole, he tossed his Ping Zing putter in the air, forgetting to retrieve it afterward. Beard, sitting on Zoeller's bag to the left of the eleventh green, immediately jumped up and raised his eyes to the heavens, possibly giving thanks for divine intervention, but more likely to keep Zoeller's putter from cracking somebody on the head. He nearly caught the putter before it landed on the green. Jackson sat stoically on Sneed's bag, seemingly in shock after being on the doorstep of becoming the first Jackson to caddie for a winner.

Zoeller and Beard had teamed to make Zoeller the first rookie winner since Gene Sarazen in 1935. Technically, inaugural tournament winner Horton Smith was also a rookie victor. There has been no first-time participant winner since Zoeller.

Zoeller forked over more than 10 percent of his fifty-thousand-dollar first-place check to Beard that day. They continued to work together through 1982, but when outside caddies were allowed to work at Augusta National in 1983, it was the end of the Beard-Zoeller team.

Originally, Zoeller was going to retain Beard over his regular Tour caddie, Mike Mazzeo. But on the Friday before the '83 tournament, Zoeller changed course.

"He told me, 'I've got to play with those guys on the Tour every week, live with them and travel with them,'" Beard said. "In other words, he was going to get some flak from other pros if he didn't go with them [on using Tour caddies]."

Caddie Jariah Beard (center) looks up as Fuzzy Zoeller (right) celebrates the winning putt on the eleventh green at the 1979 Masters. Zoeller beat Ed Sneed (left) and Tom Watson in a playoff and credited Beard with guiding him as the most recent rookie Masters winner. *Masters Historic Imagery/Getty Images*

"I'm lucky that I had a very good caddie at Augusta," Zoeller said. "We always got along well, but you see [the Augusta National caddies] only one time a year, and it's hard to build up confidence that way."

With the end of their association, it was also the finale of Beard's caddying days. He began concentrating on his full-time job, a nearly fifty-year career with Continental Can (later to become International Paper), which he had started in 1966 to support his wife and five children. "I had five kids, a great wife, a night job for many of those forty-eight years and good benefits I didn't want to give up," Beard said.

Previously, Beard would voluntarily switch to the night shift when alerted by Bennett that one of his regular Augusta National member bags would be available the next day, making for a long night of work, an early morning breakfast, and then sometimes thirty-six holes as a caddie. Caddying at Augusta National was a passion, but not an end-all. The 1982 Masters was his last as a full-time Augusta National employee.

"When I can't make the money that really counts, hey, I'll go do something else," Beard said.

He was urged by Bennett to come back to work part-time at Augusta National in the late 1990s, but Beard declined because the new caddie selection system may have relegated him to waiting around all day and not receiving a bag. Also, the policy of tipping had been forbidden, eliminating a more profitable payday. The only caddying he tried after working at Augusta National was the occasional visit to Sage Valley, a new ultra-exclusive golf club across the Savannah River in South Carolina, to work for Larry McCrary, a former Augusta National member. He was also known to tutor his playing partners during frequent casual rounds at the Patch.

For decades, Beard served as the unofficial historian for Augusta National caddies before succumbing to cancer at age eighty-two on March 3, 2023—one month before the 2023 Masters. Beard could recall caddies' given names and family members by their nicknames or recite their influences on winning players' games. He was emotional about his path and the plight of his brethren. After all, he took the usual route to the caddie yards at Augusta National: raised in the Sand Hills section of Augusta, apprentice caddie at Augusta Country Club at age eleven, "graduation" to Augusta National a few years later, and then a steady job in the Masters over nearly twenty-five years for a variety of players. He learned alongside Jackson, Peterson, and Iron Man from Pappy's everyday teachings, allowing him to quickly read a player. For Zoeller, Beard recognized that his player liked to hook the ball, a shot shape that is usually rewarded at dogleg-left-heavy Augusta National, and played largely by feel instead of by precise measurements.

"We were such a part of it, a tradition at that time," Beard said. "It was about how well you caddied. It showed in the tournament. If you pulled a bad club or read a bad green, you heard about it from the rest of the caddies. We took pride in what we did. It wasn't like just another job. It was something we really, really loved doing."

Zoeller did have a bit of a situation with Mazzeo a couple years after bringing him to Augusta. On Thursday night after the first round, a call came from one of the local hospitals at 10:00 p.m. Mazzeo had a "hot date" after one of Augusta's many Masters week parties and was headed back to his hotel room. However, his key wouldn't open the door, so he tried to kick through the plateglass window and severely cut his Achilles tendon, thereby benching him for the week. In stepped Fuzzy's older brother.

"Eddie Joe was a very weak caddie," Zoeller said with a laugh. "I drove it in the bunker on No. 1, and going down the fairway, he said, 'I ain't raking no traps, brother.' Then I hit it in the trees on No. 2, and he said, 'I'm not going in the woods. And I'm not putting any pelts [divots] back either.' Yep, he was a weak caddie. But he was cheap. I just had to pay him six cold beers a round. And we yukked it up the whole time."

Even though Beard and Zoeller saw each other only every couple of years and had a difficult breakup, they still had the bond of 1979.

When Zoeller uttered his infamous line about Woods in 1997, it was shocking to many and drew widespread criticism, but Beard saw some things differently. "He's doing quite well, pretty impressive," Zoeller was recorded by CNN saying as he stood on the back lawn at Augusta National while Woods played the last couple holes. "That little boy is driving it well, putting well, he's doing everything it takes to win. You know what you guys do when he gets in here? Pat him on the back, say congratulations and tell him not to serve fried chicken next year. Got it? Or collard greens, or whatever the hell they serve."

Beard was taking the man into account instead of just the words. "The whole thing was I think Fuzzy had been drinking," Beard said. "In the spotlight, you've got to be careful what you say. I feel like if Fuzzy had walked up to Tiger and said that face-to-face, they both would have laughed about it, as a joke, and walked on. But that should have been a private conversation, not in the public limelight."

Zoeller still contended that first-timers in the Masters should use Augusta National caddies. He is the poster boy for that advice.

"Personally, I think all first-time guys should use a caddie around here all the time just because they know the greens," Zoeller said. "I understand players have their caddies around all year long and feel like they owe it to them. But if I am caddying for a first-time player at the Masters, I step aside and become a spectator."

1

Carl Jackson

The picture of the hug on the final green of the 1995 Masters revealed their character. The years spent on the road, away from family, struggling to make a living, then making it. A soft-spoken gentleman overcoming a health scare to become an Augusta National savant. There was Carl Jackson, in the caddie outfit, on the left and towering over Ben Crenshaw.

The promise of being the next Nicklaus, the man with a seesaw golf game, respected as a historian, leader, all-around nice guy, and Hall of Famer. That's Crenshaw, filled with emotion, on the right, bent at the waist and breaking down.

It was April 9, 1995, a warm spring Sunday afternoon as dusk approached in the final round of the Masters Tournament. Seven days transformed personal hell into a triumph far beyond simply winning a golf tournament. More prominently, it was the embodiment of good men who worked hard to make things happen, and good things came raining down on them.

Crenshaw, age forty-three, came to Augusta the weekend prior with a golf game in shambles. A slightly built man at five-feet-nine, 157 pounds, he needed all parts of his golf swing in sync to manufacture the power and consistency necessary to keep up with the younger, longer hitters of the day. The long, flowing putting stroke, with his cherished putter, "Gentle Ben," had carried his game through the years, but could not shoulder this big a burden. Ben had missed the cut in three of the previous four tournaments, including a short title defense the week before in New Orleans at the Freeport-McMoRan Classic. His right big toe was throbbing from a calcium deposit suffered years earlier when he hauled off and kicked a trash can out of anger following a poor round at some far-away tournament. Crenshaw's ball striking fit a bad double bill: short and crooked.

Just as Crenshaw felt this on-course despair, his longtime instructor, Harvey Penick, passed away in Austin, Texas, their hometown, at age ninety, the

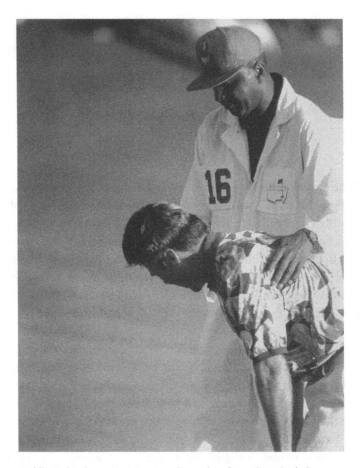

Caddie Carl Jackson gives Ben Crenshaw a hug from above in their
unlikely victory at the 1995 Masters. Jackson and Crenshaw also teamed
up to win the 1984 Masters. *Masters Historic Imagery/Getty Images*

Sunday before the Masters. Crenshaw had just completed a casual practice
round at quiet, peaceful Augusta National, with wife Julie strolling alongside,
when he received word of Penick's death. Tom Kite called from Austin to in-
terrupt the Crenshaws' dinner in the Augusta National clubhouse. It was not
an unexpected call, but still a shock to the system.

What Crenshaw, his Texas sidekick Kite, and numerous other noted golf
professionals had for years listened to in awe recently had become public do-
main. In Harvey's latter years, his down-home instructional tips were pub-

lished and critically acclaimed, most notably in Harvey Penick's *Little Red Book*, an all-time best seller that came out in 1992.

When Penick was teaching a young Crenshaw the game, he noticed the budding natural talent and sent Ben forth with an unusual rule. Ben was not to practice too much "for fear that he might find out how to do something wrong."

Penick was so basic in his teaching method. There was no technical mumbo jumbo to create paralysis by analysis in his pupils. Instead, Harvey's teachings provided guidance through the game's toughest moments. He would present adages such as: "A good putter is a match for anyone. A bad putter is a match for no one. The woods are full of long drivers" and "Arnold Palmer likes to grip the club tightly, but you are not Arnold Palmer."

On the last Sunday in March 1995, Harvey was virtually on his death bed at home. Crenshaw was over for possibly a last visit before taking off to play in New Orleans that week. The talk turned to golf and the state of Ben's game. Harvey commanded that Crenshaw go to the garage and fetch Harvey's trusty old, wooden Gene Sarazen putter. He wanted to check Ben's grip, the same grip Harvey had formed when Ben was just six years old. After a brief glimpse, Harvey simply instructed, "Just trust yourself." Ten days later, Harvey's son, Tinsley, the head professional at Austin Country Club, would present Ben the putter after his father's funeral.

The thought of Harvey's loss piled onto Crenshaw's already fragile emotions as he tried to focus on the Masters at hand. Always an emotional sort, this could create the boiling point for him.

Funeral plans were set for Wednesday, the day before the first round of the Masters. Any intense practice time to recover a semblance of a golf game would have to be compacted into two days' work.

So Crenshaw stood on the practice tee uncharacteristically beating balls on Tuesday afternoon, trying to find a simple swing key. Only hours later, a private jet would depart Augusta bound for Austin so that Crenshaw and Kite could serve as pallbearers at Penick's funeral. Frustration was setting in. Crenshaw slowly shook his head, and his shoulders stooped as he glanced toward any close-by observers.

"I just see two things," Jackson, age forty-eight, volunteered suddenly from about fifteen feet behind the golfer, perched atop Crenshaw's horizontal King Cobra golf bag. "Try something.... Put the ball back in your stance and make a tighter turn with your shoulders."

Crenshaw listened. He was used to Jackson reminding him about timing and tempo, course strategy, or the wide arc for the line of a putt, but nothing quite this technical, especially put forth so forcefully. The ball position moved back a hair in Crenshaw's stance. He concentrated on a backswing where his arms weren't separated from his body as much.

Whack...whack...whack. Magic.

"A light went off," Crenshaw said. "Two or three swings and I was making contact like I hadn't felt in a long time."

The conversation further proved that Jackson had the knowledge and timing to excel as a caddie, whether it be the range or on the final hole of a heated tournament.

"I guess you could say it was just like something Harvey would have told me, short, simple, and direct," Crenshaw said. "Carl knows me like Harvey knew me."

So Crenshaw headed to Austin for the funeral. Despite being filled with emotion that Wednesday morning, he displayed a certain glow.

"How you doin'?" older brother Charlie inquired after Penick's burial. "You've got a different kind of look on your face."

"We found something," Crenshaw said. "I can't wait to get back to Augusta and try it."

In Ben's head from the first tee Thursday onward was Penick's mantra, "Take dead aim." In his ear was Jackson, the longtime sidekick whose soothing, quiet voice belies his physical presence. No tears, no emotion, just a focus and ever-loving fun like Crenshaw had never experienced on a golf course. A first-round, 2-under-par 70 developed the confidence needed to create a miracle.

"I didn't think mechanical thoughts," Crenshaw said. "That is when I play my best, when I play by instinct."

A pack of players near the lead entering Sunday dwindled to only Crenshaw, Davis Love III, and Greg Norman, as the usual back-nine battle at the Masters transpired. Love also carried a heavy heart. He too had learned lessons at the hand of Penick, the inspiration for Love's late father, teaching pro Davis Love Jr., who played collegiately for Penick at the University of Texas. On that Sunday when he died the weekend before the Masters, one of Harvey's last acts was a couple of claps for Love's victory in New Orleans, a win that earned a last-minute invitation to the Masters. Even Crenshaw, as unconfident as he was about his golf game before the tournament began, had told Love to stay behind in Augusta and prepare for the Masters instead of traveling to Austin. Davis, he said, you're playing well, and Harvey would rather you honor him with your golf game.

Playing a few groups ahead of Crenshaw, Love finished at 13-under par and waited in the nearby Jones Cabin for Crenshaw to come home. That's when the buttery smooth putting stroke took hold again. Crenshaw converted a tricky, downhill five-footer for birdie on the par-3 sixteenth, then coaxed in a 13-footer for another birdie on the par-4 seventeenth. Two strokes clear of Love, Crenshaw prepared for his walk to glory. From the eighteenth tee on, Crenshaw was ready to crack.

"I lost concentration on my second shot to No. 18," Crenshaw said. "I was fortunate I had a two-shot lead."

As Crenshaw stood in the final fairway, from beside him Jackson spoke up again, instilling the final confidence necessary to finish the day.

"Come on buddy, we got a couple of more good shots to play here," Jackson injected as they moved to the green.

This is where the emotional picture was taken. Finally, his 274th shot of the week, a short putt for bogey, was holed on the left front portion of the eighteenth green. Crenshaw broke down, bent over, dropped his head below his knees, grabbed his face, inadvertently knocked off his Buick-logoed cap, and sobbed unashamedly. Crenshaw's face revealed a simultaneous grieving and rejoicing in one click of the camera. It could be a roaring laugh or a bawling cry. Crenshaw won the Masters for a second, and most unlikely, time.

At arm's length was Jackson, approaching slowly from the middle of the green. The strength of the six-feet-four, 225-pound man is evident, but so is his gentle nature. A caddie of lesser knowledge and pedigree would be in full celebration, rushing up to lift Crenshaw off the ground with a bear hug or to revive him with jovial reminders that the Masters title is his. But here, instead, is a friend ready to comfort, approaching slowly, respecting the moment.

"Are you OK, are you all right?" Jackson softly spoke. "How can I help?"

Crenshaw slowly lifted his head, stood upright, and acknowledged Jackson's question with a nod, then a brief hug into his caddie's chest. The gallery's standing ovation peaked once again. No other words were necessary.

"I not only gave thanks to Carl, but also thanks because we were allowed to play well on that occasion," Crenshaw said. "We had been close so many other times, and then this happened at this time. Unbelievable. All we needed to do was exchange a big, ol' hug."

The embrace was about more than just a player and his caddie, but two friends from very different backgrounds who have leaned on each other for nearly a half century. Crenshaw and Jackson formed a partnership longer than any in Masters history, dating back to 1976 and growing through their retirements from Masters play in 2015. When Ben refers to Carl in interviews or his own writings, the word *friend* usually precedes the word *caddie*.

Those decades have been like an annual family reunion at Augusta National. Crenshaw comes to town with friends and family in tow, in the role of the players' historian of Augusta National. Jackson comes back home, either staying in a Washington Road hotel or with various friends in the area, reminiscing about his youth and the other caddies from a distant past. They meet, talk about their families, trade rumors going through the sport, and then finally assess the current state of Crenshaw's game and the plan for a week of golf at Augusta National, with present-day plan to discuss the state of the game and Augusta National. They charted their path around this familiar ground like a captain and his first mate crossing the same, yet ever changing course through the ocean. In retirement, Crenshaw serves as the host of the Champions Dinner each Tuesday evening during the tournament, and Jackson hangs at the caddie facility, ready to observe and share his understated wisdom. You can depend on their convergence like the heavy yellow of the pine pollen filtering down on a warm spring day in Augusta.

"Ben and I have a bond here that will never be broken," said Jackson, who was called simply "Big Ol' Carl" by Crenshaw's late father, Charlie. "We are friends first, then player and caddie. That's unusual, I know, but that's why we have been together for so long."

To grasp the fulfillment that Jackson has experienced as a caddie and in his life, you must understand that he never knew anything but putting a golf bag over his shoulder and toting it around the course. While many of his predecessors and associates developed "holes in their pockets," lost favor with their main players, and wasted away because of alcohol abuse and other assorted maladies, Jackson took advantage of his good fortune to win two Masters titles with Crenshaw. He's not a wealthy man, but rich beyond monetary value, able to send all six of his children to college.

Jackson was born in 1947, to a single mother, Margie Jackson, and raised in the Sand Hills neighborhood. His absentee father, a local taxi company co-owner, was never in the picture, and Carl refused to reengage with him later in life. Golf was a distant pastime to the Black neighborhood boys in the 1950s, something that old, rich white men and out-of-towners came to Augusta to pursue. Carl's passion was baseball, just like many of his friends. His long, lanky frame and large feet that set a solid foundation positioned him to be quite an athlete.

That's where he developed an early nickname, "Skillet."

"I was a pitcher, at least I thought I was," Jackson said. "I wanted to be a major-league pitcher. Everybody I played with and against had the stuff to go to the majors. Some guys threw heat, BBs. But I just threw junk. I couldn't throw hard enough to break an egg. That's why they started calling me Skillet."

But playing baseball on the neighborhood playgrounds didn't bring home any money. Raised at first one block from Wheeler Road in a Mt. Auburn Avenue shotgun house—"You could shoot a gun right through the front door all the way out the back without hitting anybody or anything," said backdoor neighbor and caddie Tommy Bennett—and facing the hard times of poverty, it was essential that everybody in the household contribute to put dinner on the table. The family moved often within the neighborhood and stayed with relatives on occasion.

Margie Jackson needed help from relatives as she had nine children, including seven boys who became caddies at some point—Austin, Carl, Bill, Skip, Bud, Melvin, and Clarence—along with two girls, Jane and Margie, who died as an infant. Mother Margie Jackson worked as a waitress and maid among various other odd jobs. Carl's great-grandmother, Mamie, born in 1850 and raised during the Civil War and Reconstruction, lived next door. She couldn't read or write but had a long life and died at age 109 in 1959. Carl's grandfather, Lewis, was a painter by trade, lived with the family off and on, and helped raise fourteen children and grandchildren while working at various large homes along Walton Way in Augusta. Lewis was influential in developing Carl's character as a hard worker.

By age eleven, word had passed down through the neighborhood that caddies at Augusta Country Club could earn a decent wage by simply carrying a golf bag around for a few hours. That's when guys like Jackson, Bennett, and Buck Moore began a lifelong journey. Jackson missed a half year of school, was embarrassed by his lack of appropriate school clothing, and opted to drop out, only to earn his high school equivalency a few years later. Jackson followed his older brother, Austin, nicknamed "Tweety," to Augusta Country Club and eventually earned another nickname, "Little Tweet," simply because the caddie master, "Big Henry" Avery, didn't know Carl but knew his older brother. By 1959, twelve-year-old Carl Jackson had worked his way to Augusta National. What was first a weekend and summertime occupation had turned into a full-time job. The young Sand Hills caddies supplemented their income by gathering stray golf balls from Augusta Country Club and selling them to passersby or earned seventy-five cents per shag bag at the country club practice facility. Both occupations were much safer and more profitable than the moonshine business that creeped into the neighborhood or the trucks that came to gather neighbors on weekends to pick cotton in North Augusta, South Carolina.

"You could make more money over there," Jackson said of Augusta National. "In 1960, I was a regular caddie at the National. Some of the caddies protested because here was this boy taking money out of their pockets. 'He should be in school,' they said. But some guys backed me, 'This kid needs money just as much as you do.' After that I fit right in with them.

"I was a good student in school, but unfortunately I had to quit school to help make a living for our family."

Jackson and his caddie mates also tried to play the sport when they could find a break from the day's chores and sneak on the course.

"The only time we could get out there was after a big rain or something," Jackson recalled. "When all the members fled into the clubhouse, we would go out and play a few holes for as long as we could—until a guard came. Sometimes he'd shoot at us."

At first, the caddies thought the shots were just a scare tactic.

"We used to think he was shooting blanks," Jackson said, "until one day a bullet actually hit the tree I was standing behind. That was about it for me."

Jackson's first Masters bag was old-timer Billy Burke, the 1931 U.S. Open champion, in 1961. Only fourteen years old, Jackson probably thought he could beat Burke, who sported a white dress shirt and necktie for his rounds. Burke played in the first Masters in 1934, finishing a career-best third, and made 1961 his last Augusta start with rounds of 81-79. Burke earned four hundred dollars, with only a small portion going to Jackson.

Jackson bounced from player to player as the years progressed, namely from Burke to Davis Love Jr., Gary Player, Tony Jacklin, Bruce Devlin, Steve Melnyk, Charlie Coe, R. H. Sikes, Mike Souchak, and Downing Gray before hooking up with Crenshaw. In 1964, the twenty-six-year-old Devlin was on the verge of returning to Australia to become a plumber because of a poor season but worked with Jackson to finish fourth, earned $6,100, and stayed in the United States. His presence in the United States influenced other Australians, such as David Graham and Greg Norman and today's crop of top players, to make Australia the largest producer of PGA Tour players outside of the United States. In 1970, the esteemed Ernest Nipper dropped Player's bag in the wake of threats against Player and his native South Africa's apartheid policy. Jackson stepped in amid the possibility of protest and guided Player to a second-place finish.

Jackson's biggest early connection wasn't a Masters participant, but an Augusta National member. Arkansas billionaire Jackson T. Stephens, one of the nation's wealthiest men, would become the fourth chairman of Augusta National in 1991. He took a liking to young Carl and hired him as his full-time caddie in 1962 when he joined Augusta National. He also persuaded Carl to leave his regular duties as an Augusta National caddie and move to Arkansas in 1972 to work for him in other capacities within his powerful financial business, Stephens Incorporated.

"When I first met Jack Stephens I was only fourteen," Jackson said. "Freddie Bennett [the caddie master] let me caddie for him because the guy who normally caddied for him didn't show up that day. The next morning, I was on the practice tee waiting to see who I could work for, and Mr. Stephens's caddie didn't show up at first, and then he was late. I told Mr. Stephens thank you for letting me caddie for you yesterday, and here comes your caddie. [Stephens] told me to stay right there, told the other guy that Carl Jackson is my caddie now, and paid him. That started our relationship."

Stephens could understand Jackson's work ethic. He was a self-made man, working through the Depression by picking cotton and harvesting crops for neighbors and then, at age fifteen, becoming a bellhop, telegraph deliverer, and a shoeshine boy at night in Hope, Arkansas. Witt, his older brother, began the financial business during the 1930s, and Jack joined in after World War II to transform it from a small Little Rock investment firm specializing in municipal bonds into Wall Street's fourth-largest investment bank and one of the largest financial empires in the South.

Stephens's company became closely associated in national business circles with Arkansans Sam Walton (Walmart), William T. Dillard (Dillard's Department Store), and John Tyson (Tyson Foods). Jack and Witt were largely responsible for some of the financing to launch Walmart, Federal Express, and Tyson Foods.

Stephens joined Augusta National at age thirty-eight, just three years after taking up golf, and was a close associate of Augusta National's first chairman, Clifford Roberts, the cofounder of the club and the tournament with Bobby Jones. Stephens was influential in political circles in his home state of Arkansas and in New York, where his business ties burgeoned. Many pay quiet respect to Stephens for being able to push the relatively unknown Arkansas governor Bill Clinton from the backwoods of Little Rock into eight years in the White House in the 1990s. In many ways, Stephens is viewed as the quiet, thoughtful opposite to the often brazen, rough Roberts, who was a confidant and campaign influence on President Dwight D. Eisenhower in the 1950s and made sure that Ike became a quite public member of Augusta National in the late 1940s. Unlike the dictatorial presentation of Roberts and the easily accessible Hord Hardin, whom he succeeded as Augusta National chairman in 1991, Stephens was rarely available for comment on club or tournament issues and was not nearly as visible as his predecessors.

Stephens's status at Augusta National can be summed up by a physical presence on the grounds. Ten cabins are bunched just beyond and to the left of the tenth hole that provide lodging for members and their guests. Two of the most prominent are the Eisenhower Cabin, more affectionately called Mamie's Cabin, after the former president's wife, and the Jones Cabin, named after the esteemed Jones, both of which rest just to the left of the tenth tee. The Butler Cabin, set just behind the putting green, has had its basement used as the studio home of CBS's televised green jacket ceremony since 1964. Behind these three prominent structures, set in a semicircle just to the right as you walk to the par-3 course, are seven more cabins named after various members. The last one built in 1969 with a noticeably large back porch is the Stephens Cabin.

Stephens's mark is evident elsewhere in Augusta. Augusta National's first Black member, Ron Townsend, joined in 1991, just as Stephens was taking over the leadership role. It was Stephens who investigated building a golf facility for children after Tiger Woods won the 1997 Masters and then donated five million dollars of his own money to The First Tee, a golf industry–wide initiative to provide access to the sport for underprivileged youth, when the program was unveiled in 1997. Two First Tee facilities are open in Arkansas today. Stephens's influence on that agenda created Augusta National's public donation and partnership with the same program. In 1979, the day after Zoeller's victory, Stephens showed his loyalty to Carl by inviting him to play supposedly the first round played by a Black caddie at Augusta National with a member, playing alongside Stephens, assistant professional Mike Shannon, and co–head pro Bob Kletcke.

Officially, Carl worked in records and promotions for Independent Corporation of America in Little Rock, but predominately Stephens relied on Carl as his right-hand man, whether it be caddying at Augusta National, entertaining at the Stephens Cabin, or on business trips. "He never went into another store to shop after I moved there, I can tell you that," Carl said. Carl was often referred to by the media as a close associate to Stephens, both on and off the golf course, sometimes in a belittling fashion.

Stephens came off as a "good ol' boy" at first glance. He was slow-speaking, Southern, and pondered most questions with a long pause and a drag from a cigarette. But his business acumen and dry sense of humor revealed a highly intelligent man.

Stephens trusted Carl with classified information and wanted him within earshot when important conversations took place.

"I knew his innermost thoughts," Jackson said. "I was always by his side. If he had too much to drink and somebody called on the telephone, he made sure I was on the other phone to make sure exactly what was said. The only time he was vulnerable was when he was drinking."

Jackson remembers an early 1980s business meeting in Palm Beach, Florida, with Jack Nicklaus. Normally low-key about displaying his wealth, for some reason Stephens opted to drive his Rolls Royce to the meeting. Usually, this type of face-to-face meeting occurred with just Stephens and the other party talking behind closed doors. But not on this occasion.

"When they greeted each other at [Nicklaus's] office, I said excuse me," Jackson said. "But Mr. Stephens said, 'No, Carl, I want you to stay.' That sort of surprised Jack a little bit. Then the three of us sat down. I guess Mr. Stephens figured I was an important part of that conversation."

Jimmy Carter, the thirty-ninth president of the United States, was Stephens's roommate in the U.S. Naval Academy just after World War II. When the Georgia governor was campaigning for the 1976 presidential election, he stayed in the Stephens house, and Carl stayed put as a part of the extended family.

Stephens's children, five and ten years younger than Carl, grew close to him as they grew up. Warren A. Stephens, the younger brother, eventually also became an Augusta National member.

"We were definitely like family there," Carl said. "They always said I was their Black brother."

By 1990, that relationship had soured. Carl had married for a third time—his first wife died, and he divorced from his second wife—and he wanted to spend more time with new wife, Debra, their two children apiece from previous marriages, and their two young children together, Jason and Carlisa. Stephens wanted him alongside on various trips. Finally, Carl decided it was time to break loose and leave Stephens's employment and depart Arkansas after nearly twenty years of working for Stephens. It was a bitter parting. The two didn't talk for years.

"My kids come before anybody," Carl said. "After what I went through as a kid, I wanted to be there for my family, not away somewhere else."

They stayed apart for years, but Carl could largely attribute his Masters success to Stephens after he had toiled as a caddie for multiple players.

Following the 1975 Masters, Crenshaw was searching for another caddie from the home club. When Ben made his Masters debut in 1972, the first caddie he met when he walked onto the grounds and stopped by the caddie shack was Willie "Cemetery" Perteet, the longtime caddie for former president Dwight Eisenhower. Eventually, Crenshaw was assigned a caddie simply known as Luke, whom he described as "a great, funny man."

But Luke wasn't the answer for a promising player such as Crenshaw. The three-time NCAA Championship winner needed a steady hand to bridle his wild game. One of the first years playing in the Masters, Crenshaw faced a long second shot into the par-4 fifth hole. Luke suggested a 5-iron; Crenshaw thought it should be a 4-iron.

"Luke, I'm not sure I can quite get there with a 5," Crenshaw said in his usual aw-shucks demeanor.

"Well, hit the 4-iron then," Luke shot back fiercely with a frown on his face.

So as Crenshaw prepared for the 1976 Masters, his third Augusta start as a professional, he was seeking guidance. John Griffith, an Augusta National member and Crenshaw family friend from Fort Worth, Texas, suggested Jackson. Stephens had made a recommendation to co-member Griffith after learning of the search. They talked with Freddie Bennett, the caddie master, to work out the details. And, as they say, it was the beginning of a beautiful relationship.

"Ben hit the ball where he was looking," Carl said. "I told myself, if you think you're a good caddie you're gonna find out now."

Their first year together, 1976, Crenshaw may have finished eight shots behind the record-setting Raymond Floyd, but he was in second place. Over their first twenty years together, Crenshaw and Jackson recorded two wins, eleven top-10 finishes, and missed only two cuts.

"It was just incredible how well Carl knew the greens," Crenshaw said. "He thought his way around like a player, which I really appreciated. He has great imagination. It was very strange also because he very seldom relied on yardages. We were a team right from the start."

Jackson had learned the secret of Augusta National from Pappy Stokes. Every green had a tendency for putts to break toward Rae's Creek, a fact that was lost on many of the outside caddies from 1983 on, and Jackson would share that intel only with Crenshaw. Bruce Edwards, Tom Watson's longtime caddie, continually asked Carl about the particulars of the greens. Steve Williams, Tiger Woods's New Zealand–based caddie for three of his five Masters wins and a four-time Masters winner (also with Adam Scott in 2013), said he would get Jackson's shoe size and try to appease him with an offering of some brand-new shoes each spring.

"Carl is such a gentle-natured guy," Williams said in 2017. "Very smooth. Very gentle. Unlike a lot of caddies, who were sort of fidgety, jumpy, grumpy. He was probably the complete contrast to what a caddie would be."

But many of the caddies didn't pay attention to what was right there in front of their faces. In spacious caddie facilities adjacent to the tournament practice facility, simple framed maps of green complexes hang on the walls. On every drawing, there is a distinct red dot, showing the direction of Rae's Creek from that green—and the tendency for putts to break to the lowest point on the property when it's not evident to the naked eye. More and more caddies through the years have denoted that red dot in their personal Augusta National yardage books. Crenshaw indicated that the spot to eyeball is the wooden structure that covers the dam on Rae's Creek just left and behind the eleventh green.

Perhaps even more important was the sense that these two were meant for each other on this hallowed ground. When Crenshaw won his first Masters in 1984, he was in the middle of a divorce from his first wife, Polly. Much like 1995, Jackson took the focus of the week and placed it solely on the golf course.

"He brought the golf out of me," Crenshaw remembered. "He started the week by saying let's work real hard on the little approach shots, the kind of thing you can overlook at Augusta National. When you play in the Masters, your first priority is to drive the ball the best you can. But as we went through the practice rounds that week, Carl just guided me around. He'd say, 'Hit the ball from here. Take an approach putt from here because the pin is gonna be here this week.' Carl is so good at that. He got my mind ready to play to the point where I didn't feel the suddenness you sometimes feel when the Masters starts on Thursday. My long game and short game were in sync."

When the back nine came on Sunday, Crenshaw drained a memorable sixty-foot birdie putt on the par-4 tenth hole, his third consecutive birdie, only to turn around and bogey the eleventh. As they stood on the tee of the treacherous par-3 twelfth hole, Crenshaw was the leader. And in his ear was Jackson. They picked a 6-iron.

"Don't worry about that bogey," Jackson whispered before the tee shot. "You're playing well. We'll get through this thing."

A subsequent birdie on the twelfth secured his lead, and Crenshaw went on to capture his first green jacket.

"I was reading an article in a magazine when they talked about the ghosts out there that year," Jackson said a few years after the 1984 win. "There was something special going on that week. I'm going to tell Ben it wasn't ghosts, it was angels. We just sort of knew it was going to happen."

Their teamwork was awe-inspiring to many of Crenshaw's competitors.

"There's a guy [Jackson] that can read those greens," Nick Price said in 1989. "I have the greatest admiration for that man. There aren't too many that know the greens as well as he does. When you have two brains like that working together that's why Ben holes so many putts. I remember what he did [in 1988] in one round here with his putter. In the first seven holes, Ben hit one green and was 1-under par."

The Masters relationship expanded to the PGA Tour in the early 1990s. Jackson was on Crenshaw's bag when he won a second Southwestern Bell Colonial at Fort Worth in 1990. He stayed on in 1991. But the stress of being away from family, coupled with the absence of that Augusta magic, put an end to the weekly association. Jackson's green-reading didn't have the same local knowledge effect at places such as Riviera or Doral as it did at Augusta.

Still, the link with Crenshaw enabled Jackson to take routes in life he would never have previously considered. Rumor has it, though Jackson won't confirm it, that the 1995 caddie payday from Crenshaw far exceeded the usual 10 percent and a fat tip for the winning caddie. Some say it soared to nearly ninety thousand dollars. "Let's just say that Ben did me right," Jackson said. In the late 1990s, Jackson partnered in a golf company, Diamondized Golf, that developed specialty wedges. Jackson was titled Director of Tour Operations and moved to Atlanta. Even though the venture wasn't successful, it allowed him to spread his wings.

Then came a move to the North Carolina mountains in 1999, first to Hendersonville and later to Asheville. Jason was tall and rangy just like his father had been some forty years before and was a budding football star as a tight end and one of the leading tacklers at outside linebacker for the Asheville T. C. Roberson High Rams, an athletic trek that led to a scholarship to Southern Methodist University. He also excelled off the field, being recommended for honors classes and participating in ROTC. Both young children were excellent students and college bound, with Jason going on to earn a degree from Southern Methodist University, a master's degree from Prairie View A&M, and currently working in the business world in Dallas and Carlisa obtaining a degree from Loyola–New Orleans and entering the title design field in Little Rock. Both completed high school after Jackson's return to Arkansas.

They followed in the footsteps of their older half brothers and sisters, all of whom are college graduates. Carrethia, the oldest child, attended the University of Arkansas and went into the insurance business. Carl Romeo, the oldest boy, attended Clark-Atlanta University and became a school principal. Jonitha is a University of Arkansas–Little Rock graduate who went into nursing. Crystal earned a University of Chicago degree and became a psychologist.

Six college-graduate children successful in a variety of fields, and five grandchildren—not a bad record for Jackson, who had to cut short his education to work.

"I got a great education in a different way, which didn't come with any type of certificate," Jackson said in 2023. "I got a great education working for Jack Stephens. I worked with him for a long time. He just put me out there to manage different aspects of his business here and there."

The gypsy lifestyle of being a caddie persisted for Jackson into the early 2000s. He would occasionally depart for a few weeks at a time, cruising to Durham, North Carolina, to pick up Tommy Bennett at his residence and drive around the eastern part of the country looking for open golf bags on the PGA Tour or a secondary circuit. When Crenshaw turned fifty in 2002, he asked Jackson to pick up his bag on the PGA Tour Champions—with little success. Crenshaw had a similar yearning to stay home because of his three young daughters and a burgeoning course design business.

Jackson and Crenshaw continued to team up at Augusta for another twelve years, until one of them—or both—couldn't go any longer. Jackson insisted that he wouldn't make a sudden move to a young Masters hopeful, such as a Charles Howell III, unless Ben gave his total, unsolicited blessing.

Mostly, the Carl Jackson of the early 2000s was "Mr. Mom" at home in Asheville, making sure the kids didn't spend too much time on the phone, hovering over their school lessons, or proudly attending football games. That's not too far from Crenshaw's MO of helping to raise three daughters while building a widely respected course architecture business.

"We've got two computers in this home," Jackson said with a laugh. "We're busy all the time, going here and there. The expenses build up. But that's a good sign of the times. All my kids are doing well in school. That's my commitment in life."

Life is something that Jackson cherishes because he is simply here. In February 2000, he was diagnosed with colon cancer, the second-most common cause of cancer death in the United States. He was so weak after chemotherapy treatments early that year that he told Crenshaw to find a replacement. Their twenty-fifth anniversary pairing at the Masters would have to wait. Linn Strickler, Crenshaw's regular Tour caddie, stepped in. The signs were not good regarding Jackson's diagnosis. Colon cancer is treatable if discovered in its early stages, but when it spreads to other organs, the survival rate lessens, especially for a man in his early fifties. Caddies, tournament officials, and players called Jackson and sent their best wishes.

"I walked in to see the doctor, and he told me I needed immediate surgery," Jackson said. "When he said I've got colon cancer, I just prayed about it."

Crenshaw prayed, too, because he knows illness. In 1985, he mysteriously lost thirty pounds. Doctors diagnosed him with hyperthyroidism and prescribed four months' worth of radioactive iodine treatments, which gradually got his condition under control. Crenshaw was so concerned about Jackson's condition that he called him every day at one point, especially when the Masters date closed in. He offered financial assistance. You could almost hear the tears pouring over the telephone in Jackson's hospital room.

"Hey, you take care of your own business," Crenshaw said. "Those doctors there know what it is. Tell them to go ahead and fix it."

"That was a great lift," Jackson said. "When Ben tells you something, he means it."

Jackson credits his doctor and the use of liquid oxygen for his recovery. "I feel better than ever, like I was never sick," he said in 2001. He gladly goes to local charity tournaments when invited, proudly professing himself a cancer survivor.

He also points out the role that herbal medicine played in his healing. Jackson first heard of alternative medical care more than twenty years before his diagnosis when he traveled from his home in Arkansas to a religious rally held by Tennessee pastor Mamon Wilson. He watched as Wilson magically worked an inoperable baseball-sized tumor lodged in a man's mouth out the side of his face with only the slightest bit of damage. He heard of other "healings" where people with tumors were treated and miraculously survived. In 2002, Jackson spent hours in classes studying herbal medicine and continued for years to pursue avenues to get some of the herbal medication into the marketplace. He is as passionate about this effort as he is stalking a ten-foot putt at Augusta National.

As Jackson pursued his family and religious beliefs, Crenshaw was inducted into the World Golf Hall of Fame in mid-November 2002. It was an honor particularly poignant because Penick was enshrined at the same time during the ceremonies in St. Augustine, Florida.

Not to be lost in this ceremony was Crenshaw's Hall of Fame collection of memorabilia that was on display during and after his induction. It included a replica of "Little Ben," a Masters green jacket, and, right there in the middle, the Masters caddie jump suit that Jackson wore when winning the 1995 tournament.

The story gets even better from here.

As Jackson aged, his relationship with Stephens was refreshed and Stephens's son, Warren, built a new, exclusive club in Arkansas, the Alotian Club. Jackson became the caddie manager when the club opened in 2004 and moved south with his family, one year before Jack Stephens died at age eighty-one in the summer of 2005. Carl and Debra divorced in 2006, burdened by the strains of the seesaw finances and traveling life of a caddie.

"God put some good people in my life," Jackson said. "It's all about respecting people. You have to give every person a chance, give them respect up front. That is how I viewed my life. Everyone is equal until they prove otherwise."

In 2008, Jackson was inducted into the Arkansas Golf Hall of Fame, with Crenshaw present for the October induction in Little Rock.

"When you think back, the first caddies were slaves," Jackson told the *Arkansas Democrat-Gazette*. "This has come a long way. I hope other caddies will pick up on that for years to come."

As even more of an everlasting legacy, Jackson figured by 2014 that it was time to reveal his own Masters secret. Prior to the 2014 tournament, he spent time with Michael Greller, the caddie for Jordan Spieth, a Texan and former University of Texas star just like Crenshaw. Greller is a former middle-school math teacher in Washington who played small-college golf and developed a passion for caddying—and the extra summer wages to supplement a meager teacher's salary—at the recently opened and nearby Chambers Bay Golf Course in suburban Seattle. Chambers Bay would be the site of Spieth's 2015 U.S. Open victory with Greller on the bag at his hometown course, less than three miles from the school where he taught. Greller's caddying career took off after an introduction to Spieth at the 2011 U.S. Junior Championship in Washington and a spectator visit to the 2012 Masters, a cross-country venture that cemented his focus on carrying a golf bag as a career. Shawn Spieth, Jordan's father, asked Greller to caddie fulltime for Spieth in the winter of 2012.

Jackson went through his weathered yardage book, schooling Greller on the intricacies of Augusta National. They sat outside the caddie facility at picnic tables and went hole by hole as the Monday practice round in 2014 was rained out. Greller wrote down important information to carry him forward during that midmorning session and resumed their discussion on Tuesday morning before practice rounds resumed. The result: a runner-up finish in 2014 and a record-tying victory in 2015 for Spieth.

"The young man [Greller] humbled himself," Jackson said in 2014. "He asked if I would help him. They're good people, and both Ben and I appreciate that.

"I took his yardage book and marked it for each hole. I told him to understand where the slope is going on every green. Know where the pull of Rae's Creek is on every hole, that's the key, and then judge things. That's the low area on the course that I always leaned to in figuring out the course.

Caddie Carl Jackson (left) was honored with Carl Jackson Day in his hometown, Augusta, Georgia, in 2015, a ceremony attended by Ben Crenshaw. The duo would compete in their final Masters later that week, which was Jackson's fifty-third as a Masters caddie. Jackson was the first nongolfer and first Black person to be so honored by the city during Masters week. *Still frame from* Loopers: The Caddie's Long Walk

"Ben came in and sat down while I was doing it. We have seen guys misreading speeds on putts all the time. Ben would say the pull got him. We kept that to ourselves all these years. I taught it to Ben, and he used it and knew how to use it."

"It was unbelievable the wisdom he has about this place," Greller said, referring to Jackson as "Mr. Jackson." "The things he emphasized were to tell Jordan to trust his instincts and for me to always find out where Rae's Creek is from every hole. That's a real key."

That interaction continued through 2019 as Jackson offered a refresher course to Greller as Masters week came, sitting down to review Greller's "homework" and offer some refinements. Jackson also hung out at the lavish caddie digs, unofficially labeled the Carl Jackson House by Jim "Bones" Mackay, Phil Mickelson's former caddie and current caddie for Justin Thomas. Jackson touched base with old friends, met new ones who respected his life's work, and talked with various international media outlets. All this despite feeling slighted that he didn't have access to more Masters tickets that would be consistent with his Augusta National history, success, and connections.

"It used to be the caddie and the player and no one else [to discuss strategy]," Crenshaw said in 2015. "Now, it's the caddie and the player and a legion of people around that player. There might be a teacher. There might be somebody from their team. All of them got teams now. So, that can be a little delicate as well and I think if a team is smart—if they have a good caddie—they go to the caddie and say what do you see when the player is not around?"

When Spieth won the 2015 Masters title, it didn't come as a surprise that the week also offered the final walk for Crenshaw and Jackson. Early in the week, Jackson was the city honoree at the mayor's Masters Reception in downtown Augusta, becoming the first nonplayer and first Black person honored on Monday of Masters week. He was also given a crystal key to the city on what was declared to be Carl Jackson Day.

"Being honored here is something I never imagined, because this is a long way from where I began and I am profoundly grateful and humbled to be standing here," he said during a public ceremony in downtown Augusta, where Crenshaw also spoke. "I was fourteen years old at my first Masters. I remembered being in awe of the Augusta National Golf Club—a boy among men."

Jackson couldn't caddie in 2015 because of a rib injury and recent surgery for colon cancer, so his brother Bud stepped in to carry for Crenshaw during the first two rounds. Carl had already begun to focus on helping underprivileged youngsters via his foundation, Carl's Kids (www.carlskids.org), an organization started in 2009 and run by his younger brother Jimmy Wright in Durham, North Carolina. The organization, which benefits children learning the game and faith-based morals to go through life and sports, was planning a facility and annual kids' camps in Newberry, South Carolina, in early 2023.

When Bud, who still caddies some at Augusta National, worked for Crenshaw, he became the fourth Jackson brother to caddie at the Masters, following Carl, Bill (runner-up in 1979 with Ed Sneed), and Austin. When Crenshaw came home on the eighteenth hole on Friday afternoon, missing the cut by a large margin, Carl was waiting at the back of the green, wearing his caddie jumpsuit to celebrate a lengthy career, standing with Augusta

National chairman Billy Payne. It completed fifty-three Masters on the bag at Augusta National.

When play finished, Jackson came onto the green, and the two embraced, like they had in 1995.

"I said, 'I love you,' and he said, 'I love you,'" Jackson said. "That's all that needed to be said."

1

Burnt Biscuits

Tommy Bennett was talking on his cell phone in between shots on the golf course, playing his own game in the Tidewater area of Virginia. Only hours before, one of his most recent bags on the PGA Tour, New Zealand's Michael Long, missed the cut in the 2002 Michelob Championship at Kingsmill.

"I had to play, just had to," said Bennett. "It's in my blood."

It was just another day on the PGA Tour for the fifty-four-year-old Bennett, an Augusta native and former Augusta National Golf Club caddie. For most of his caddying career, Bennett went from bag to bag, crisscrossing the country by car on different tours to try and find a steady paycheck. He estimated that he had toted for more than fifty players, beginning in the 1969 Atlanta Classic when Allan Henning earned $184 for a seventy-second-place finish. His longest tenure came in the late 1990s when he worked with Tom Pernice Jr. for just over two years.

Bennett has never won on a Tour bag, with a best Masters finish of fourth in 1987 working for Jodie Mudd, and a handful of seconds in other Tour events. Jobs seem to last as long as under-par scores and a prompt arrival at the golf course. He is the poster boy for the caddie on Tour—a gypsy.

But Bennett holds one claim to fame as he turned seventy-five in 2023. He was Tiger Woods's first Masters Tournament caddie. That came in Tiger's 1995 Masters debut when the raw nineteen-year-old reigning U.S. Amateur champion and Stanford University freshman made headlines at Augusta National.

And just think: Bennett didn't want Tiger's bag.

Bennett hoped to work with Dicky Pride, an up-and-coming twenty-five-year-old Alabaman who had won his first PGA Tour event the previous year as a rookie in the FedEx St. Jude Classic at Memphis. A good Masters show-

Caddies Jariah Beard (left) and Tommy Bennett participated in a question-and-answer session following a 2019 showing of the documentary *Loopers: The Caddie's Long Walk* in Augusta, Georgia. *Photo by Ward Clayton*

ing by Pride would mean a nice paycheck, while Woods's ability to ante up and make the cut was debatable.

"I wanted to caddie for the Masters champion, and I figured Dicky Pride had a better shot than Tiger Woods, the amateur," Bennett said. "But Jack Stephens [the former Augusta National chairman] said he wished I would caddie for Tiger in the Masters. That made it a done deal."

Bennett was picked to loop for Woods during the practice rounds for the 1995 Masters "because I was the only caddie on hand with PGA Tour experience and local knowledge," he said. Still, Tiger wished that his mentor and father, Earl Woods, would tote for him. The nation's Black population, whether golfers or not, was watching, as were the caddies at Augusta National. Tiger was the first Black amateur in the field. Tiger pointed out that he often had friends or family caddie for him; witness the victory in the 1994 U.S. Amateur at the Tournament Players Club at Sawgrass in Ponte Vedra Beach, Florida, when navy captain Jay Brunza, a sports psychologist and family friend, was on the bag.

Bennett was selected to tutor Tiger in the practice rounds and then step aside. He carried thirty-six holes on Monday of Masters week, in a group with Nick Faldo in the morning and Trip Kuehne, the 1994 U.S. Amateur runner-up, in the afternoon. Raymond Floyd, Greg Norman, Fred Couples, Nick Price, and Gary Player also joined Woods during practice rounds on Tuesday and Wednesday and during the Par 3 Contest. They wanted a glimpse of what they would have to overcome in the future. Lee Elder, a special invitee twenty years after breaking the player color barrier at the Masters, made a special effort to speak with Tiger and follow just about every shot.

But questions arose about Earl's on-course role as the tournament grew closer. Was he physically capable of this task? Butch Harmon, Tiger's instructor, wasn't sure. Other observers echoed Elder's comment, "I think it's a mistake."

The usually self-confident Earl seemed ready . . . to a point.

"We have an excellent relationship," Earl said of his son. "I know how to interface with Tiger. Most fathers couldn't do it because you have to have a role reversal. He's the boss. You are nothing but a peon out there. Most fathers couldn't make that transition. With us, it's no problem.

"I don't know how a sixty-two-year-old is going to handle those hills down there. I don't think I'm going to like that white uniform. It looks hot just to look at it."

On Tuesday night, Tiger and company decided that Bennett would be the man for the week. Bennett said they didn't let him know he would carry in the tournament until Wednesday afternoon's Par 3 Contest was completed.

"I really didn't have a job until then," Bennett said. "It was all evaluation until they told me to get ready for Thursday."

Lucky for Bennett, as Pride would shoot 79–73–152 to miss the cut by seven strokes. To date, that has been Pride's only Masters appearance.

Bennett's most lasting impression of Tiger occurred on the first tee Thursday morning. It was a rainy, cool first day of play. Paired with defending champion José María Olazábal and with nearly the entire Masters gallery craning their necks to watch this new phenomenon, Tiger walked to the first tee sporting his Stanford cap, shook hands with the Augusta National members who serve as starters, and mentally prepared to tee off. To the right of the tee box, Bennett was getting set also. He counted clubs, checked his yard-age book, and then bent down to the ball pocket of Woods's small carry bag to retrieve a ball. He searched quickly in the pocket of the bag and swallowed hard. His eyes got big as he sidestepped over to Tiger.

"We've only got three balls in here," Tommy quietly and incredulously told Tiger as he prepared to hand over the driver.

"We've got three balls. That's all I need," Woods said straight-faced.

"I just thought, 'Man, you're at Augusta National in the Masters for the first time. Whew, who you kidding?'" Bennett said. "But that's all we took onto the golf course all week, three balls, no more, no less. He was that con-fident, even then."

In 2020, on the twenty-fifth anniversary of his Masters debut, Woods sec-onded the story about the golf balls, even adding that he used only one ball all day and had two unused balls.

"In college, I didn't really have a whole lot of golf balls," Woods said. "And I didn't really switch golf balls that often. That's what amateurs do. . . . In col-lege, our coach would give us a dozen balls per event. Otherwise, we didn't have any new balls. So, you saved them."

Bennett said that Woods listened to his advice about the golf course but that he was his own man, soaking in the atmosphere and the precision nec-essary to play Augusta National. Every morning, Bennett would meet Har-mon at the driving range, just before Tiger warmed up, and Harmon would dole out some simple instructions for the day.

"He was an easy man to work for. Anybody could work for Tiger," Bennett said. "Tiger knew what he could do on the golf course. But when he came to the Masters, he didn't know anything about this golf course. He learned pretty fast."

Tiger dazzled the crowd with his prodigious length off the tee, hitting no more than an 8-iron into the five-hundred-yard par-5 fifteenth every day and no more than a 7-iron all week into any of the par-4s. In Friday's second round, Bennett recalled Woods's second shot from 232 yards (250 to the hole) on the par-5 thirteenth hole. From a sidehill lie in the right trees, Woods cut a 3-iron into the green to within fifteen feet and two-putted for birdie.

But Tiger struggled with distance control on his irons, blowing the ball over a few greens and spinning it off the front on others, and shot three even-par rounds of 72 and a third-round 77 on the way to a tie for forty-first. He had the usual rookie embarrassments, beginning with a thirty-foot birdie putt on the first green in the first round that rolled off the green and down a slope on the left side, some fifty feet away from the hole.

"When I first played it, I thought this was one of the shortest and most open golf courses that I thought there was," Woods said in 2020. "It was just a driver and a wedge everywhere. There really wasn't a bunker off the tee that was in play. The first time I played here, I drove a 3-wood into the bunker on 10. Obviously, the tees have been all lengthened and it's a very different golf course. The fairways were all cut down grain at the time."

Still, he captured Low Amateur honors and made a statement that Augusta National was a course he could overpower. Tiger averaged 311.1 yards per drive, number one in the tournament, and nearly five yards more than the second-place finisher in driving distance, Davis Love III.

"That's where all this talk about changing the golf course at Augusta National began," said Bennett, pointing to the addition of more than 350 yards from 2001–2003 and comparing the 6,925-yard course with 7,545 yards in 2023. "They rebuilt the golf course because of what they saw coming at them that year. There's no doubt about that.

"See, that's why they called him Tiger. Because he was going to be feared."

Woods made a point to connect with the mostly Black Augusta National employees, particularly the caddies, that week. He signed autographs daily as he walked under the large oak trees behind the clubhouse, in the clubhouse, at the bag storage area on the north end of the clubhouse, and around the driving range entrance. He invited Bennett up to the Crow's Nest, the traditional amateur quarters at the top of the clubhouse, for a hamburger after one round. It was Bennett's first trip there.

After making the cut on Friday, Tiger, Earl, Bennett, and Brunza hopped in a car and drove twenty minutes over to Forest Hills Golf Club, one of the city's best and most historic public courses. Tiger put on a clinic for a small group of junior golfers and caddies at dinnertime on a driving range tee nearly devoid of grass. About twenty caddies were on hand to watch Tiger show his stuff, particularly a hilarious act where he zoomed 3-irons over Earl's head as the elder Woods casually stood about twenty yards away serving as the emcee. Afterward, Bennett served as a tour guide as the foursome drove through Bennett's old Sand Hills neighborhood up above Augusta National where "we just visualized how things used to be."

"Just knowing that Tiger came to hit balls for them is enough to get some of these kids playing golf," Beard said. "As for the caddies, we deeply appreciated it. We have been the forgotten men of the Masters, but maybe Tiger will help us be remembered."

For Bennett, a cousin of longtime Augusta National caddie master Freddie Bennett, the experience was unforgettable. It was one of the last times he would caddie at Augusta National and his last Masters appearance. By 1997, a year after CaddieMaster Enterprises took over the Augusta National caddie corps, Bennett was gone, he said, because "they didn't like my attitude." He wasn't cast to follow in the footsteps of boyhood neighbor Carl Jackson, who has served a long courtship with Ben Crenshaw. By 1996, Brunza was on Woods's bag at the Masters. Then for the historic victory in 1997 in his professional debut, Mike "Fluff" Cowan had been hired to work for Woods, followed by Steve Williams in 2001, 2002, and 2005 and Joe LaCava in 2019. Bennett did get a picture in *Sports Illustrated* in 1995 with his five-year-old son Donte and Woods. And Earl forked over "a pretty decent" $1,500 for the week's caddie fee. Plus, a large, fading mural still adorns the wall of the former Sand Hills Grill in his old neighborhood, depicting Bennett carrying Woods's bag in 1995.

"Oh, I still see him around," Bennett said of Woods. "I'll speak to him sometime. But he's in another world now."

Bennett trudges on in a career that came to him because "it was our lunch money for the week." He and Jackson lived in back-to-back shotgun houses when they were growing up, playing baseball and caddying at Augusta Country Club and Augusta National by the early 1960s, working at the elbow of legendary Willie "Pappy" Stokes. Bennett worked hard to make it to the level where he could caddie in the tournament.

"If there were one hundred caddies at Augusta National, I sure didn't want to be number one hundred," Bennett said.

Bennett owns one of the most unusual nicknames, "Burnt Biscuits," among Augusta National caddies. It has nothing to do with his caddying skills but came about when he tried to sneak through a window at his grandmother's house to confiscate some freshly baked biscuits. Upon jumping out the window when his grandmother came running, Tommy kicked a pot of boiling water off the wood-burning stove, started a house fire, and burned his legs. Of course, in a tight-knit neighborhood everyone soon heard about the incident, and the nickname stuck.

He lived in Durham, North Carolina, for most of the late 1990s and into the early 2000s after meeting a woman from that central Tar Heel state city.

Bennett played casual rounds of golf at Hillandale Golf Course, the city-owned municipal course, with "a few hustlers." Bennett and Jackson, who lived about four hours west in Asheville, would carpool to tournaments, staying on the road for as much as a month, trying to find an available hot bag.

Bennett had a few big opportunities in his Tour caddying during the early 2000s but then watched it wash away. Augusta native Charles Howell III hired him at the end of the 2001 season for a handful of events. He also worked for Matt Kuchar for a few events in 2001 when Kuchar earned his Tour card for 2002. Neither relationship with very promising young players lasted very long. Bennett was tardy a few times and put the nail in his coffin by asking Howell if he could borrow money on the first tee the night after a cash deficit in a casino during the Las Vegas stop.

"I've lost a few dollars there," Bennett said of Vegas. "All the caddies go through that in Vegas. You can win some and lose some. Every time I go there, I lose some."

Today, Bennett has settled down a bit. He left Durham following a breakup with his girlfriend in 2002 and spent a few days in an Atlanta jail for driving without a license, according to Jackson. Following the Tour as a caddie was his way of life. Bennett believed he would find a steady bag, but it didn't happen solely because he had been an Augusta National caddie.

Today, he is back home in Augusta, making frequent playing appearances at the Augusta Municipal Course, caddying at ultra-private Sage Valley Golf Club in South Carolina, and reminiscing with old caddying friends, but still hesitant about Augusta National.

"I couldn't work there again," Bennett said. "There are too many memories there. That walk down memory lane would be tough."

1

The Place

1

The Neighborhood

One of the most recognizable gathering spots at Augusta National during the Masters is under the ancient branches of a sprawling live oak tree on the back lawn of the clubhouse and overlooking golf's most famous piece of property as it trundles from the nearby first tee down to Amen Corner and Rae's Creek. The tree, estimated to be at least 175 years old and sentinel of the 1850s-erected manor house before it was a golf course clubhouse, is held in place by cables attached to long, low-hanging and thick branches, and its base is secured by cement placed in a hole in the trunk years ago. This place has shaded nearly a century of golf gatherings among players, celebrities, worldwide golf officials, members, and media and been witness to past and future Masters champions marching from the clubhouse across the lawn to the putting green or first tee. Many titan business deals have been formulated in this place, not all of them related to golf.

Masters attendees gather outside of the ropes, adjacent to the first tee, both for watching tee shots and to turn around to see how many famous folks they can spot nestled under the tree whose branches reach out toward the tee. As mobile phones aren't allowed on the grounds, a common rendez-vous point at an agreed-upon time for those coming on the grounds goes, "I'll meet you at the tree."

Similarly, but in a completely different context and time, there is another prominent set of trees in a historic neighborhood just two and a half miles by road from the back lawn of Augusta National. Out of the pearly front gates at Magnolia Lane, hang a left on Washington Road. After passing the Augusta-logoed water tower on the left, take another left on Berckmans Road moving through the expansive grass and gravel lots where circa 1950s homes once rested but now hold a wide-open vista where free parking is of-fered during the Masters. Then enter neighborhoods and cross Rae's Creek

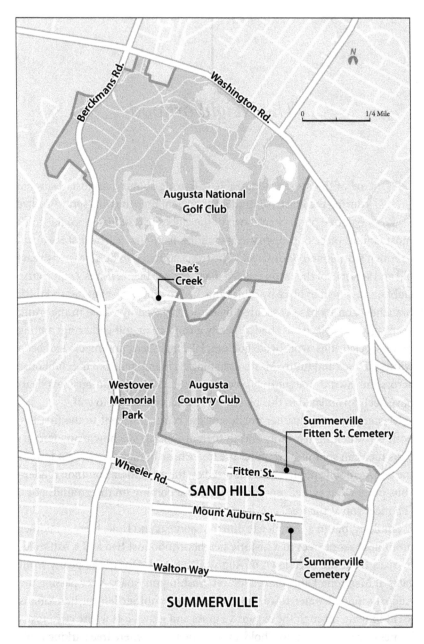

The Sand Hills neighborhood in Augusta, Georgia, is situated between prominent landmark golf courses Augusta National and Augusta Country Club, centuries-old cemeteries, and historic Walton Way. *Map by Robert Cronan, Lucidity Information Design, LLC*

The park and sitting area at the corner of Wheeler Road and Fleming Avenue in Augusta, Georgia, is where former caddies and area club employees regularly gather in the Sand Hills neighborhood. A next-door reminder of their caddying history is depicted by an artist's rendering of Tommy Bennett caddying for Tiger Woods at the 1995 Masters. *Photo by Ward Clayton*

as it flows into the Augusta National property at the thirteenth tee before winding up to Surrey Center on the right with its numerous restaurants and shops packed with Masters attendees. You come to a stop light and intersection with Wheeler Road. Sand Hills surrounds you here, to the left past Westover Memorial Cemetery and skirting Augusta Country Club, straight up Highland Avenue for a bit almost to Walton Way and to the right nestling around Surrey Center. This is where many prominent Augusta National caddies were raised—not all of them, but the majority who rose to fame from the 1930s to 1980s, simply because of proximity.

Pappy, Iron Man, Carl Jackson, Beard, Johnnie Frank Moore, Leon Mc-Claddie, Eddie McCoy, Herrington, Joe Collins, Hop Harrison, Jim Dent, and many others who carried in multiple Masters were all from here.

Others came from Atlanta, located 150 miles down Interstate 20 West, or downtown Augusta, where neighborhoods such as Laney Walker and

Harrisburg are in the throes of redevelopment with the support of Augusta National and its corporate partners, with a first investment of ten million dollars in 2021 and more to be announced. In June 2022, the Hub for Community Innovation opened, two new buildings that house five nonprofits, including a new Boys & Girls Club headquarters. Also, Augusta National donated funds for a Lee Elder Scholarship at Paine College, a historically Black college (HBCU), to fund one male player and one female, thereby starting the school's women's golf program in the fall of 2022.

The Sand Hills lot with the non–Augusta National trees is to the left down Wheeler Road, across from the Sand Hills Community Center at the corner of Fleming Avenue and Wheeler Road. The large trees, an oak and a magnolia most notably, shade the empty lot and a half dozen picnic tables, circular tables, and surrounding chairs and benches scattered about the sandy yard. The barren street corner has been a centralized gathering spot for Sand Hills residents for decades, similar in tone and probably much longer in duration than the more revered trees on site at Augusta National. Today, the area is usually reserved for the older and mostly male set, all Black, with many being current or former Augusta National or Augusta Country Club caddies or workers. It is here where you can find at least a dozen or more folks at any given time and take in the skinny on national and local sports, political and social issues, the golf that is going on next door, or any other state secrets during seemingly endless card games. Outsiders are questioned about their intentions or what they can "contribute" financially, but just listening will teach valuable lessons. Opinions flow freely and loudly here.

Occasionally there are alcoholic drinks in hand, but a NO DRUGS sign is affixed to a tree in the center of the sitting area with smaller type reading: COOLING OUT BY THE TREE. BEST CADDIES IN THE WORLD. UPTOWN – SANDHILLS.

Very little untoward or unlawful occurs, even though there have been a couple of complaints over recent years from new landowners who either judge from a distance or don't know the neighborhood's heritage. The objection is often quickly shot down by local law enforcement and political leaders.

Next door, across Fleming Avenue, are the former Bea's Pool Hall and Sand Hills Grill, which are closed and barely standing. That building still wears the faded painting of an Augusta National caddie carrying a golf bag, viewed from behind to display the green cap, uniform, and name plate of the player. The model for this image was Tommy Bennett, a son of Sand Hills

The sitting area where former caddies and area club employees gather in Sand Hills has a sign indicating proper behavior and who usually congregates in this spot at the corner of Wheeler Road and Fleming Avenue in Augusta, Georgia. *Photo by Ward Clayton*

and the first caddie for Tiger Woods at the 1995 Masters. Bennett toured Tiger and his father Earl around the neighborhood during that year's tournament so they could gain a sense for where the caddie resource developed.

The entire Sand Hills community, known more simply by locals as "The Hill," earned its name because of the sandy and hilly terrain different from the usual red clay composition of most Georgia soil in the region. It also holds a notable place in Black culture that should be restored for its social values beyond just its golf connections.

Summerville, a historic summer retreat for prominent white Augustans and northerners more than a century ago and still a bastion of large homes and the well to do, abuts Sand Hills in the Walton Way periphery as one of the Central Savannah River area's highest geographic points. The residents, from some of Augusta's most prominent white families, once owned the Sand Hills land.

Soon after the Civil War ended, many Black families, some of them previously enslaved or close kin of the enslaved, settled in the area, primarily toiling as laborers and domestic workers at the nearby larger homes in Summerville, which they could easily reach by foot. Many prominent white families deeded small tracts of land in Sand Hills to Black families to closely position butlers, maids, gardeners, carpenters, and other workers to their own homes. After Augusta annexed Summerville in 1912, an ordinance was passed in 1913 to impose racial zoning, leading more Black families to move to Sand Hills in closer proximity to Summerville jobs—some who had been free for generations and lived near the often-flooded and much hotter lower lands adjacent to the Savannah River in downtown Augusta. The remains of the spacious Bon Air Hotel, now a senior-living residence, is a few blocks away on Walton Way and was the city's centerpiece hotel through the 1950s. Most Masters participants and officials stayed there during the tournament, and it employed many service industry workers.

Businesses, churches, restaurants, and social establishments came about in Sand Hills with the incoming population—places like Mr. Smalley's Shoe Shop, Tate's Grill with its tasty sausage dog, Gene's Barbershop, and Bea's Pool Room. Historic churches dot the landscape, including still-existent Greater Mt. Canaan Missionary Baptist, Elim Baptist, the circa-1890 Rock of Ages Christian Methodist Episcopal Church, and Cumming Grove Baptist, built in 1867 and rebuilt in 1915 but recently purchased by Augusta Country Club for undisclosed purposes.

"Most of our parents worked as domestics in Summerville," said Gwen Clayborne, who grew up in Sand Hills between the Beard family and the family of Eddie "E. B." McCoy, who caddied for Gary Player in 1974 and 1978 Masters victories, moved to Connecticut in the early 1960s, and is now back as an Augusta resident. "A lot of the Black kids who grew up in downtown Augusta had never been in white people's homes. We were in white people's homes all the time. When you were in the home of successful Black people, their homes were decorated differently because they were exposed to people who had money.

"We were poor, but we had fireplaces in the living room and bedroom as our only source of heat. Our friends played and worked on the course at the Masters. We were poor, but we never knew it.

"We lived in a community where we loved each other. That sums up what it was like."

A Chinese community emerged in Augusta in the late 1870s when approximately two hundred male Chinese laborers were brought in to widen and deepen the Augusta Canal, a seven-mile-long waterway that provided water and power to downtown factories. The canal work was conducted alongside formerly enslaved Black people who became businessmen and offered to help with the hot work if paid a similar wage as other work, which Augusta city officials agreed to, according to Augusta historian Dr. Ed Cashin. The Chinese community, one of the oldest in the eastern United States, took root, and more Chinese families arrived by the 1920s to support more than forty Chinese grocery stores located around inner-city Augusta in the 1930s, including three Chinese groceries within a couple of blocks in Sand Hills. The total presence was much larger than Chinese grocery representation in Atlanta or Savannah. Groceries such as W. T. Woo and K. F. Wong were prominent in offering credit to the mostly Black Sand Hills customers and hiring young Black men—after a trial period of observation by the Chinese grocery owners—to serve as delivery agents for food. White grocers would not serve Black customers, so the Chinese grocers saw an opportunity. The Chinese families mostly resided in the back of the grocery stores.

It was a growing place for two communities that weren't accepted by the majority white population but were tolerated at completely different levels, according to a 2023 PBS documentary, *Blurring the Color Line*. The Chinese children were allowed to attend white schools but not interact with their white classmates, while the Black youth had separate schools during segregation.

Famous names also began to emerge from the inner-city Black neighborhoods by the 1950s and 1960s, including the "Godfather of Soul," James Brown, and opera superstar Jessye Norman. They were predated by prolific author Frank Yerby, who was born in the Sand Hills neighborhood in 1916 and wrote thirty-three novels, selling a total of fifty-five million copies, and was the first Black person to write a series of novels and then have many of them purchased by Hollywood for film adaptations before dying in Spain in 1991. Another prime influencer was the gospel music group, the Swanee Quintet, which originated in Augusta in the 1930s and sang all over the world.

The Summerville Cemetery, with Revolutionary War and Civil War–era dead and prominent white Augustans buried within, and massive Westover Cemetery with similarly historic and mostly white inhabitants, frame the neighborhood. Of much lesser notoriety but more importance to the Sand

Hills community is Summerville Cemetery-Fitten Street, founded as a Black cemetery two blocks from the main Summerville Cemetery and adjacent to Augusta Country Club's seventeenth hole. Often overgrown in past years, it is now maintained by the city and researched by historian Joyce Law. Former Augusta National caddies and workers are buried in all three locations.

The Federal Emergency Administration of Public Works funded the 1936 building of the Weed School on Mount Auburn Street, two blocks from the community center. Named after a white 1880s minister and Black education supporter, the Reverend Edward Weed, the school met the need to educate the infusion of youngsters in a facility that closed in the early 2000s but still stands. The segregated school was the centerpiece of the community for decades, and most kids encountered the powerhouse English teacher Hattie Pearl Scott, who taught there for forty-eight years and lived across the street. Just about every caddie who went on to Augusta Country Club and Augusta National had Ms. Scott in their ears, especially since her boyfriend was Edwin Dove, the longtime locker room attendant and expert shoeshiner at Augusta National. She would hear about the young caddies' conduct or share her perceptions with Dove.

"You had to know your lessons for her," said Lawrence Bennett, whose father, Freddie, the longtime Augusta National caddie master, settled his family on the periphery of Sand Hills in the 1950s despite objections, such as bottle throwing, from some white neighbors. "If you didn't know your work or cut up in class, you had to stay after school and write on the board how many things you did wrong. She wrote on the board Thomas Paine's famous line, 'These are the times that try men's souls.' She had perfect handwriting and put railroad tracks on the board with the names of local prisons to emphasize that unless you do your work you might end up in one of those prisons. She was tough."

Lawrence Bennett said most of the single men in the neighborhood who didn't have full-time jobs worked as caddies or held other jobs within the two clubs. Many of those who did have full-time jobs found a way to caddie on the side at either course to earn extra money and a chance at notoriety, especially in the spring around Masters time. Those who worked night shifts would leave work at daybreak and find their way to Augusta National in time for the 8:00 a.m. start of the caddying rotation, a routine that Beard followed for years.

"Back in the 1950s when I started caddying, you could make three dollars, four dollars, five dollars a day at Augusta Country Club, and that was pretty good back then," Beard said. "And for two weekend days at Augusta National, you could make twenty-five dollars, thirty dollars, or forty dollars, and that was really good."

The path to both courses was a short walk from Sand Hills. If you eyeball a map of Augusta, the neighborhood rests just south of the border of Augusta Country Club, which was founded in the late 1800s as Augusta's first golf course.

At golf's infancy in Augusta around the turn of the twentieth century and with the pomp and circumstance of Bobby Jones's Augusta National Golf Club opening, there was a prominent mention of caddying and its connection to the Black community in Augusta. Under the headline, "Golf Club Reorganized," in the October 3, 1900, *Augusta Chronicle*, plans were being prepared to sort out the new sport in Augusta at the recently built Bon Air Golf Club, a smattering of holes designed in 1897 with browns (sand) instead of greens near the Bon Air Hotel, in proximity to where today's Augusta Country Club course sits and just more than one mile from Sand Hills. Palmetto Golf Club in Aiken, South Carolina, had formed in 1892, and Bon Air was right on its heels. Augusta was so entrenched as a winter retreat prior to Florida's emergence that English golfer Harry Vardon made the Bon Air course one of his many national exhibition stops in early 1900, therefore bringing more luster to Augusta and golf.

Toward the end of the October 3 article, among names thrown about as officers and with high expectations for the winter season, was a note about how to incorporate some of the younger, albeit looked-down-upon set in Augusta, many of whom worked labor jobs at Bon Air. That one paragraph stated: "Col. Phil North, the eminently practical city treasurer, has a good idea for a connection with golf. He says that while the rage is on to teach negro boys useful accomplishments by which they can earn a living it might be a good idea to add a 'school of caddies' on to the curriculum of the negro schools. Caddies are in demand and the more prevalent golf becomes the greater the demand for caddies will become."

Little did the colonel know, but this possibly set forward a mindset among the Black youngsters that caddying could be a profession where they were accepted—at least in some regard.

That perception didn't change much three decades later when Augusta National was slated to have its official opening in January 1933. More than one hundred visitors traveled from the North and East, particularly those on a special train commandeered by Clifford Roberts to bring business and media leaders from New York, Philadelphia, and Baltimore to the course opening. Jones and superstar sportswriter and member Grantland Rice were listed as the hosts.

Previewing the gathering, the Friday, January 13, 1933, *Augusta Chronicle* predicted "a touch of the Old South will be given to visitors today" with a mention of barbecue to soothe the golfers' hunger pangs. Most notable in the description was the reception that the participants would experience:

> As the visitors come into the grounds, they will find awaiting them a horde of red-clad negro caddies and two chipper boys in flaming red uniforms standing at the door of the old plantation home converted with only slight alterations into the clubhouse.

Even more disconcerting was a narrative that rankles many who have some knowledge of Augusta's Old South history and how it is often connected to golf, particularly at Augusta National:

> An old tavern was erected on the plantation during the days of the Revolution and from then until about 1853 the story of the plantation was about the same as that of the others throughout the country. Slaves did the work as the masters took their ease under the trees which now provide hazards for unwary golfers.

With all this in mind, it was a natural progression for young men to wander next door to Augusta National for work, much like kids in the Bronx growing up in the shadow of Yankee Stadium would dream of being bat boys, playing the outfield, handling concessions, working in the ticket office, or doing any odd jobs that were available. To draw another baseball parallel, the Sand Hills kids aspired to spend their minor-league days at Augusta Country Club and then graduate across the creek (Rae's Creek) to major-league Augusta National.

The sixteenth and seventeenth holes at Augusta Country Club run parallel to Fitten and Gardner Streets, and severely sliced shots can end up in the neighborhood. For years, just a buffer of bushes and trees and a makeshift fence that was easy to get under separated Augusta Country Club from Sand Hills. Jackson said he would walk from his home to the dead-end Weed Street and enter Augusta Country Club. A pathway skirted Augusta Country

Club's eleventh and tenth holes near the Westover Cemetery at Berckmans Road to form a shortcut to Augusta National. A sizable hole in the fence from the woods adjacent to Augusta National's thirteenth tee provided an entryway to the grounds.

Jackson said many young Sand Hills caddies would swim in Rae's Creek, often jumping off Nelson Bridge in front of the thirteenth tee box on hot summer days when Augusta National was closed. They would also fish there and prepare their catch via makeshift fires on the banks of Rae's Creek at spots hidden in the woods on the bordering area of the club property—to stay out of view of club security. Today, that buffer from Augusta Country Club includes a sturdier chain-link fence occasionally topped with barbed wire hidden among trees and shrubbery and a part of the extended area behind the thirteenth tee that includes a service road around the Augusta National property.

Also close by Sand Hills was the Augusta Municipal Golf Course, a 1928 course built for the public, albeit on hardscrabble land with tiny greens and so closely situated to Daniel Field, the private- and small-aircraft airport, that planes occasionally overrun runways and interfere with the course. The current par-3 tenth hole is at the southern end of a runway, and if you time it correctly, a high, short iron shot could slam into the side of an approaching plane, or at least startle golfers if they didn't realize a plane was about to touch down. In 1993, Dr. Trey Holland, a rules official at the Masters and a future United States Golf Association president, careened his small plane into a pond at the public course's fourteenth green, which lines up with the runway descent, exited the plane on his own, and was only slightly injured. During Masters week, Daniel Field changes from a small southern airport into a big-city rush hour with a cavalcade of planes and jets owned by well-to-do members, players, and Masters attendees soaring in and out.

The course is more commonly referred to as "the Patch" for two reasons—longtime pro Lawson "Red" Douglas grew cabbages in a garden patch outside the small clubhouse and close to the tenth tee, and the course was usually in less-than-stellar condition.

However, the course just three miles from Sand Hills was off limits for its residents. Until the early 1960s it was a segregated course. In May 1964, one month after Arnold Palmer won his fourth and final Masters, prominent Augusta civil rights attorney and future judge John Ruffin Jr., and friends Clois Herndon, John Elam, Raymond Jenkins, and Dr. Maurice Thompson became the first Black people to play the Patch as they walked on. That started a pro-longed legal process and eventually opened the doors for many Augusta National caddies, including future successful pro Jim Dent, to enjoy the course. Dent, who grew up in Sand Hills, perfected his short game at the Patch on a strip of land sandwiched by the eleventh fairway and the runway since there was not a driving range at the time. Dent, who turned eighty-four in 2023, had caddied in the Masters for Bob Goalby and went on to win twelve times on the Senior PGA Tour from 1989–98. Today, Dent's sons and cousins operate the course with a road leading onto the grounds titled Jim Dent Way. If you want to find some of the old Augusta National caddies, the driving range, putting green, or the restaurant at the Patch are good places to start.

In 2023, Augusta National announced it will partner with the Patch, Augusta Technical College, and the First Tee of Augusta in a "model for other communities" to elevate public golf in the Augusta area. Augusta National Chairman Fred Ridley, who grew up playing public courses in central Florida, cited the Augusta National mission statement, spelled out on a laminated green card that members carry in their Green Jacket pockets, that reads, "We are committed to our community as one of our underlying principles." He also noted the "wonderful bones" for the rolling land where the Patch lies and key words such as "affordable" and "welcoming pathway" for the project.

The trio of programs is slated to bring course management and workforce programs to the Patch property and incorporate the next-door First Tee facility into the concept. The Patch and the First Tee, located alongside the third hole at the Patch, will be the beneficiaries of a master plan and renovation of the courses, with thoughts of bringing their conditioning up considerably by the time Augusta Tech takes over operations of the Patch by 2025.

"While in its early stages, this partnership can help produce the next generation of golf's workforce and make the game more accessible and inviting to youth and residents throughout the community," Ridley said. "I commend Augusta Technical College, the Patch, the First Tee of Augusta, and all leaders involved in this project, and we look forward to supporting their partnership and this exciting new chapter for public golf here in our city."

There was hope at the Patch in April 2023 about the announcement but also apprehension within its own clubhouse, since outside agents with deep pockets had previously defaulted on making the Patch whole. Would the Patch's low-key, inclusive atmosphere and low-cost green fees remain (a maximum of $37 in 2023)? A wait-and-see attitude prevailed as fall came in Augusta.

The news about the Patch cast the spotlight back on these neighborhood kids who are now mostly in their seventies—and those from other surrounding communities—to bring a parallel to another lot of underappreciated figures at a similar athletic event in the South. The Kentucky Derby in Louisville, Kentucky, began in 1875, and the early heroes were singularly the horses. Just like the all-Black caddie corps at Augusta National went largely unnoticed during the first four decades of the Masters, most of the early jockeys were local young Black men from Louisville or Lexington who didn't get their due respect. Thirteen of the fifteen riders in the first Derby were Black, and winning jockeys in fifteen of the Derby's first twenty-eight races were Black before Jim Crow laws in the early 1900s halted their success. One of the most successful Black jockeys was an Augustan, Willie Simms, who is the only Black jockey to win all three Triple Crown races (all in the 1890s) and who died before Augusta National was founded. In the past twenty years, and particularly recently, these jockeys have been duly recognized at the Churchill Downs racetrack and adjacent Kentucky Derby Museum in southern Louisville with various displays honoring their participation.

When Augusta National allowed outside caddies to work at the Masters in 1983, it not only dissolved many Masters week caddying jobs, but it took some of the enthusiasm out of the Augusta communities, with burgs such as Laney Walker and Harrisburg among other inner-city Black neighborhoods that had their own proudful businesses, gathering spots, and parties. The Golden Blocks in the downtown Laney Walker neighborhood were a notable example of Black businesses thriving despite segregation and Jim Crow laws that required racially designated blocks with banks, insurance companies, theaters, and other businesses becoming quite successful where James Brown and Laney Walker Boulevards meet. Harrisburg is located adjacent to the Augusta Canal just west of downtown and east of Augusta National and was largely populated by workers at the adjacent mills in the early and mid-1900s, with many of those being Black families.

"During the Masters week we Black caddies at that time were celebrities. The news media used us all the time. We were celebrities that week. We were the talk of the town. We gave parties, we had fun," said Beard, who grew up in Sand Hills and resided there until his death at age eighty-two in early 2023.

"We did it because we had a long-standing pride in what we did. You don't know how much money that took out of the Black community. It devastated a lot of guys because they depended on that money to hold them over when the course closed in May for the summer until it opened again the next October. That just wore a lot of guys out."

In many ways, the Black community in Augusta had more to celebrate when neighborhood caddies worked in the Masters than it did even when Tiger Woods emerged a quarter century ago.

Tiger is a point of pride in that he reached the pinnacle of what was once an all-white sport and has undoubtedly brought more people to the game who previously had no interest in playing golf, much less watching the sport. The First Tee, a national program focused on offering access to golf for those who previously had not received the opportunity, sprang up in 1997 at the same time Woods won his first Masters. Augusta has the beautiful First Tee small course and clubhouse located on Damascus Road, a little more than a block from Forest Hills Golf Club and adjacent to the Patch's front nine on the former site of low-rent apartments and the planned partnership with Augusta National. Beard was one of many community members who have tried to infuse more interest and involvement from within the young Black community of inner-city Augusta.

For years, the Monday after the Masters always began a huge week of celebration in Augusta's Black community. All the Augusta National employees, including the caddies, waiters, ground maintenance, cook staff, attendants, and other workers received their paychecks on the Monday after the Masters. Cab drivers, hotel workers, and other employees around the periphery of the tournament also welcomed the week after when they could relax. It was a time to celebrate their contribution to Augusta's most visible event. Usually at the center of the celebration was Augusta's winning caddie, first because he had become famous the previous Sunday and second because he had garnered the largest paycheck.

"Black businesses thrived that week too because it was time for everybody to celebrate," Beard said. "When less and less caddies started to work the tournament and less of us came from Augusta, it was absolutely all gone."

As a result, the Sand Hills' caddie story became more history than current events in a neighborhood that has far too many lots and homes that are overgrown or in shambles among property largely made up of 1950s and 1960s bungalows and a drug problem that is documented over nearly three decades, all despite being on the National Register of Historic Places since

1997. For a half century, Augusta Country Club has slowly purchased small Sand Hills lots and has indicated an interest in creating a buffer, more space for membership parking, and an expanded golf practice facility, a buying-off of adjacent land similar on a much smaller scale to what Augusta National procured during recent decades on its public-facing western and northern perimeters.

But there is promise, even though there are echoes of previously forsaken undertakings. In September 2021, city officials revealed that a master revitalization plan was ready to kick off. Concerns about gentrification—like those that the Patch supporters have voiced—were addressed at the outset, with Augusta commissioner Jordan Johnson promising this wasn't an effort to attract wealthier people and push out longtime residents but instead a focus on preservation to protect longtime Sand Hills residents with property tax freezes and inclusionary zoning. Gentrification has been a topic of concern for residents dating back to the 1990s.

Another element of the neighborhood work was a plan to erect a historic marker or artwork honoring the Black caddie corps that made Sand Hills so proud. That plan was approved in 2020 and is currently awaiting further action, as it was delayed by a change in political leadership and the pandemic. Following the 2023 Masters, more people became involved in the discussion about the potential makeup of the piece—artwork with a symbolic theme or a marker with names and dates—and where it would be placed in the community. The conversation was long overdue, as it occurred forty years after the caddie ranks were opened to outsiders and a few years since there was initial approval by city officials. Time moves on . . . slowly.

1

The Caddie Masters

Freddie Bennett never had to travel very far to reach another world. It was in his backyard.

He was practically born on the golf course in 1930, growing up just off the sixteenth fairway at Augusta Country Club in the Sand Hills neighborhood. He swam in Rae's Creek as a child, right in front of the twelfth green, and remembers the cows grazing on the Augusta National grounds during World War II. When it came time to retire as the caddie master at the Augusta National Golf Club in 2000, all he had to do was mosey a mile or so away, to his current home located a block above a cemetery and three blocks from Berckmans Road. In between, he made a name for himself for more than fifty years as a caddie and, more prominently, caddie master.

During a forty-one-year career at Augusta National, the only person you had to call to make something happen was Freddie. "I went to see Freddie," was the ringing endorsement many Masters participants uttered when they needed a change of caddies or advice about hiring a caddie. He paired most of the Augusta National caddies with the players and members. Some became long-term relationships, others simply year-to-year or day-to-day partnerships. He recruited extra caddies for the tournament or for member play by occasionally driving his station wagon into various Augusta neighborhoods and transporting potential caddies back to the Washington Road course. He had a backup plan if a caddie had to be fired or didn't show up, helped store the players' golf gear, laundered the famous caddie jumpsuits (five sets of one hundred uniforms at one time in the late 1960s), found some minor medication for players' queasy stomachs, and, in a pinch, could even repair a player's broken equipment. He even got his son, Lawrence, a job as a chauffeur for Augusta National members, guests, and Masters participants, a job Lawrence held for more than forty years. In other words, he did everything, all on a flat salary with no commission.

Freddie Bennett was the caddie master at Augusta
National for forty-one years before retiring in 2000.
Bennett was responsible for many of the memorable
Masters caddie pairings and oversaw the esteemed
Augusta National caddie corps. *Photo by Frank Christian
and Lawrence Bennett*

"I love it, but I'm getting steadily gray, got an ulcer, and it is a worrisome
job that'll just get tougher because caddies are disappearing," Bennett, then
age thirty-seven, said in 1968.

In the later years of his Masters duty, he could often be found perched atop
a stool in the bag room that sat adjacent to the first fairway and attached to
the clubhouse, separated by a thin passageway from the course side to the
parking lot. He greeted players, caddies, Augusta National members, and
various international officials. The roster of celebrities he greeted included

Presidents Eisenhower, Nixon, Ford, Reagan, and Bush, Bob Hope, and Michael Jordan.

Bennett had a gruff exterior and booming, baritone voice that could rattle even the most experienced caddie. "Freddie's a nice guy," said Edward White, who remained for years after Bennett retired as the club's man in charge of the bag room and cart fleet. "He's got his ways. When he acts like he's mad, he's just trying to throw you off. He gets steamed up every now and then. But with Freddie, today is today and tomorrow is tomorrow."

The caddie master job has been significant in the development of caddies for ages, which is important to understand when examining Bennett's position. In recent years the term *master* has been changed at most places to *caddie manager* to avoid any type of racial stereotyping. The manager title is used by the Western Golf Association, which administers the Caddie Hall of Fame and Evans Scholarship.

Blurry history lessons—no matter how far-fetched and more than likely pure hyperbole—have often said that caddies first were heard about in the 1500s when Mary, Queen of Scots went to France as a young girl. The king of France had the first golf course outside of Scotland built for her. The king hired cadets from a military school to guard Mary as she played golf or simply to carry her belongings. When Mary returned to Scotland from France at age eighteen, she brought several of the uniformed lads back with her. Mostly, they toted her bags and other goods. But one of their supposed duties back home in Scotland was to follow Mary around the links and carry her clubs. Most Scottish golf historians debunk this myth, though they do find it amusing since that storyline has been spread for centuries.

In French, *cadet* is pronounced "ca-day." Cadets soon became "caddies," simply because of the Scottish pronunciation. A legend was born.

Roger McStravick, a St. Andrews, Scotland, historian, author, and two-time winner of the USGA's Herbert Warren Wind Book Awards said, "The greatest myth about caddies is they came from Mary, Queen of Scots. I read it in all the history books. They are outlandish stories." McStravick indicates they were likely just porters for baggage, not golf clubs, and eventually were roped into toting clubs.

One of the earliest written references to caddies appears in the record of Andrew Dixon, a golf ball maker in the early eighteenth century who lived near Edinburgh, Scotland, and worked for Mary's grandson, the Duke of York (future King James II).

Caddie masters became a necessity in the late 1800s as caddying and club and ball making developed into more established trades for the working classes in golf-mad Scotland and Ireland. The caddie master was often selected from among the caddie ranks to make sure the rambunctious caddie corps behaved properly and performed its duties to meet the expectations of the higher class of golfers.

The first documented caddie master was Old Tom Morris, who grew up extremely poor in St. Andrews, Scotland, and became a revered golf figure. He came home after a stint at Prestwick to work at St. Andrews in 1864 as the champion golfer for three of the first five Open Championships. He was hired to shape up the rugged Old Course as its "Keeper of the Green" and tasked with overseeing the caddies.

"Caddies were an unruly bunch, unkempt, frequently drunk, more curse words than any words in a sentence. They were of the lower classes," McStravick said. "[Old] Tom Morris was a caddie and became the greatest golfer of his era, but his circle of friends and environment was caddies. That was his class, his people. In 1864, Tom Morris was put in charge of the caddies. A code of conduct was developed—caddies had to be older than age eleven, attend Sunday School, and no drinking. You could see Old Tom's influence. From then on, there was a person to look over the caddies. And from that point forward we've had a caddie master."

Until 1963, the United States Golf Association rules for amateur status considered a caddie, caddie master, or anyone who worked at a golf club cleaning or repairing clubs to be a professional. As a result, until 1975, all four major championships banned the use of outside caddies.

Donald Ross, the famed course architect, moved to Massachusetts from Scotland in the late 1800s. Soon, he was hired in Pinehurst, North Carolina, in 1900 to serve as the resort's professional and caddie master. He supervised the all-Black caddie corps and vastly improved their facilities, designated a caddie shack for women, established a standard for academic and health guidelines, conducted child-labor law discussions with state authorities, and demanded ample food services through the 1920s, according to author Brad Klein's book, *Discovering Donald Ross*.

The caddie master's role can be close to the heart for a club or course, much like the individual caddies. For example, at Canterbury Golf Club in Cleveland, Mike Kiely served as the caddie master for fifty-four years through 2021. His son-in-law, Trey Anderson, stepped into the role upon

Kiely's retirement. Kiely was named the Caddie Master Emeritus, and club members decided Kiely would receive a salary for the remainder of his life. The membership raised approximately $400,000 in his name and created an Evans Scholarship to honor his time at Canterbury.

In golf's best-known movie, the 1980 comedy *Caddyshack*, the fictional Lou Loomis, the gruff, gambling caddie master played and scripted by Brian Doyle-Murray, was based on another Lou—Louis Janis, the caddie master at Indian Hill Club in the northern Chicago suburb of Winnetka from the late 1950s to the 1960s. Janis and his brothers took the bus from their home to caddie during the 1940s at another suburban Chicago club, Sunset Ridge Country Club. Louis went on to Northwestern but didn't like being cooped up in a business office. The caddie yard is where Janis learned from a veteran caddie master the mantra "Watch the ball, keep up with your player, and never bet the gray horse at the racetrack."

So, Janis was happy to banter with his caddie corps or wager on just about any member's golf game, card games, college football, or horse racing, like the more famous Lou Loomis.

Janis's persona led to the movie's famous line by caddie master Loomis/Doyle-Murray: "I'm going to put it right on the line. There's been a lot of complaints already. Fooling around on the course, bad language, smoking grass, poor caddying. If you guys want to get fired, if you want to be replaced by golf carts, just keep it up."

Ed Murray, the oldest of the six famous Murray brothers and the model for *Caddyshack* lead caddie Danny Noonan, first met Janis while serving as an altar boy when Janis was attending Mass one day and asked if anyone had ever caddied. Ed pursued the new gig, as did the other five Murray brothers, including comedian, actor, and golf icon Bill. That established the background for the movie.

Bennett also came by his job by being in the right spot at the right time and was deserving of the promotion. He was a caddie at heart, first serving in the Masters as a sixteen-year-old in 1946, toting for Billy Burke. Jackie Burke Jr., Frank Stranahan, Peter Thomson, Jay Hebert, and Chick Evans would follow. Evans was the founder of the Western Golf Association's Evans Scholarship for caddies in 1930.

Stranahan's story is particularly memorable. The wealthy amateur grew up in Toledo, Ohio, as the son of the founder of Champion Spark Plug and was one of the first golfers to train with weights. He carried himself confidently, evidenced during a 1948 Masters practice round when he had a verbal confrontation with the Augusta National superintendent, Marion Luke. It seemed Stranahan was playing more than one ball in his practice rounds, chipping and putting excessively to learn all the nuances of the course. Playing more than one ball was forbidden in those days and remained so for years to come, evidenced by the small signs that were placed on the first and tenth tees during the practice rounds stating, "One ball only." But tournament officials put up with it if the player didn't abuse the policy and play a bucket of balls on each hole.

But Stranahan kept on and on during a particularly wet day at Augusta National. Finally, Augusta National officials asked him to leave the course on the eighth green. He had been disqualified after some of the members were kept abreast of his actions.

"He said, 'I only hit two balls,'" Bennett remembered. "There were balls all over the green, but Frank didn't explain they were there for putting. On No. 6, he asked me if they were still following him. I told him they were. When he got to No. 8, they said, 'Get off the course.'"

John Henry "'Leven" Williams was the original caddie master at Augusta National. He became a caddie as a youngster and was assigned to lead the caddie corps after World War II, earning his nickname either because eleven was his caddie uniform number or he was the eleventh of eleven children. 'Leven sported a uniform that resembled an old-fashioned cab driver's, complete with a large cap, and gave many of the caddies of the 1940s and 1950s their nicknames. He was also known as an excellent club repairman.

Bennett served in the military for two years in the late 1940s and then took a bricklayers' course. After laying bricks for a couple years, Bennett figured his passion was working at Augusta National. He came back to the club in the early 1950s to work on the maintenance crew.

Williams died suddenly on October 16, 1959, at age forty-five, suffering a cerebral hemorrhage while working his summertime gig at the Broadmoor Golf Club in Colorado Springs, Colorado, for former Augusta National head professional Ed Dudley. Bennett, who was in his late twenties at the time, was quickly named caddie master just as the club opened for the 1959–60 season. Golf was reaching new popularity as golf enthusiast Eisenhower was in office, Arnold Palmer was becoming "the King," and Jack Nicklaus was a young amateur making his way toward history.

Bennett's position running the caddie corps at Augusta National came

John Henry "'Leven" Williams was the caddie master at
Augusta National through the late 1950s. *Masters Historic
Imagery/Getty Images*

with high prestige. Billy Ricks, a former Augusta National caddie, said when
the group would hit a bar downtown after a long day caddying, they would
invite the caddie master along. Buying him a beer would, in their minds, be
a good way to try and get an angle on a bag for the next day.

"The caddie master never bought a drink, no sir," Ricks said. "Hey, but that
didn't necessarily mean you'd get a bag either."

The caddie master's most arduous task was assigning caddies for players
or members. In the 1950s and 1960s, your caddie knowledge got you a long
way. Bennett knew his men's strengths. If a player needed help with club selection, Bennett might choose Ernest Nipper, a good player and yardage

man, to work the bag. A player yearning for some help on Augusta National's difficult greens might get Matthew "Shorty Mac" Palmer, renowned for his keen sense for reading greens. Looking for a reliable, steady hand who could work with anyone? How about Joe Collins. For members, meshing personalities was just as important as caddying ability. The player had to know where to go and when and how to interact with the member.

Bennett recognized his best caddies by offering them the best player bags or the highest-paying members' clubs. One way that you could tell his best caddies was by the wear and tear on their "tenni-pumps." Bennett estimated that a good caddie would wear out approximately forty pairs of shoes during a season as a "winter club" from mid-October when Augusta National opened until late May when it closed for the summer.

Bennett worked with a crew of thirty-five to forty caddies most of the year. Having a car was a luxury for many of the caddies, and 8:00 a.m. was the magic hour where the first-come, first-served policy rewarded the drivers or those who lived within walking distance who could arrive before the other caddies who had to ride the 8:00 a.m. Augusta city bus that dropped them at the entrance to Augusta National. On many occasions, caddies for member play made their mark beginning on Friday afternoon when they would be assigned to a member's party that arrived for either nine or eighteen holes, which carried over to multiple rounds on Saturday and a concluding eighteen holes on Sunday morning if the player-caddie relationship worked. The number of caddies at least doubled with part-timers coming on in the weeks leading up to the Masters in hopes of becoming famous in the tournament. School-age boys would volunteer to caddie just that week at no charge. Bennett watched out for his year-long regulars by making sure they received first dibs on a Masters bag.

In the late 1960s, caddie fees for member play were three dollars for nine holes and six dollars for eighteen, increasing to fifty-five dollars per eighteen by the early 2000s and nearly one hundred dollars by 2023. Most make tips equal to the fee and sometimes lots more. A Masters caddie fee in the late 1960s was ten dollars per day, but most earned at least one hundred dollars from the tournament on fees alone.

Today's Masters-winning caddie can earn at least $250,000 with the usual 10 percent cut for a win and the $2-million-plus first-place prize. In 2023, Masters winner Jon Rahm earned $3,240,000, giving caddie Adam Hayes at least a $324,000 payday. Normally, caddies at the highest level of professional golf are paid with the "ten-seven-five" concept: ten percent of the player earnings for a win, seven percent for a top-ten finish, and five percent for anything else after the cut. Additionally, there's a ballpark minimum salary per week to allow for some return should the player not make the cut, which is at least $1,500.

In 1968, Bennett described the caddie selection process for the Masters: "Julius Boros's caddie of last year, Henry Jenkins, got a little old, so we gave him a job sticking decals and gave Boros to Rufus Whitfield. See, we try to give the new, good players our best available and our best available try to get the good players. They can read, they know who they are."

When one caddie was picked for a group of member play, that caddie had the option of picking three more to join his foursome, creating an atmosphere of camaraderie and tutoring. When CaddieMaster Enterprises took over operation of the caddies in 1996, the caddie system became a lottery. Each caddie had his own number, which was drawn out of a bag. Each caddie in the foursome was chosen by this drawing instead of the previous system by which the fit caddies survived. No one was guaranteed a day's work, even though the basic benefits for caddies improved.

"I think it was good for the caddies because they had a salary," Bennett said. "They may not have made quite as much money. But they could go on unemployment in the summer when the course was closed [from May until October]."

Being the caddie master also fostered unusual relationships, which often depicted racially insensitive role-playing. Club photographer Frank Christian and club officials persuaded Bennett to take part in a comical club film one year in the early 1970s, to be shown during the members' annual early spring Jamboree weekend, the largest member gathering of the season where members play in two-person team competition. The film portrayed a gorilla running all over the grounds at Augusta National, stealing clubs and causing havoc. The man inside the suit was Bennett, even though the conclusion of the film revealed that it was supposed to be Roberts, who had a hard-edged reputation among members.

Another odd club film the following year had Roberts walk out on a hidden plank at the sixteenth hole pond as if he could walk on water, a similar inside membership joke as the previous year's gorilla script. The following caddie, unaware of the prank, misstepped and went directly into the water beside the short walkway that was built especially for the occasion and just a bit under the water surface. The undisclosed caddie had to be rescued by club staff since he couldn't swim. Christian snapped an image of Roberts, seemingly walking on water, looking back at the caddie, who is trudging in with water at thigh level. The image was published in Christian's 1996 book *Augusta National and the Masters: A Photographer's Scrapbook*, and was similarly unnerving.

Both were demeaning, but something the caddie master had to endure while working with an all-Black workforce at a club that didn't have its first Black member until Ron Townsend joined in 1990.

When Roberts died by suicide on the grounds in 1977, Bennett had theories about what happened. He remembered Roberts coming on the club grounds for that visit with fresh one-hundred-dollar bills in his wallet, and the chairman was empty-pocketed when his body was discovered on September 29 near Ike's Pond on the Par 3 Course. Bennett contends that the eighty-three-year-old Roberts was too frail and it was too dark that night for him to walk down to the Par 3 Course. He thinks Roberts paid an overnight guard to drive him to the short course and then drop him off. Roberts was discovered with a fatal bullet wound to the head.

Bennett's life in the early 2000s was far removed from the fast pace at Augusta National. He was a persistent visitor with old friends in the Sand Hills area, sitting on a porch early in the morning or getting a cup of coffee at a neighborhood restaurant. He would occasionally go fishing, a longtime passion before he passed away in late 2006, with burial in Westover Cemetery, almost within view of the Sand Hills home where he resided for forty years.

He was drawing close to his retirement in 2000 when CaddieMaster Enterprises took over in 1996. That took all the responsibility of choosing caddies out of Bennett's hands. Tom Van Dorn was brought in by the caddie corporation to run the show, leaving Bennett hanging out at the end of the clubhouse to talk about the old times when he ran the show at Augusta National.

"I won't be here," Bennett said in 2000 about coming back to Augusta National (even though he would visit). "I'm gone. That's it. I won't be back. I've seen enough."

Top 10

When Freddie Bennett retired as caddie master at Augusta National in 2000, he provided his top-ten list of the Augusta National caddies to *Sports Illustrated*:

1. Willie "Pappy" Stokes
2. Nathaniel "Iron Man" Avery
3. Willie "Pete" Peterson
4. Carl Jackson
5. Eddie "E. B." McCoy
6. Ernest "Snipes" Nipper
7. Jerry "Bubba" Beard
8. Matthew "Shorty Mac" Palmer
9. Leon McCladdie
10. Mark "Banks" Eubanks

1

The Caddie Shack

Peek behind the bushes located to the right of the first fairway's landing area, just up from the gigantic scoreboard. The area is off-limits to tournament patrons, but it's where the soul of the Masters and Augusta National resided for decades. For most private golf clubs in America, the caddie facility was home base as caddies weren't allowed to enter the clubhouse.

During tournament week, the smell of freshly grilled hamburgers, fried chicken, and French fries wafted through the tall pines. You could walk around the parked semis that hauled in an assortment of goods, including the on-course concessions of pimento cheese sandwiches, ham sandwiches, etcetera. The smell from the grill served as a guidepost for the noses of approaching caddies, the police force, other security personnel, and various volunteers who knew of the throwback to another day. Picnic tables sat to the side as another busy Masters round was in progress.

Appropriately, the cook's name was Herbert Fryer, himself a former caddie, who asked for orders in rapid-fire succession, occasionally missing the details of an order, but who cared when it tasted and smelled this good? Fryer shared the grill duty with Horace Avery, the brother of Iron Man and Big Henry. A window where the orders were taken was hidden behind the semis as a line of a dozen or so people waited patiently—most caddies but some tournament-week employees and media from the nearby press building. A makeshift sign hung near the order window:

Hamburgers and cheeseburgers, $1.50
Chicken strips, $2
Fries, 50 cents
Soda, 50 cents
    Diet Coke

Root Beer
Lemonade
Orange

Hands down, the best meal on the grounds was prepared here, with a good helping on a simple paper plate, eaten on an adjacent green picnic table. Compare the fare that was six dollars cheaper than the same burger you could order in the more famous grill room at the clubhouse.

Step inside the caddie shack, just to the right of the grill window, and you would find a basic, square room with green lockers against the walls, giving the appearance of the visiting locker room at a middle-sized college football stadium. The facility was built in 1994. The caddie master, Tom Van Dorn, holed up in an office just to the left of the main, glassed entrance. Boxes of white Foot Joy athletic shoes were stacked to the ceiling, awaiting the fittings like at the shoe store at the local mall. Of course, just about everything was green or white.

This is where all caddies came to get fitted for the traditional white jumpsuit. Professional caddies, such as Stevie Williams, Tiger Woods's famous caddie, came by here daily to don the jumpsuit. Caddie novices also checked in here, such as Jane Storm, the mother of English amateur Graeme Storm. She worked for her son in the 2000 Masters and needed quite a tailor's job to make the suit fit properly on her slight build. Friends and relatives of players, even the small children who work the Par 3 Contest, also dropped by to deck out in the suit. Longtime Augusta National caddies still in the caddie corps hung out here just in case somebody needed an emergency caddie. This is also where the daily ritual of determining who earned a bag during regular member play was carried out. You wouldn't find the Masters participants' golf bags here, however. For years, they were stored in an extension to the clubhouse that is located just to the right of the first tee beside the members' golf shop.

This was a vast improvement over the first caddie shack, which by 1941 was located approximately one hundred yards from the Augusta National golf shop, near where the main walking corridor, concessions, restrooms, and a humongous golf shop are now packed with fans during Masters week. That caddie shack wasn't more than a small room, which at one time had a makeshift potbelly stove for cold days and a dirt floor before concrete was added after World War II. The second building at the same location included a pool table, a deep fryer for making all sorts of meals, tables set up for all-day card games, a shower, restroom, lockers, and a refrigerator. It was where the Augusta National caddies hung out in the infancy of their glory days.

"That pool table didn't last too long," said Lawrence Bennett, the son of former caddie master Freddie Bennett. "Guys would get caught up in their pool games, gambling, talking, and they would just about miss their members' tee times. There had to be priorities."

One sense of history did prevail in the third facility, located farther up the hill and to the right of the landing area at the first fairway. Pictures of the "Masters Caddie Hall of Fame" adorned the walls above the lockers inside the locker room, albeit just the caddies who worked there since Caddie-Master Enterprises took over in 1996. The framed pictures displayed the photos and accompanying nicknames of Bull, Hop, Skinny, Po Baby, Day Break, and many more. There were more showers, an enlarged restroom, and cafeteria-style dining.

One feature of the first three caddie facilities was a book that Lawrence Bennett simply called "The Due." If caddies didn't have enough cash to pay for a sandwich or drink, the spiral-bound book came out, and what a caddie owed was documented, with amounts subtracted from caddying wages till the balance was even.

"Some guys were in the hole because they never saved their caddie money in order to eat," Lawrence Bennett said. "There was also a lot of betting going on, especially when they had that pool table, so there were some guys in debt."

Six of the regular crew who were still on staff in the early 2000s had worked there for more than fifty years, guys like Frank "Skinny" Ware; Johnny Garrett, better known as "Harrisburg," who first caddied here in 1940; and Johnnie Frank Moore, who caddied for Gay Brewer's win in 1967. They formed an encyclopedia of greens-reading knowledge.

"Some of those guys were here when Ike's Tree was just a baby," said Joe Collins, himself a veteran caddie dating back to the 1960s. "They're living history."

Today's modern caddie facility isn't a shack; it's a palace, more than making up for the lack of accoutrements over the years. The building is formally labeled the Golf Services Building and has been located a few steps right of the expansive Tournament Practice Facility since the practice area and building rose from an old parking lot in 2010. Together, they form the greatest practice facility and caddie shack in all of golf.

The practice area contains two separate fairways, one moving left, the other a slight dogleg right to mimic the actual course. It's more than a four-hundred-yard poke from the tee to the large Press Building at the back of the driving area. A putting green and two elaborate chipping greens with five bunkers are also close by, with patrons streaming in on the left to get a first view of the grounds before they turn right to the golf course. The new practice facility is only in use during the Masters and for special member events. Members and guests most often use the previous, more tightly confined and shorter practice facility, set just behind the new area and next to Magnolia Lane.

Caddies can easily enter the grounds off Washington Road just a few yards from Magnolia Lane, step into the caddie facility, and feel as if they are decades away from the previously pedestrian caddie digs. Lockers are reserved, jumpsuit sizes remembered, and the green carpet rolled out.

An extra-large closet is filled with more than one hundred white jumpsuits, with sizes ranging from 36, suitable for kids caddying in the Par 3 Contest, and up to 62 regular. Uniforms are washed nightly across Washington Road by club staff at a specially arranged laundry facility and hung alphabetically by player name in the caddie facility. Club staff also handles the cleaning duties during regular play from the club's opening in October until its closure for summer in late May.

Another room has electronically operated metal bins that hold all the Masters week participants' golf bags, with ample security nearby.

The biggest feature may be the large dining area, with food prepared as if the caddies are in the highfalutin company of wealthy Masters members, patrons, and players, even though the atmosphere is more laid back. The biggest compliment comes from the players who often spend more time at caddie central than they do at the clubhouse's locker room and dining spaces because of the proximity to the practice area, the relative quiet, the ease of getting a fine meal, and the close-by parking lot for players' courtesy Mercedes-Benz SUVs, which are located behind the tee and hidden by a row of trees. The walls are full of caddie photos from past Masters tournaments and diagrams of all the greens, with red dots on each showing the direction of Rae's Creek from every putting surface. Even the towels are deemed exceptional.

"We call it the Carl Jackson House, even though it's not officially that," said veteran caddie Jim "Bones" Mackay.

1

The Jumpsuit

The most famous caddie garb in the world is also closely associated with painters and chicken and pig farmers, but at Augusta National, the bright white, long-sleeved, full-length uniforms are the tuxedo of all caddie dress.

"I wore it with pride," said veteran Masters caddie Carl Jackson, who began caddying at Augusta National in 1959. "It was a uniform that showed you were a professional. Mr. Roberts wanted everything to look the best that it could—the golf course, the players, and that included the caddies. We wore those uniforms to look uniform."

Walk into International Uniform in the 1200 block of Broad Street in downtown Augusta—about five miles door to door from Augusta National—and you are in the middle of a typical midsized city's uniform store. Uniforms hang throughout the store for the medical and culinary fields, along with coveralls for all types of industrial and blue-collar jobs. But in one corner, just to the left of the front door, is a hint that this isn't the typical uniform supplier. There is the logo of Pinehurst Resort and Country Club in North Carolina on a caddie bib and, just down the wall, the bright white jumpsuit with the forest green lettering, "PALMER," on the back.

This is the origination point of the famous caddie jumpsuits worn every day by Augusta National Golf Club caddies, made particularly famous during the Masters. The white coloring is particularly bright, in similar tone to the white sand in Augusta National's bunkers, with the all-green Augusta National logo on the right breast pocket, the caddie number in green on the left breast pocket, and the player's name Velcroed on the back—all originating right here in downtown Augusta.

Any ol' Joe can walk in this door, plunk down his $27 (that 2002 price had climbed to $50 by 2023), and walk out with what some think is a piece of history. The white "coveralls," as they're called in the industry, are specifically

Fred Daitch (right) and manager Jennifer Todd stand before a host of caddie uniforms and bibs, including a historic No. 105 from the Masters, at the International Uniform store in downtown Augusta, Georgia. *Photo by Ward Clayton*

made for painters and chicken and pig farmers who need the white coloring to make sure infection doesn't spread from one area to another in their work, and for "clean-room" inspectors who also require a sterile environment.

"I sell blank coveralls all the time, and some of the people that buy them I know aren't our typical customers. They probably put logos on it, sell it, whatever. But I can't control that. I would never do anything illegal or unethical," said Fred A. Daitch, the third-generation owner of International Uniforms.

The jumpsuit that Daitch made for Augusta National is the vastly improved ancestor to the suits initially worn at the Masters in 1946 when a handmade, hand-sewn herringbone jumpsuit debuted for the first Masters after World War II, worn by caddie Thomas Evans who worked for Herman Keiser. In the first eight Masters, caddies usually dressed like the gallery: with a coat and tie, some type of fedora or pancake hat stylish in that day, and, for a few of these years, a simple cut-out number pinned on their backs to identify the players. In the first Masters, 1934 winner Horton Smith's caddie, whose name was not identified, was dressed in a jacket, sweater, and ball cap. The *Augusta Chronicle* listed the pairings for the 1938 Masters and gave corresponding numbers for each caddie, with Pappy Stokes wearing No. 12 as he would do again in 1948. But the first photograph of a caddie wearing a number came when Pearly Dawsey, working for winner Craig Wood in 1941, wore No. 30—and had a live baby rabbit tucked in his overall pocket for good luck during that year's final round.

Attending fans identified the players by accessing their one-page pairing guide to connect the caddie number with the player's name. Many caddies also dressed like farmers' hands, with denim coveralls, or in woolen jackets and casual clothing, something akin to what Jed Clampett wore in the 1960s television comedy series, *The Beverly Hillbillies*. The dress was not standardized as even the hats differed; witness the tall, silk hat that Gene Sarazen's caddie, Stovepipe, wore in the 1935 Masters. Therefore, with Augusta National having a penchant for uniformity, the uniform was born, with discussions and experimentation beginning prior to World War II.

Daitch's grandfather, Philip, formed Daitch Dry Goods Company in 1930 to provide industrial uniforms to the public and opened a store in downtown Augusta—in the same space that was still operational in the 2020s. To help family members and fellow Jewish community residents, Philip Daitch allowed people to sleep in the new store so that they could get their feet under them, usually on a soft bed of blue jeans.

The business was first developed by Fischel Levy, a Jewish man who immigrated from Poland to the Augusta area in 1899 through Ellis Island and began by peddling pots, pans, and dungarees house to house from a wagon. Once he made some money, Levy purchased a horse to hook to his wagon. Levy's daughter, Sarah, married Philip Daitch. Along the way, probably in the 1940s, he and his son, Irvin, started providing Augusta National with various items for the tournament, particularly vinyl raincoats and, eventually, the simple, white coveralls with no logos. At first, Augusta National caddies wore the prescribed uniform of green denim coveralls topped by a green cap with a yellow button in the center that included the caddie number during regular member play and then evidently wore the sportier white uniform during Masters play before the white suit became the year-round calling card in the 1950s.

The Daitch family's business spirit was like that of the all-Black caddie corps, as Jewish people made up a small percentage of the Augusta population in the twentieth century, is still a small community within one of the oldest cities in the South, and has experienced anti-Semitism in various scenarios, Fred Daitch indicated. The plight of Jewish people worldwide and for centuries as a minority population and a disparaged group draws parallels to the Black community's efforts, and especially that of the Black caddie corps, to make their mark.

In its April 12, 1950, edition, *Golf World* reported that "the Negro caddies were clad in white coveralls and green baseball caps, plainly numbered in green across their backs."

Irvin and sons Gary and Fred would fill a U-Haul with raincoats, truck them out to the tournament, and if the seal on the trailer was broken, Augusta National would have to buy raincoats.

"We, of course, prayed for rain at the Masters," joked Fred.

Fred, who changed the business's name to International Uniform after his father passed away in 1995, is not a golf junkie, even though he was born and raised in Augusta. He has attended the Masters for years and once made a brief visit to the Richmond County Jail for attempting to scalp a Masters Series Badge as a college student in the early 1980s. He does cherish the 1960s handmade caddie jumpsuit that for years was on display in Neil Ghingold Antiques two doors down from his store. Fred made informal overtures with Neil to purchase it, simply because it may have been one of the first caddie jumpsuits his family provided to Augusta National. Eventually, Neil relented, and the old jumpsuit, with No. 105 and precise chenille fabric processing for lettering, numerals, and green bordering, became one of Daitch's most cherished keepsakes for a price of more than one thousand dollars. It is believed that Amos Washington wore the suit when caddying for Claude Harmon in 1962, the only year that the field exceeded 103 players (Masters-high 109 players that year).

Fred just took up golf in the early 2000s. He most often rents his home

One of the most historic caddie suits is owned by International Uniform's Fred Daitch. The suit was believed to be worn by Amos Washington with Claude Harmon at the 1962 Masters, the only time the Masters field exceeded 103 players. *Photo by Ward Clayton*

during Masters week and takes his family on vacation. And he doesn't know most of the world's most famous golfers by name.

But he does know a good business deal when he sees one.

That's the reason he cherished the Augusta National business connection. In 1996, when CaddieMaster Enterprises began supervising the caddies at

Augusta National, Fred didn't get a caddie jumpsuit order from Augusta National early that year. Curious why, he called the club and was told it had changed plans for the supplier of its caddie jumpsuits. Fred quickly inquired about the price with new Augusta National caddie master Tom Van Dorn and was told $27 per order. He replied that he could provide the same product for $19, and produce it locally, including other area vendors in the process. He kept the Augusta National account and gained a slew of Caddie-Master Enterprises clients as the word spread about his business.

"The reason I price like I do is I want to own the market," Daitch said. "My goal really and truly is to own the golf market as far as caddie wear is concerned."

In the early 2000s, his caddie wear business thrived like "a snowball rolling slowly downhill," Daitch said. After attending the PGA Merchandise Show in Orlando in 2001 and 2002, his line of caddie jumpsuits, bibs, sandbags, and belts grew from 10 percent of his business to 25 percent as of the fall of 2002. His biggest concern at the first Merchandise Show in 2001 was not simply getting enough business but how his small operation could handle an ordering feast where he wrote ten thousand dollars worth of business in the first two hours of the show. He was able to phone home to his wife after the first day of the show and tell her to go ahead and purchase a new car, with cash. By 2022, Daitch was preparing hundreds of jumpsuits and bibs for caddie programs internationally, with one in ten being jumpsuit orders. One of his largest customers is Sage Valley Golf Club, an ultraprivate club near Aiken, South Carolina, that opened in 2001 and is modeled after Augusta National, including the white, long-sleeved jumpsuits worn by the caddie corps, many of whom are Black and former Augusta National caddies. The success allowed him to put his store on the real-estate market, with a proposed move to nearby Greene Street by the mid-2020s. The growth allowed Daitch to promote Jennifer Todd into a role overseeing the caddie business as the golf management and sales manager.

The thing that caught everyone's eye at the early 2000s Merchandise Show in Daitch's simple ten-foot-by-ten-foot booth was the mannequin display with the Masters caddie jumpsuit. Golf pros stood two and three deep to get a glance at this new vendor. One of those onlookers drawn in by the crowd was Dave Spencer, the former longtime cohead professional at Augusta National. Concerned that the Augusta National name was being commercialized, Spencer requested that the logo be taken off the jumpsuit, and Daitch quickly complied. Ten minutes later, Spencer returned.

Gnomes are among the most popular items for sale at Augusta National during Masters week. The gnomes are often dressed as caddies for the tournament. *Photo by Ward Clayton*

"The white coverall is symbolic of Augusta National and the Masters," Spencer said, according to Daitch. "I'd appreciate it if you would take the whole white coverall out of the booth."

Daitch removed the white jumpsuit, with quick apologies to Spencer. Clubs such as Pinehurst Resort and Dallas National had emphatically requested that their emblems be displayed in the booth. They wanted their name affiliated with the product.

But the show had proven that Daitch's calling card was the Augusta National–branded jumpsuits. By 2003, one of Augusta National's most popular items was the sale of commemorative Beanie Babies in its on-site stores. That was nothing new since the club had previously sold the small items, first as pure green bears. But this time the small bears were dressed in a caddie jumpsuit, with the No. 1 on the front breast pocket, a Masters name tag on the back, and the green baseball cap on the head. Customers rushed to buy the product as word spread among collectors. The same held true in the 2000s when commemorative garden gnomes were sold, changing the garb every year, with the caddie outfit being one of the most popular when the main golf shop was expanded in 2018.

Daitch has even endured a couple of incidents when Augusta National officials called to complain about the slightest flaw in his work. In 1998, Daitch was laid up in an Augusta hospital suffering from a recurring gastrointestinal disorder, probably stirred up by stress, which resulted in internal bleeding. He had already rented his home for the week and was planning another family vacation. It was the evening of the first Masters practice round, and Daitch's cell phone rang in his hospital room. Woozy from medication and with IVs in his arm, he answered to the sound of an angry Augusta National employee berating him because the green lettering of approximately ten player names from the back of the jumpsuits had bled onto the rest of the garment when they were washed. They needed replacement name tags, pronto. Daitch never mentioned he was in the hospital or that this was normally a two-week process. He called his secretary at home, coaxed the printer out of a son's Little League baseball game and into working overnight, and then he promptly fell asleep, exhausted. When he woke up the next day at approximately noon, Daitch nervously called his secretary and heard the great news that the new suit and corresponding nameplates had been hand-delivered to the caddie shack that Tuesday at 7:00 a.m., just in time for the first players out for a second day of practice.

"I've been to hell and back for them," Daitch said. "But that is what has made us the best in the industry. We have to come up to the standards of Augusta National. Our name tags have to be level and can't be one-quarter of an inch off. Augusta National would notice and send them right back. Being forced to come up to their standards makes anything we do acceptable to anybody else. I have never had a complaint from another caddie-wear customer. These clubs rant and rave about what we do. If Augusta National put these challenges in front of most companies, they would probably think some of their requests were ridiculous, too picky. It's been a blessing in disguise."

Daitch hasn't provided the Augusta National uniform since 2016, mainly because CaddieMaster began working with a vendor that supplied caddie uniforms for many of its hundreds of Troon Golf–affiliated clubs around the world. Troon Golf purchased CaddieMaster in 2015. Daitch still provides Augusta National with sand and seed bags—large shoulder bags filled with sand and fertilizer used to fill in divots during play—and caddies and golf fans will stop by his business to purchase a similarly designed uniform.

Daitch's company heritage had been formulated by producing the basic, no-frills jumpsuit for regular play at Augusta National and the more famous version for the tournament, complete with all the logos and an ever-improving system of using Velcro to stick the player's name on the back of the uniform. In the early years of the jumpsuit's use through the 1980s, the name and Masters logo were stitched on and prone to break loose and flap in the breeze. Augusta National receives sizes X-small to XXX-large to better fit the gamut of caddies from English amateur Graeme Storm's tiny mother in 2000 to 7-foot-1 San Antonio Spurs center David Robinson, who caddied for friend Corey Pavin in the Par 3 Contest. Augusta National might have to do some on-site tailoring, but at least the sizes are close.

Most tied the uniform to the buttoned-up look that flight attendants or Disney World employees wear as customers arrive, similar in context to how Augusta National members first wore green jackets so that Masters attendees could identify whom to ask questions. Some may have also at first thought that the outfit was demoralizing as it was universally worn by only Black employees with no name tags for themselves, just the associated names of white players. However, as time passed, the knowledge and skill of the caddies turned this traditional garb into a symbol of excellence.

The complaint by many caddies is that the jumpsuits are hot or simply too bothersome. They differ from the standard wear of a professional caddie today—sneakers, shorts, and golf shirt covered with a simple sleeveless bib that bears the tournament sponsor's name and comes with a pocket in the front for placement of pencils, scorecard, and yardage book. The Memorial Tournament, Jack Nicklaus's PGA Tour event in Dublin, Ohio, is the rare exception to that dress. Caddies at Jack's event wear a similar jumpsuit—giving a nod to the Golden Bear's affection for the Masters—but with a lighter-weight material and short sleeves because of the Memorial's usual early summer play date. In recent years, the pants portion was eliminated, and the Memorial caddies wear short-sleeved jackets atop shorts, a look similar to a traditional barber's jacket.

For years Augusta National's caddies were also instructed to wear the FootJoy brand shoes, white with a touch of green outline, instead of their normal athletic shoes. Outside caddies have the option to wear their customary footwear but are asked to use white shoes. Still, shoe boxes used to be stacked ceiling high in the former caddie shack, awaiting the odd foot sizes, from the very small for children of players to the very large to fit the large dogs of caddies such as Carl Jackson or Robinson. Once, years ago, the caddies even wore the canvas, high-top Converse basketball shoes, more famously called "Chucks" for inventor Chuck Taylor.

Until 1999, caddies on the PGA Tour were required to wear long pants during tournaments. After lobbying for a softening of the policy, shorts were allowed on the Tour if the heat index reached one hundred degrees. That was broadened even further to allow for shorts in any event but with the stipulation that they be Tour-dispersed navy or blue with the Tour logo on the bottom. That too was eventually altered to today's standard, allowing any color but no cutoffs, cargo shorts, or gym shorts.

Many caddies wear bare bones under the Augusta National jumpsuit, usually a pair of gym or standard shorts and a T-shirt or golf shirt. Some have taken a dare and worn nothing but underwear—or even less—under the jumpsuit to get better "ventilation." When the weather gets cold, the jumpsuit is welcomed as another layer to hold off the elements. But when Augusta gets hot and humid . . .

"Quite a few guys wore nothing under them," said Donnie Wanstall, a former Tour caddie who worked for Mark O'Meara for years and toted for Japan's Tsuneyuki "Tommy" Nakajima in the 1983 Masters. "If it was cold, I might have worn a long-sleeve T-shirt and some jeans under them. But when it was hot, it was nothing. When I got through for the day, I just got dressed in the caddie facility privately and then put the suit in the dirty laundry. I wasn't telling anybody that I wasn't wearing anything underneath."

That's exactly the reason that Beard always wore his normal clothes underneath. The former Augusta National caddie said, "I wanted to be sure that everything was clean. Who knows who wore it before I did?"

Daitch said that the jumpsuits' current 65 percent polyester–35 percent cotton makeup is more heat resistant than 100 percent cotton or even the shorts, golf shirts, and bibs that caddies wear most of the year and more comfortable than the herringbone makeup of the early suits. He also said that the caddies shouldn't wear clothes underneath the jumpsuits, which the majority do, but just underwear and, at most, an accompanying T-shirt. He said the polyester component doesn't wrinkle easily, a very important factor to Augusta National officials.

Daitch's association with the caddie jumpsuits has spread simply by word of mouth, and his business has continued to grow, especially among private clubs and with Masters participants. Scott Verplank, a veteran PGA Tour member, called to get his son Scottie a custom-fitted version in time for a caddying stint in the Par 3 Contest several years back. Daitch didn't set a fee for that request. He just asked that Scott send golf memorabilia for various charitable auctions, which he did. Some players who get their young children to join in the casual atmosphere of the Par 3 Contest on Wednesday have followed suit.

A new client club in Jamaica called one time to order jumpsuits, and Daitch suggested they get short sleeves because of the hot weather in the Caribbean. However, the club insisted on the Augusta National–style long-sleeve version.

But perhaps the coolest takeaway is that the winning caddie can obtain the jumpsuit he wore when his man won. All the winning caddies must do is write a letter to Augusta National making the request, and it will be shipped to that home address a few weeks later. Damon Green, the winning caddie for Zach Johnson in 2007, has the flag for the eighteenth green, the plastic pin pole, the green hat, a yardage book signed by Byron Nelson, and the suit on display at his Florida home.

Funny, how far a simple, white outfit has come as the tuxedo or green jacket parallel for caddies.

1

Picking the Numbers
of a Masters Champion

The unlucky numbers for the Augusta National caddies are 1 and 13. Sometimes.

Every caddie is assigned a number to assist the fans in determining the names of players, using that day's Masters pairing sheet as a reference for the number, which is Velcroed onto the left breast pocket of the jumpsuit. The numbering system began before the caddie jumpsuits were first used in 1946. The first recorded numbering of caddies, according to Augusta National Golf Club documentation, was in 1941 when caddie Pearly Dawsey wore No. 30 pinned to the back of his overalls, which housed a live baby rabbit during the entire final round, bringing good luck to winner Craig Wood. However, there is also a photo from the late 1930s of Sam Snead posed with his regular caddie, O'Bryant Williams, who is wearing a number on his back. In those early days, no player names were worn, only numbers. The only identifying element was a makeshift piece of paper with a number taped to the back of the caddie's jacket or shirt.

The only player who receives a designated number is the defending champion. The No. 1 is always reserved for him. The remainder of the numbers given to caddies and their players are determined by the order in which the players check in at registration during tournament week, which begins the Saturday before. Fans can usually assess which players have put in the most practice time at the course during tournament week by checking out the single digits and teens on their pairing sheets.

Veteran players such as Jack Nicklaus or Tiger Woods usually wear high numbers, unless they draw the defending champion's No. 1, because they limit their tournament week on-site preparation. Nicklaus used to be famous for coming to Augusta the week before the Masters to get in his practice time uninterrupted, usually playing regularly with member Billy Morris, the former publisher of the local newspaper, the *Augusta Chronicle*, and then returning a couple days before the tournament competition began. Woods would usually drop by a couple weeks before the tournament to quickly determine the course characteristics that year and then work out in Augusta National–like conditions at his home course in south Florida or on holes at his home.

Ben Hogan combined those two strategies. He prepared at Seminole Golf Club, his home course in south Florida, in the weeks leading up to the tournament, playing matches against the likes of Claude Harmon, the head pro and 1948 Masters champion. Hogan would travel to Augusta as soon as the week before the tournament to hit balls in the practice area and develop a game plan. When Hogan won in 1951 and 1953, caddie "Pappy" Stokes wore No. 6 and No. 2, respectively.

The numbering system even inspired a nickname. John Henry Williams, the caddie master from just after World War II until his death in 1959, was simply called "'Leven" because that was the number he wore as a caddie before becoming caddie master.

It should come as no surprise that No. 13 was the first number to concern the Masters participant. In the 1938 photo, Williams was given the No. 13. The jovial Snead posed for a front-page *Augusta Chronicle* photograph as he pinned the unlucky number on his caddie, who was dressed in dark trousers, jacket, and hat as if he had just walked out of a church service. Snead joked that the number, which resembled the size and material that track-and-field athletes wear, would result in "the worst nine I've ever played since joining the professional ranks."

Snead shot a 2-under 34 on the front nine in the first round but then played poorly on the back nine to shoot 44 for what would be his worst nine holes in tournament history.

"Iron Man" Avery turned No. 13 into his own lucky number. After wearing No. 85 in Arnold Palmer's first Masters victory in 1958, Avery wore No. 13 for 1960. Palmer birdied the last two holes to win the tournament. Two years later, in 1962, Iron Man again sported No. 13 for a second Palmer win. Avery wore No. 82 during Palmer's last Masters victory in 1964.

The No. 13 phobia, triskaidekaphobia, was documented in the mid-1950s when players were registering for the 1954 Masters, according to the *Augusta Chronicle*. Cary Middlecoff and Lloyd Mangrum showed up at the same time to register, and Middlecoff filled out the entry log just before Mangrum in tournament headquarters. Helen Harris, Augusta National's longtime office manager, gave Mangrum the option to skip line 13 and go to 14 in the log for his number, but Mangrum, with a positive spin, said, "That's just what I wanted." He finished tied for fourth. The previous year's No. 13 registrant, Canadian amateur Bill Mawhinney, withdrew just before teeing off for the 1953 Masters.

The number 13 is one of twenty-three numbers that caddies have worn to multiple Masters titles. The numbers 6, 12, 52, and 89 have each been worn a record three times each by the victor. Stokes and Hogan (1951), caddie Johnnie Frank Moore and Gay Brewer (1967), and non–Augusta National caddie Nicholas DePaul with Seve Ballesteros (1983) all wore No. 6. Pappy Stokes had No. 12 for wins with Henry Picard in 1938 and Claude Harmon in 1948, and Fred Searles also wore that number with Byron Nelson in 1942. Ernest Nipper won in 1961 and Eddie McCoy in 1978—both with Gary Player—and Carl Jackson with Ben Crenshaw in 1984 with No. 52. Jack Nicklaus won his sixth Masters title in 1986 with oldest son Jack Nicklaus II wearing No. 89, the same number worn by the caddies of Danny Willett (Jonathan Smart) and Sergio Garcia (Glen Murray) in 2016 and 2017.

No. 1 has been quite superstitious also.

When Nicklaus returned to Augusta in 1966 to defend his 1965 Masters title, the Golden Bear refused to take No. 1, the defending champion's number. Nicklaus was aiming to become the first man to repeat. He opted instead for No. 90, the number caddie Willie Peterson wore in 1965.

"A No. 1 has never won this tournament, you know," Nicklaus said the week before the 1966 Masters as he went through his usual pre–Masters week practice routine. "The fact of no repeaters doesn't bother me, really it doesn't make one bit of difference. I would just like things to be like last year."

Nicklaus jokingly said the plan was to take the superstitious attitude beyond the golf course. "I'm going home [to Palm Beach, Florida] Saturday. I'm going to try and leave at precisely the same moment that I did last year. I've even told the lady we rented the house from to put the same dirty sheets back on the bed."

Peterson wore No. 49 in 1963, No. 16 in 1972, and No. 76 in 1975 before Jackie took over the bag in the mid-1980s.

Peterson's 90 is the highest number a caddie has ever worn to win the Masters. On three occasions, in 1957 (101), 1962 (109), and 1966 (103), the

The defending Masters champion receives the number 1 for the caddie suit. Only Jack Nicklaus in 1966 has chosen not to wear No. 1 the following year. Willie Peterson wore No. 90 the year that Nicklaus repeated. *Photo by Ward Clayton*

field pushed into triple digits, bringing on the higher numbers on the back of the jumpsuits.

The two back-to-back champions since have broken the No. 1 curse. Nick Faldo's caddie, Fanny Sunesson, took No. 1 when Faldo repeated in 1990, although Andy Prodger was Faldo's caddie in 1989. Tiger Woods's caddie, Steve Williams, wore No. 1 in 2002 after displaying No. 71 in 2001.

If No. 1 was originally unlucky, then No. 32 was very lucky for Tom Watson. Leon McCladdie took Watson's bag in 1977 and wore No. 32. Watson won his first Masters that year. When Watson won the 1981 tournament, McCladdie once again wore No. 32.

"Any number you win with is lucky," McCladdie said in 1981. "This is the first time since [Watson] won in 1977 that we've had it again. I knew we would win."

1

The End of
an Era

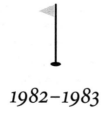

1982–1983

Thursday, April 9, 1982, began with a cool, damp morning and went downhill from there. The miserable day all but ended the exclusivity of Augusta National caddies in the Masters. Weather was a factor, but inattention to detail was the biggest fault.

Thursday's first round has been among the most difficult days in tournament history. Rain halted play at 4:30 p.m., with thirty-six players still on the course. A continuous drizzle hit the players all day, and the temperature never reached more than forty-eight degrees. The new bent-grass greens, being used for the second time in Masters competition, were even faster than normal because of the cool weather. Conditions were so difficult that Fuzzy Zoeller's even-par 72 led the field of those who completed first-round play. Frank Conner shot 89 and Jim Thorpe 88. Herman Keiser, the 1946 Masters champion making his farewell appearance, withdrew after a 93.

"Hell no, let 'em play. I think they'll enjoy it," Zoeller cracked about calling off play after completing his round.

"It'll be cold [on Friday]," two-time champion Tom Watson said. "The lakes will be frozen. We won't have to worry about carrying those holes. We'll be able to drive No. 10 [where there was casual water on Friday] and No. 11. We won't have to worry about Rae's Creek on twelve and thirteen."

As the rain-delayed first round resumed at 7:30 a.m. on Friday, many players were literally left holding their bags, scurrying for last-second caddies. David Graham's wife was forced into duty on the driving range, shagging balls as her husband prepared to complete his first round. Some players' clubs and bags were even still wet from the day before, left stacked at Augusta National in the caddie master's area, making the resumption of play even more harried. Some Augusta National caddies had presumed that the first round was washed out, with players retaining their same tee times for Friday. LeRoy Schultz said his boss, Tom Weiskopf, even told him that his tee time for Friday would be the same as for the first round. Some caddies stayed out late Thursday night partying and were still asleep when play began, and others simply arrived late, unaware of the early start.

However, the *Augusta Chronicle* story on Friday morning, posted on the front page, clearly stated, "The 36 left on the course will tee off at 7:30 a.m. today. At the completion of the first round, new three-man pairings will be made, and second-round play will begin around 11:30 a.m. from both the No. 1 and No 10 tees." Note that this information was inserted the night before in time to make the newspaper.

"The problem was that they didn't show up," Watson said in 1983. "What do you do? Carry your own bag? Use pull carts? Some of us had to take whoever was available as caddies."

At tournament's end, Watson was most notable among the players who wrote Augusta National chairman Hardin about instituting a change. Watson, the 1977 and 1981 champion with Leon McCladdie on the bag, also spoke with Hardin about the request.

"Suppose you had to go into your biggest trial and you were told you couldn't use your own legal secretary? That's what it's like for us at Augusta," Watson told Hardin, a retired attorney.

"Mr. Watson, you plead a very strong case," Hardin responded.

"Through maybe no fault of their own, but that was the straw that broke the camel's back when we went to the committee and said this is one of the most important events, golf events, in the world, and not to have reliable caddies is not the way we should go," Watson said in a 2015 interview for the *Loopers* documentary, noting he made $1.25 per bag as a kid in the early 1960s caddying at hometown Kansas City Country Club. "And they relented and said you're right."

The movement by Tour players to bring their own caddies to the tournament had been building for years. Until 1962, the United States Golf Association considered a caddie, caddie master, or anyone who worked at a golf club cleaning or repairing clubs to be a professional. Until 1974, all four majors banned the use of outside caddies.

Some caddies tried to usurp the rule, such as when "Creamy" Caroline, Palmer's regular Tour caddie, tried to bribe Canterbury Golf Club caddie master Mike Kiely with five hundred dollars weeks before the 1973 PGA Championship at the Cleveland, Ohio, club so that he could become a local caddie and Palmer would have a better chance to win his only missing major championship. That failed, only because of Kiely's dedication to his own caddie group and the PGA Championship rules. Still, Caroline hung around the gallery ropes that week to offer caddying tips and interact with Palmer as Kiely indicated that Palmer drew a "local nervous kid who was a so-so caddie." Palmer missed the cut.

By 1975, the PGA Championship at Firestone Country Club in Akron, Ohio, and the British Open at Carnoustie, Scotland, had opened their doors to outside caddies. The U.S. Open followed suit one year later. Ironically, the U.S. Open first allowed caddies who were not attached to the host club for the 1976 tournament at the Atlanta Athletic Club, Bobby Jones's home course. Of the 150 players in the field at that U.S. Open, 104 brought their own caddies. For the 1976 British Open, Nicklaus's longtime caddie for the overseas event, Jimmy Dickinson, pulled up lame in a practice round, and Jack's oldest son, fifteen-year-old Jack II, stepped in to tote for his dad, ten years before the miracle Masters of 1986. Jackie even played the role of the lucky caddie on the morning of the final round by—unbeknownst to Jack and Barbara Nicklaus—donning the clothes he had worn weeks earlier in capturing a junior golf tournament in Columbus, Ohio.

Only the Masters and Western Open remained off limits to Tour caddies by 1982. The Masters held fast simply because of its tradition of providing caddies. The Western remained true because of its long-standing charitable effort via the Chick Evans Scholarship Foundation, a program of providing college scholarships for caddies that began in 1930 and prominently continues today. Chicago-area caddies alone worked at the Western Open until 1986, but by 1987 Tour caddies were allowed.

For the players who wanted to bring their own caddies, there was quite a bit of piling on. "My caddie had been with me through all the good finishes I had there, so I can't say he's a bad caddie, but he showed up late twice last year," Tom Kite said at Augusta in 1983. "My Tour caddie has worked for me four and a half years, and he's never been late."

"The caddies at Augusta have gotten progressively worse," said Raymond Floyd, the 1976 champion. "Most of them take a week off from their regular job to caddie. They're not caddies, and they don't know yardages. The caddie I won with [Hop Harrison] is a mill worker who's been taking the week off to work at the National.

"I can accept going into one or two tournaments a year [not using his own caddie], but last year when most of them didn't show up to complete play...that killed them. A lot of players had been very vocal about it for a long time. The seed was planted. When they didn't show up last year, that did it."

"There's no question the Augusta National caddies aren't as conscientious as they used to be," said four-time Masters champion Arnold Palmer.

Even Lee Elder, who made his historic debut as the first Black man to play in a Masters in 1975 and died in late 2021, had gripes about the caddies. He was welcomed enthusiastically by the entire caddie corps when he came to play practice rounds and during tournament week. Henry Brown, a thirty-six-year-old Augusta cab driver, was given the job, much to Elder's pleasure...at first. Brown, who professed to have worked at Augusta National since 1952, was a cross-handed golfer who sported a 1 handicap and was invited to play in an Elder pro-am event in Virginia in May 1975. Brown had also caddied for Roberto De Vicenzo when the Argentine golfer incorrectly signed his scorecard in 1968, thereby losing by one stroke to Bob Goalby. However, Elder later revealed that the caddie didn't show that much skill carrying the bag.

"Henry was a very personable guy, but his idea of caddying was the wrong way for me," Elder said in 2021 upon being honored at Augusta National as an honorary starter, only seven months before his death at age eighty-seven. "We didn't hit it off very good because he caddied by sight. I usually played by yardage. He wanted to hand me the club instead of us figuring out how far we were away. That wasn't the way I was expecting to receive the work those caddies were supposed to be so famous for. I liked yardages and told him so. He said he would change, which was nice of him to do."

PGA Tour caddies were grumbling behind the scenes at the 1982 event that they were considering a class-action discrimination suit against Augusta National or the sponsors of the tournament. They argued that you had to be Black to caddie in the Masters and they were being denied the right to work.

One undisclosed Tour caddie attended the 1982 Masters and voiced his displeasure over the Augusta National caddies' performance: "My player would hand his ball [for the caddie to clean] after marking on the green, and there wasn't anyone there," the caddie told *Golf World*. "He was told not to help my man read greens but tried anyway and didn't know from beans. He got real active when we got to the televised holes. One day my man had to awaken his caddie, who was fast asleep on the bag at the putting green....I talked to Augusta caddies, and they said they had to caddie at the club at least two weeks in one year's time to be eligible for drawing assignments in the Masters. Two weeks won't teach you a thing. Then I asked if I could put in two weeks, and the unison reply was, 'Man, you are the wrong color.' If this is true, then that sure as heck is discrimination and restraint of trade."

As Augusta National opened for membership play in October 1982, one of Hardin's first orders of business was to finalize a new caddie policy. Some members disagreed with allowing outside caddies; they wanted to be true to their home caddies. Hardin called the decision-making process "traumatic," with the players' wishes winning out.

On November 10, 1982, the closing bell rang on the exclusive use of Augusta National caddies in the Masters. Hardin made the following statement about why the caddie force was opened:

> The advent of the golf cart has made caddies a dying breed. Many clubs have none at all. That fact, coupled with the enormous growth of the professional circuit in this country and elsewhere, has created a new phenomenon—the Tour caddie.
>
> The latter normally works for the same professional wherever he plays, frequently is an accomplished player in his own right, knows his man's swing characteristics, and has been known to provide helpful advice in that area during play. He knows his man's preferences as to caddie procedures and is careful to comply herewith. Perhaps more importantly, he works week after week under highly competitive tournament conditions. In fact, he and the player are a team—a partnership.
>
> Despite the general excellence of our Augusta caddies, the players are absolutely convinced that their own performances will be better if they can use their regular caddies. We have concluded therefore that it is very important to the player competing for one of golf's four major titles that he be comfortable with his caddie.

Before the 1983 tournament, Hardin addressed the issue further: "We're not naive enough to say we have eighty caddies who can be classified at the same level as Tour caddies," he said. "If I were a player under today's conditions, and I think Bobby Jones would agree, I would want to bring my own caddie."

Hardin also noted that caddies would continue to be a tradition within the membership ranks. "We had ninety-six members of three hundred on hand for our recent party, and everybody had a single caddie," Hardin said. "We had carts, but they [aren't allowed to] put golf bags on the carts."

That decision may have been the reason many of the longtime Augusta National caddies despised Hardin and cherished the old realm of Clifford Roberts. They said that Hardin didn't show them due respect in the transition. Roberts was noted for creating a charitable foundation at Augusta National and using funds from it to support former caddies who were having a difficult time. He also encouraged guests to pay the caddie "what you think he's worth" during a round, usually urging them to pay more than the standard fee. This was an important piece of Augusta National lore as displayed in the late 1930s on the Augusta National scorecard, at the top left, where it denoted "Caddy Fee 75 cents."

"Our members are gonna take care of us," Hop Harrison said in 1983. "I've called one member before who lives three hundred miles away, needing money, and he has sent me three hundred dollars or four hundred dollars. They're gonna take good care of us. They'll take better care of us than our chairman."

But the deed had been done, and the 1983 Masters had a new feel to it. There was some friction in the caddie shack, usually an uncomfortable silence when outside caddies came in to get their jumpsuits. Willie Peterson, Jack Nicklaus's caddie, had a confrontation with Jack Tosone, amateur Jim Hallett's caddie, when Tosone was the first caddie to register for the tournament and got locker No. 1, a position Willie believed he deserved.

Augusta National changed many things for the new caddie corps. Yardage books were available for the first time to accommodate the outside caddies who weren't quite as familiar with Augusta National. Previously, the Augusta National caddies went by their trained eyes. They had used rudimentary yardage guides that were prepared by the superintendent or checked a diagram of the hole location for that day that had been placed on each tee box.

"When I first started caddying, we didn't use yardages, we used our head and our eyes," Beard said. "It was an art back in those days. When you caddied for a new player, you learned how far he could hit particular clubs. He would hit a 7-iron, and it would go 150 to 155 yards. I would ask is that the best you can do with that? He would say yes. There weren't any markers in the fairways or anywhere. You marked yourself with a tree, top of a bunker, that type of stuff. We called it judging distance. There was a lot of memory involved. I had been to spots thousands of times and knew them."

"Gorjus" George Lucas, a former PGA Tour caddie and experienced course surveyor, was hired by the club to visit Augusta National and precisely measure the course to devise his creative, hand-drawn, wallet-sized yardage guide.

Lucas was a former caddie for many players, including Palmer, from the early 1970s until the early 1980s. He earned his nickname in the 1970s when Lanny Wadkins's caddie, with whom he roomed on the road, noticed the large supply of toiletry items that George was carrying in his suitcase and dubbed him, "Gorgeous," after the famous professional wrestler. Lucas shortened the moniker to "Gorjus" to fit on a vanity license plate. Lucas's calling of creating yardage books began in 1976 and was starting to become a trademark on the PGA Tour—and continues today through other caddie sources—as caddies were provided with more and more guidance as they prepared their players.

Lucas met with Hardin and other club staff members in the chairman's crowded office to review the process. Lucas used a wire cable to precisely measure the golf course. (He used a laser gun and reflective prisms in later years for the more than one thousand courses he has measured in more than twenty-five years on the job.) He did not charge for his initial services on the prestigious grounds "because it would have been like charging to go to church." Instead, he was offered a tournament badge and a parking pass for the players' lot during that year's tournament.

Lucas's books give exact distances from various spots on the holes, utilizing the usual places such as sprinkler heads and trees and the unusual landmarks such as abrupt changes in elevation, to enable caddies to calculate distances. He also denoted the depth and rolls in the greens and added the subtle, humorous references such as "J.I.C." (just in case) for odd positions on the course, "Granddaddy Choco-Drop" for mounding in the fifteenth fairway and "H2O" with a fish figure for water hazards.

One of the first books, with the standard green cover including the Masters logo and YARDAGE in block letters, gave attribution to Lucas inside the front cover as follows: "The distances contained in this book were compiled and measured by George L. Lucas II. Although the information is believed to be correct, the Augusta National Golf Club does not guarantee its accuracy."

Players had compiled their own books prior to Augusta National's initial supply. Using a scorecard circa the mid-1960s, Palmer trimmed pages from

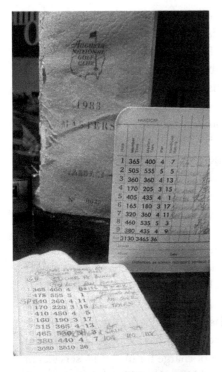

Yardage books are a valuable tool for caddies and players at the Masters to figure out distances and slopes. Raymond Floyd's locker in the World Golf Hall of Fame displayed his 1983 yardage book, the first provided by the tournament (left). The first books also had a disclaimer on the information (bottom left), and current-day books have a simple cover (bottom right). The books have developed in detail over the last sixty years as shown via diagrams of hole No. 12 (facing page), from Arnold Palmer's homemade 1960s yardage book (facing page, top left), George Lucas's first tournament-provided yardage book (facing page, bottom left), and the current-day graphically presented book (facing page, right). *Photos by Ward Clayton*

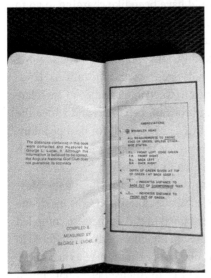

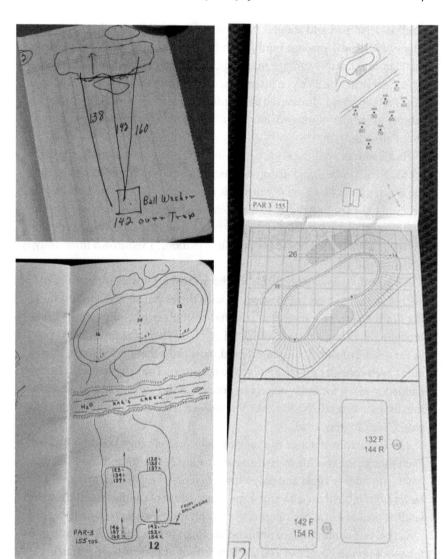

a yellow legal pad and stapled them inside the scorecard to build his own Augusta National yardage book. Each hole was drawn in ink with greens, bunkers, and notable yardage markings, including penciled-in math on one hole. Cori Britt, the vice president at Arnold Palmer Enterprises and a long-time Palmer friend, discovered the yardage book while searching through a cabinet in Palmer's Orlando, Florida, office in mid-March 2017, six months after Palmer's death.

Nicklaus was credited with beginning this documentation. In the early 1960s, Nicklaus began charting Augusta National by yardage, and in 1963 the Golden Bear had a small notebook jammed in his back pocket. He was believed to be the first player to use such a system in a major championship.

Still, most players acclaimed the new books when the caddie ranks opened. Even Nicklaus started to use the new information. "I've thrown mine away," Nicklaus said.

Range balls were also available for the first time, with six different brands offered so that players could warm up with their accustomed specifications. Previously, players wanted the true feel of their own equipment, so they brought a shag bag. Old, out-of-round golf balls that were provided by public ranges didn't satisfy the players, and most clubs that hosted tournaments didn't even consider practice balls to be necessary. The range tee was also expanded to allow for more players to practice at the same time and extended the distance to a tall, backing net that deflected balls from bombarding adjacent Washington Road.

The dangerous practice of shagging balls on the range was also banned. Even though the routine offered an extra caddie fee, it was tortuous. Imagine having no catcher's gear and only a towel to fend off a golf ball traveling like a bullet from more than 150 yards away. The custom of caddies standing in the landing area of a practice range as players hit their own balls in their general direction was commonplace until the late 1970s in the United States and into the 1980s on the European Tour. When dozens of players were practicing at the same time, it was almost comical to the spectators and quite frightening for the receiving caddies dodging balls hit by other players as they eyed their own man. Before the creation of the current short-game practice facility on the south side of Magnolia Lane, both sides of the famous entryway to the clubhouse were utilized for practice with all clubs.

Caddies would step back toward the far end of the range as their players progressed through the bag toward their drivers. Many used towels or even an occasional baseball mitt to flag down balls on the fly—therefore the base-ball term *shagging*—while others took the safer route of one-hopping balls. Some players practiced diagonally so that their caddies could be situated on the edge of the practice area, thereby eliminating some of the friendly fire. Others simply found a schoolyard or park for warm-ups instead of subject-ing their caddies to bombardment. Legend has it that Hogan's caddies ad-justed their towels from one hand to the other only when the extremely accurate Hogan was practicing a draw or a fade. But many a caddie de-veloped battle scars from being drilled in the stomach, shoulders, or even around the head, especially on cloudy days when the white golf ball was dif-ficult to follow against the backdrop of clouds.

In all, twenty-two current or former Augusta National caddies had jobs in the eighty-one-player field for 1983, including eight with former champions and five of the nine amateurs in the field. That included Peterson with Nick-laus, Jackson with Crenshaw, Matthew Palmer with Casper, McCoy with Player, LeRoy Schultz with Weiskopf, Robert "Cigarette" Jones with Calvin Peete (the only Black player in the 1983 field), and Ben Bussey with defend-ing champion Craig Stadler. Leon McCladdie, Watson's caddie in his two Masters victories in 1977 and 1981, even got a bag with amateur Robert Lewis Jr. Brian Edwards, the younger brother of Watson's caddie, Bruce Edwards, got a job working for Jack Renner. Judd Silverman, Stadler's regular cad-die, worked as a reporter for the *Toldeo (Ohio) Blade* as Bussey carried for Stadler.

"Since I won with him, I thought he deserved another shot," Stadler said of Bussey.

Even though McCladdie got another bag, he was distraught. "In January and February it's bad out here [at Augusta National]," he said. "You can't make nothing. We caddie once or twice a week then. The Masters gives us a chance to make some money and catch up on bills. But there's nothing we can do about it."

One of the surprise changes was Zoeller going with his regular Tour cad-die, Mike Mazzeo. Fuzzy had planned on retaining his Augusta National caddie, Jariah Beard, but relented on the Friday before the tournament. Seve Ballesteros, who won in 1980 with Marion Herrington on his bag, won in 1983 with his regular Tour caddie, Nick DePaul, who also carried for Seve's 1984 Open Championship victory at St. Andrews.

"Some guys, my best friends, say it doesn't feel like the Masters anymore,"

Jackson said in 1984. Jackson also indicated that the changeover could have had a positive effect on Crenshaw's first Masters victory in 1984. Crenshaw finished at 11-under-par 277, two in front of Watson. The 1984 and 1995 wins by Crenshaw are the only wins by a caddie with Augusta National ties since 1982.

"I think it could have cost Tom Watson the '84 Masters," Jackson said. "He had a good caddie, Bruce Edwards. But Leon McCladdie was a great caddie, too, and really knew this course. We played with Tom on Saturday [in 1984] and because they didn't know a few things, that local knowledge, it helped us a few shots."

Crenshaw also saw that coming. "You can see the players when they come in for the first couple of years," Crenshaw said in 2015. "They had hundreds of putts out there in different situations, and you just have to know them. There's a lot of putts that defy what they look like. It's something that's acquired over a period of time."

A handful of veteran caddies say that Augusta National caddies would still be in service if Roberts were still around. Even if Roberts had remained their leader, it was inevitable that the ever-changing makeup of caddies would eventually come to the Masters and the doors would be flung open to all caddies. Many Masters veterans still say it would be beneficial for young players and first-time Masters participants to hire an Augusta National caddie to fully digest the subtle breaks of the greens and where to best hit approach shots.

"It really hurt when they did that to us," Beard said. "We lost a lot of pride. I know this would have eventually happened. But the way it was done was disrespectful. It could have been handled a whole lot better. That's all we asked.

"I had no problem with the outside caddies coming on. But make them earn their way like we did. Make them learn the course first, learn the greens. Some players even came in and brought their mommas, their daddies, their brothers to caddie for them. All we wanted was an equal chance."

1

The First
Female Caddies

lizabeth Archer was a nineteen-year-old student at Stanford University majoring in American studies and international relations when she became the first female caddie in tournament history in 1983.

"I hadn't planned to do this," said George Archer, Elizabeth's father, in 1983. "But when mother and daughter go to work on you, you know who is going to win.

"My wife pushed it. And I gave in. So, I wrote Mr. Hardin, and he just wrote back, 'What's her shoe size?'"

Elizabeth started caddying for her father, George, the 1969 Masters champion, in 1980 on a suggestion from her mother, Donna. It was a way to get closer to her father, who traveled quite often on the PGA Tour. She had the athletic ability to tote a fifty-pound golf bag around the hilly Augusta National course; she stood five-feet-eleven and threw the javelin and discus for Stanford's track and field team. To better prepare for those sports, she had begun a weightlifting program in college.

Their first time together, in the 1980 Canadian Open at Royal Montreal Golf Club, George set his watch incorrectly for the earlier time zone, gave it to Elizabeth, and then was late for his tee time the next morning. He was assessed a two-stroke penalty.

"Before I became his caddie, my father and I were never really close," Elizabeth said. "Then I got to see him do what he does best, and we started a friendship that first summer. How many kids get to know what their fathers do for a living? That's the neatest thing about it."

Even with two summers under her belt caddying on the PGA Tour, George was concerned about putting Elizabeth on his bag for the first Masters that allowed outside caddies.

1969 Masters champion George Archer (right) with his daughter, Elizabeth, who became the tournament's first female caddie in 1983. *Masters Historic Imagery/Getty Images*

"My first thought is it would be rocking the boat," George Archer said in 1983, "especially since it is the first year that golfers have brought their own caddies."

Archer recorded a tie for twelfth finish in 1983. Two years later, younger daughter Marilyn became the second Archer daughter and second woman to work in the Masters.

Today, Dr. Elizabeth Archer Klein is a Presbyterian minister with a doctorate in theology working under the title of Evangelist in the Presbytery of Olympia and chaplain of the Woodbrook Hunt Club in Lakewood, Washington. She also became the first female Presbyterian minister at three Northwest United States churches over the years.

"There were not any women I knew who had such a calling," she told Masters.com in 2019, comparing being the first female caddie at Augusta with becoming a minister.

"While I resisted the call for many years, I eventually dug deep into the original translations of the Bible, found many, many instances of women in leadership, and agreed that doing what God intends is the best path to follow."

Women caddying in the Masters have been a rarity, usually reserved for kin such as the Archer daughters. Daughters, wives, sisters, and mothers of players have all worn the famous jumpsuits.

Nicole Stricker caddied for her husband, Steve, and Sheryl Calcavecchia for then-husband, Mark. Both had caddied off and on for their husbands on the PGA Tour.

Shelley Green drew the spotlight in the 1986 Masters when she caddied for younger brother Ken in his Masters debut. Ken shared the first-round lead with Bill Kratzert and became a big story because of his off-beat personality (evidenced by acts such as throwing his putter to his caddie, sneaking friends into the tournament in the trunk of his car, and wearing lime-green shoes) and the partnership with his twenty-nine-year-old sister. Shelley had left a bookkeeper's job in Connecticut a couple years before the 1986 Masters to move to Florida and be closer to her brother and warm weather. Ken gave Shelley, his full-time caddie that year, some credit, in an odd sort of way, for the quick Masters start. He would eventually fade during the week, which was highlighted by Nick Price's course-record 63 in the third round and Jack Nicklaus's comeback on Sunday to win his sixth green jacket.

"She has no clue out there," Green said of his sister. "If she suggests something, I always do the opposite.

"She wasn't interested in learning about golf. That's the way it should be. I don't want a caddie that can make me second-guess myself. Too many caddies control the players sometimes, and I don't think that's right. I've seen too many caddies alter a player's decision."

Jane Storm became the first mother of a player to caddie in a Masters tournament, working with son Graeme, the British amateur champion, in the 2000 Masters. Jane's small stature forced the Augusta National staff to make some alterations on the scene. They had to cut six inches off the arms and pants legs of her caddie jumpsuit so that she could have a snug fit. In the process, Jane tried on three different suits.

Graeme resisted hiring an Augusta National caddie because his mother had always been there for him.

"It just happened really," Graeme said. "She would drive me to the golf tournaments as a young player [in England] and then stay around and caddie for me. She was going to have to be there to take me home anyway."

Fanny Sunesson has been the most successful female caddie and one of the winningest caddies in Masters history. The Swede was on Nick Faldo's

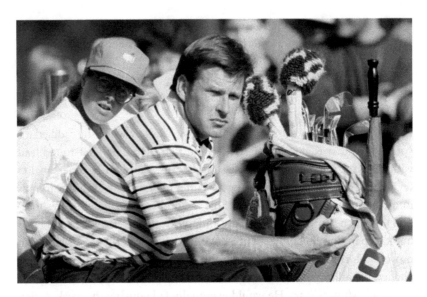

Fanny Sunesson (left) with Nick Faldo at the 1990 Masters. Faldo won that Masters as Sunesson became the first female to carry the winning bag. *Masters Historic Imagery/ Getty Images*

bag during two of his three victories, in 1990 and 1996. Before 1990, she had never visited Augusta or even seen the course on television.

"I don't like doing anything. I don't like being in the press," Sunesson said after Faldo won the 1990 Masters. Faldo had a stoic on-course demeanor and wouldn't divulge much to the press, perhaps because of the usually rumor-filled British tabloids. He also disliked the spotlight, at least until he retired and went into television, a trait reflected by Sunesson.

Fanny was noted as a good player (5 handicap, began playing at age seven) who could give input on Faldo's very technical swing mechanics. She would regularly listen in on the range as instructor David Leadbetter gave Faldo some swing thoughts for the day. She was also famous for being a tireless worker, spending multiple hours walking a course before a tournament began.

"Fanny goes too far even for me," Faldo said. "We don't need to know every blade of grass out there. She'll spend six hours walking the course and getting yardages. But she has to do it that way. She finds it very difficult to do it any other way."

Fanny Sunesson caddied for four of Nick Faldo's six major championship victories and is an international broadcaster and golf coach today. *Still frame from* Loopers: The Caddie's Long Walk

She also offered the camaraderie that was so instinctive in the Augusta National caddies.

"She's a rattler," Faldo said. "We were walking up the fourteenth hole at St. Andrews [on the Sunday of the 1990 British Open]. I was leading by three or four when she turns to me and said, 'So, are you going to get a dog?' I knew what she was doing. She was trying to get me to switch off. It was a great little pressure relief."

Fanny worked with Faldo for four of his six major victories, missing only his 1987 British Open and 1989 Masters titles. She worked with Faldo for ten years until leaving in late 1999 to caddie briefly for Sergio García before the temperamental Spaniard axed her ahead of the 2000 Masters. By 2001 the Faldo-Fanny duet was back together.

Their close relationship was so in tune that they were each married on the same day (July 27, 2001) in separate cities.

Back issues caused her to reconsider a full-time caddying career by the 2010s. After that she used her knowledge of motivation to assist European golfers and amateur teams on the best way to tackle a golf course and dabbled in broadcasting for professional events in Europe and the major championships. She parlayed her caddying knowledge into a business as a sports psychologist.

"In the beginning, when I started, no one wanted me because I was a girl,"

1

The First White Caddie
at the Masters

When Jack Tosone checked in at Masters headquarters on the Saturday before the 1983 Masters, he became the answer to a trivia question. Tosone caddied for amateur Jim Hallet, a Bryant College (now Bryant University, Smithfield, Rhode Island) golf teammate, and became the first non–Augusta National caddie and first white caddie in Masters history. He just beat Tommy O'Toole, the caddie for amateur Jim Holtgrieve, to the punch.

The first day for Tosone was akin to being the nerdy freshman on the initial day at the new high school. He and Hallet were twenty-three-year-old college kids in the company of older professionals, both players and caddies. After checking in at registration, Tosone went to the pro shop and was directed to see caddie master Freddie Bennett about acquiring the standard caddie jumpsuit. Bennett refused to give him one, saying that non–Augusta National caddies couldn't start until Sunday. When Tosone showed Bennett the rules he had received in the mail, Bennett promptly sent Tosone to the caddie shack.

He also got a chilly reception when he reached the facility. "I walked in and there were about fifty or sixty guys, all playing cards or just sitting around," Tosone recalled in 2003. "It was a smoky room. They all looked around at me, and there was dead silence. All the guys were Black. I just thought to myself, 'Oh, shit!' It was like a scene from some movie, and I was the guy in the middle."

Finally, he pleaded his case and got the caddie supplies he needed.

"I think it was more of an economic thing than racial," Tosone said. "I emphasized to them I was amateur Jim Hallet's caddie, not the caddie of a pro golfer."

Since he checked in first, Tosone was assigned caddie locker No. 1. None other than Willie Peterson, the five-time Masters winner on Jack Nicklaus's bag, usually got that position and wasn't too happy about the outsider's new spot.

"He came up and said he wanted locker No. 1," Tosone said. "He was really the only one who gave me any trouble."

Peterson denied what occurred, but it was true to form for one of Augusta National's most outspoken caddies.

Hallet said he even heard from Peterson about the situation. "Willie got up in my face and said, 'How dare your caddie take my locker,'" Hallet recalled in 2003. "I couldn't believe a caddie was doing that to a player."

Hallet said that he hired Tosone because of their successful relationship in previous tournaments. Tosone was on his bag when Hallet reached the semi-finals of the 1982 U.S. Amateur and earned a spot in the Masters field. Plus, Hallet admits he didn't know much about Masters tradition.

"I was more of a hockey player," Hallet said. "I didn't know too much about Augusta at that time. I probably knew more about [Boston Bruins hockey great] Bobby Orr than I did about Bobby Jones."

Tosone knew more about the caddying business. He began caddying in New England as a sixth grader and told Hallet that it wouldn't be possible for him to work the Masters because he was not an Augusta National employee.

"I'm not Black," Tosone remembers telling Hallet.

"We'll get you there somehow," Hallet came back. "I'll write a letter."

By the fall of 1982, Hallet learned of Augusta National chairman Hardin's change in policy for caddie hiring. He ran down the hall of his Bryant College dormitory with an Augusta National press release in hand to inform Tosone of the news.

"I'm there," Tosone quickly said.

Tosone's reception warmed up greatly when tournament play began at the 1983 Masters. Hallet, making his only career Masters appearance, was one stroke off the lead after a first-round 68. Through twenty-eight holes, he held the lead at 5-under par. Walking down the eleventh fairway in the second round, Tosone pointed to the leader board to the left of the green and noted the HALLET at the top. Playing with Arnold Palmer and Seve Ballesteros, he kept his cool until the par-3 sixteenth. His 8-iron tee shot landed inches from the right-front hole placement but spun back quickly, down to

Jack Tosone stands in front of an image from the 1983 Masters where he caddied for friend Jim Hallet. *Photo by Jack Tosone*

the lower tier and into the pond. Hallet wound up with a double bogey and fell from the lead.

He would go on to finish in a tie for fortieth at 9-over-par 297 and earned Low Amateur honors. Hallet turned pro soon after and played on the PGA Tour through the mid-1990s.

"When I walked in [after the first round], they were all shaking my hand, saying I did a good job," Tosone said. "I got more of that after the second round. The caddies there give you credit for doing a good job. I guess they realized I wasn't taking money out of their pockets. It was a great experience."

Tosone said the most difficult thing he found about the Augusta National course was reading the greens. Matthew "Shorty Mac" Palmer, Billy Casper's caddie, even helped him on some of the specifics during a practice round.

The 1983 Masters remains Tosone's only trip to Augusta. He has served as the head professional at various New England golf clubs, coached the golf team at Massachusetts College of Liberal Arts, and given skiing lessons. In

2023, he was serving as the general manger at the Weekapaug Golf Club in Westerly, Rhode Island, downstate from his hometown in Barrington.

He still has some Masters trinkets, including two coveted Masters caddie hats, one with the cursive caddie name and the other with a Masters logo.

"Some guy called me right after that tournament and said they were going to put my name in Trivial Pursuit," Tosone said of the game, which made its official introduction in 1982. "I don't know if it ever happened. But it was supposed to say, 'Who broke the last color barrier in professional sports?' I'd love to have that card if it happened."

1

Today

SIGNS OF THE TIMES

The significance of Augusta National caddies in the Masters Tournament has clearly diminished over the forty years following the last Masters to use only Augusta National caddies. The caddie shack is still busy because the new facility has an enlarged footprint and more centralized location that draws in the entire field, but it isn't the same bustling, behind-the-scenes center of activity among locals that it used to be during the first full week in April. The banter in the nearby Sand Hills neighborhood, usually reserved for who was caddying for whom in the Masters, changed to topics of other sports and politics. The men on the bag for Masters contenders hail from places away from Augusta, including distant reaches like Canada, New Zealand, and Japan. There is diminishing knowledge of the band of men who made the jumpsuits famous.

It is left to displays at Augusta National memorializing the caddies' contributions, such as the one that occurred in 2003, the twentieth anniversary of allowing outside caddies to work in the Masters. In the exhibit area on the left of the entrance corridor from the main gate during that Masters week, a mannequin fitted with a caddie jumpsuit and topped with a green caddie cap was presented. Behind glass was a golfer's bag, weighing approximately fifty pounds, for viewers to lift. A short printed passage on a display explaining the history of the caddies and their duties and mentioning Stovepipe, Cemetery, Iron Man, and Pappy was adjacent to the bag. The caddie display was so popular that it was scheduled to be shown again in 2004, near the annual displays of tournament anniversary remembrances and trophies and crystal that Masters participants can win.

Occasionally, there is still an actual glimpse back to the emotions and thrills that caddying in the Masters used to bring to these men who grew up with a tournament that has been Augusta's calling card for nearly a century. Such a moment took place in 2002. A group of four caddies with Augusta National ties looped in that tournament, with none of the players making the cut. Jackson worked with Crenshaw for the twenty-sixth time, record longevity for a Masters caddie (it reached thirty-nine Masters with Crenshaw's and Jackson's retirement from Masters play in 2015). Buck Moore, a former Augusta National caddie who worked the PGA Tour for a variety of players, got a last-minute bag when Paul Azinger's regular Tour caddie, Terry Holt, couldn't reach Augusta because of the birth of a child the previous weekend. Azinger missed the cut by a stroke in his final Masters appearance. Jesse "Gray" Moore was on the bag of U.S. Mid-Amateur champion Tim Jackson. Louis Laurence was hired by Tommy Aaron to carry a Masters bag for the first time.

Carl Jackson and Buck Moore are from the old school, Black men who learned to caddie out of necessity, first at neighboring Augusta Country Club as preteens and then, as they "graduated" to Augusta National, tutored by Stokes and Nipper. They caddied because it was a resource for money, first on the weekends and then full-time. They made associations with the game's best players and eventually decided to make a living on the road caddying for a variety of journeymen or promising young players on various Tours.

Laurence and "Gray" Moore are white, a noteworthy description since the first white caddie didn't pick up a bag in the Masters until 1983. Both men are Augusta natives who grew up in the shadow of the Masters during the 1960s, watching Palmer, Player, and Nicklaus dominate. They weren't brought up in the game as caddies but instead played the game in hopes of following in the footsteps of "the Big Three."

They learned golf at two local municipal courses: the Patch and historic Forest Hills Golf Club, a Donald Ross design that was the site of Bobby Jones's thirteen-stroke victory in the 1930 Southeastern Open, his final tournament start before he went on his Grand Slam run. At these courses, they mixed with Augusta's finest players, many of them Black men, including Jim Dent, himself a former caddie at Augusta National. Often, they played high-stakes gambling matches.

Two of these men, Buck Moore and Laurence, had particularly prudent stories to tell as the 2002 golf season rolled from the West Coast to Florida and up toward Augusta. They were the past and the present.

For Buck, all eyes were on his chance to restore some of the lost glory of the Augusta National caddies.

Charles Howell III, the hotshot twenty-two-year-old Augusta native, was coming off a Rookie-of-the-Year season on the PGA Tour in 2001. Charles, the son of an Augusta pediatric surgeon, was a self-proclaimed golf geek who grew up next door to the Masters. One year, Ernie Els and Tom Watson were neighbors in rental homes during Masters week, with Charles sharing a casual shootaround of driveway hoops with Watson. Charles first played Augusta National as a twelve-year-old, shooting 79. He learned the game at Augusta Country Club, the course that neighbors Amen Corner, and during his teen years regularly visited swing guru David Leadbetter in Florida to hone his game.

Howell's proximity to both Augusta National and the neighborhood of many of the caddies was particularly striking. Howell's neighborhood and private high school, Westminster School, is just beyond the Sand Hills as the area transitions into a prominent white residential area.

With a qualification for his first Masters all but in hand as 2001 wound down, Charles quietly pledged to make it a real Augusta affair, paying homage to the Augusta National caddies by hiring one of their own for the Masters. Picture this first-time scenario: a son of Augusta winning the Masters with another type of son of Augusta on his bag.

Charles was still searching for a regular caddie on the PGA Tour after Tony Navarro opted to remain with longtime boss Greg Norman early in 2002. In a small town like Augusta, everybody knew Charles's potential, particularly the caddies at Augusta National. Charles liked their association with his backyard tournament and their local knowledge, plus he had grown familiar enough to call them by their first names over the years by playing casual rounds at Forest Hills or Jones Creek Golf Club in neighboring Columbia County. In turn, the caddies favored Charles because of his bubbly personality and respectful nature; he often ended sentences with a "Sir" or "Ma'am" when he first joined the Tour. He didn't act like the spoiled rich kid that he could have become. Most folks just remembered him as "Little Charlie," a slight, bespectacled kid who had a knack for golf.

The tryouts for Howell's bag began the year before when Tommy "Burnt Biscuits" Bennett worked for Howell during the tail end of the 2001 season. Bennett had been Tiger Woods's first Masters caddie when Tiger made his amateur debut in 1995 and had bounced around various players on numerous Tours since leaving as an Augusta National regular.

That relationship was very short. Howell claimed that Bennett showed up for work all too often with beer on his breath. Then came the morning at the Las Vegas Invitational late in the fall when Tommy began the morning's conversation on the first tee with an under-his-breath request to borrow five hundred dollars and pay back a gambling debt from too long a night in the Vegas casinos. Bennett said the lure of the casinos is a problem all Tour caddies have in Vegas.

"Charles needed some chemistry, and they didn't have it," said Dr. Charles Howell Jr., Charles's father who also served as a close follower and confidant for his older son's career.

Joe Collins was considered next, but "Joe has a raspy voice and it didn't work out. They couldn't find an understanding," Dr. Howell said. Joe never worked a tournament with Charles.

The Howells thought about talking with Jackson, but Carl's long and close association with Crenshaw prevented them from even making a serious inquiry.

"The first time I met him in person was at the New Orleans tournament in [the spring of] 2001," Jackson recalled of Howell. "I was caddying for Brad Fabel. And Charles just looked at me one day on the range, introduced himself, smiled, and said matter of factly, 'You and I are going to win the Masters one day.' I said let's do it. But nothing ever came of it."

Then came Buck Moore. A husky man with gray around the temples at age fifty-five, Buck once hoped to make it professionally as a pitcher in baseball but injured his shoulder playing high school football at Augusta's oldest Black high school, Lucy Laney. Buck is laid-back, speaks in a Southern baritone, and once supported his family by doubling as a truck driver and caddie. He began caddying at Augusta National at age twelve in 1966 and worked in more than thirty Masters, with a best finish of sixth with Ed Fiori in 1980. On the advice of the late LeRoy Schultz, Tom Weiskopf's former Masters caddie, Moore left Augusta National in 1988 to caddie for an assortment of players on the PGA Tour, including Kelly Gibson, K. J. Choi, Grant Waite, Fiori, and many others on a weekly basis. He had a number of runner-up finishes but didn't win until 2005 in Boston with Olin Browne and again in 2011 when Browne won the U.S. Senior Open.

"You can't get rich being a caddie," Moore said, "but you can live comfortably if your player does all right. I'd rather hit the lottery, though. I ain't got to have that much. I ain't greedy."

Buck pokes out his chest proudly for the well-known accomplishments of two of his children. Older son Otis played defensive tackle at Clemson University in the 1980s and was an all–Atlantic Coast Conference selection in 1989. After bouncing around a few NFL teams in the early 1990s, Otis completed his playing career in the Arena Football League, playing the 2002 season as a six-foot-four, 270-pound, thirty-five-year-old two-way lineman for the New Jersey Gladiators. Younger son Ricky was the starting point guard and inspirational captain on the University of Connecticut's 1999 NCAA basketball championship team. Buck took a week off Gibson's bag to accompany his wife, Dorothy, to the Final Four in St. Petersburg, Florida, that year, where UConn beat Duke, which also had an Augusta presence—William Avery, the great-nephew of Iron Man Avery. Ricky, who at one time attended the same elementary school as Howell, tried his wares in Europe in hopes of one day making an NBA roster before turning to coaching. Even more proudly, Buck notes that Ricky earned a degree in four years at the Storrs, Connecticut, school, went on to be a college assistant, and now coaches AAU basketball and high school basketball at Northwest Cabarrus High School in Kannapolis, North Carolina.

"I know all those guys," Howell said of the Augusta National caddies at the Players Championship in March, one month before the 2002 Masters. "They keep urging me to hire one of them. If I do, I'll have all of them in my court. If I don't . . ."

Howell prepped for the run toward Augusta by hiring Buck at the Phoenix Open in February. He called to inquire about Buck's availability a few weeks before.

"What are you doing now?" Charles asked.

"Starving," Buck replied.

"Come work for me, and you won't be starving anymore," Howell said.

Charles earned $24,933 at Phoenix. At the Nissan Open two weeks later, Charles finished tied for sixth and carried home $123,950. The first stop on the Florida Swing came next, and Charles won $10,798 at Doral but shot 73-75 on the weekend. Total payout: approximately $160,000, with Buck earning more than $10,000 with the standard caddie payment arrangement.

In the middle of this stretch, Howell became disgusted with his short game, particularly his putting, and felt a twinge of uncertainty about his working relationship with his caddie. Buck wasn't viewed by the Howell Camp to be the necessary wise voice who would spur on a young player in a tight situation or provide the needed motivation when uncertainty struck, even though Buck admitted later, unsolicited, at the Masters that "Charles is the kind of player who needs talking to, a player where you've got to get in his head and tell him he's good, keep telling him that." Charles also insisted from the outset, in his own kind way, that Buck not spill the beans about a possible Masters job just yet. This was still just a trial. The next week, one of the golf weekly magazines carried a small news item where Moore was quoted not only talking about working the Masters but also possibly getting Howell's bag for the rest of the year.

"I have a hard enough time sticking my foot in my own mouth," said Howell, who had quickly become a media favorite for his candid interviews. "I didn't need two feet in my mouth."

Before the second stop in Florida, on the Monday of the Honda Classic, Buck received a phone call from Dr. Howell. It was five weeks before the Masters.

"I thought everything was going just fine," Buck said. "Then the phone rang, and Charles' father just said, 'Charles and I think we need a change.' I asked him why Charles hadn't told me himself. He just said they had been thinking about making that decision for a couple of weeks."

Rumor was that Buck was hot about being laid off. He said he had only a passing "hello-hello" exchange with Charles since the parting. But come Masters time, Buck had evidently had a chance to cool down.

"No bad feelings," Buck said. "I wish [Charles] all the best. Ninety percent of the people here in Augusta were pulling for me to caddie for him. But it just didn't work out."

Perhaps Buck's anger lessened because he got a bag on Monday of Masters week when Azinger was looking for a practice-round replacement for his sidelined caddie. Buck, on the grounds just as a spectator, was hanging around the clubhouse area, in the right place at the right time. When Azinger told his regular caddie to stay home with the newborn, Buck worked the tournament, even though Azinger didn't reach the weekend.

"I just guess the good Lord does some mysterious things," Buck said.

Howell hired Bobby Conlan, a career caddie based at Pebble Beach Golf Links and Cypress Point Golf Club who had previously worked on Tour for Bobby Clampett, David Edwards, and Clarence Rose and won on Dave

Eichelberger's bag at the 1999 U.S. Senior Open. Howell met Conlan on the Monterey Peninsula and used him on the bag at February's AT&T Pebble Beach National Pro-Am, where he finished twelfth earlier in the year, and then rehired him for the Bay Hill Invitational and the Players Championship before his first Masters appearance. Conlan's love for and knowledge of the course architecture of Dr. Alister MacKenzie, the designer of Cypress Point and Augusta National, was a main selling point.

Howell's first-round debut was highlighted by his clothing. The Swedish fashion designer Johan Lindeberg had put Charles in some offbeat golf clothing during most of the season, but for the Masters' first round, Charles sported white pants, flared at the bottom, with a forest green stripe down the sides. It looked like either the prison clothes Paul Newman wore in the film *Cool Hand Luke* or, more appropriately, the pants that Augusta National caddies sported in the old days of the jumpsuit.

Howell made the Masters cut by one stroke and finished tied for twenty-ninth at 3-over-par 291.

"I don't think Charles has found his full-time caddie yet," Dr. Howell said as the muddy weekend progressed at Augusta National.

By late summer, Howell had changed caddies again, hiring Brendan McCartain, who worked for José María Olazábal in his 1999 Masters victory. McCartain worked the 2002 Masters with Argentina's José Cóceres, who was paired with Howell for the first two rounds. Howell said he and McCartain developed a friendship and mutual respect during those rounds. In the fall, McCartain was a key component when Howell captured his first PGA Tour title at the Michelob Championship at Kingsmill in Williamsburg, Virginia.

McCartain's proactive attitude may have brought on the victory. He was used to watching Olazábal's outstanding short game and was insistent on improving Howell's. He watched as Howell devoted more time to his game around the green. He helped Howell choose a new putter. Two weeks before the Michelob victory, McCartain grabbed Howell's sixty-degree lob wedge out of his bag and took it to the Callaway Golf trailer on-site at a tournament and had most of the bounce shaved off the bottom of the club. "Trust me, this will work," McCartain said. Howell went on to finish second in putting for the week.

"I spent a lot of time talking to Brendan about absolutely nothing," Howell said of his first victory. "We had conversation about some of the stupidest things, and he kept it going, which was the best thing ever. You know, Brendan won the '99 Masters with José María Olazábal, and I felt that anyone who can win that golf tournament has something to him, has some serious guts, and it showed today. He never blinked, his expression never changed. Where I was nervous as a cat on a hot tin roof at times, Brendan stayed the same, and I wouldn't have known if I was in first or last place."

Laurence took a much lower-key approach to achieving a childhood dream of walking the Augusta National fairways. The fifty-four-year-old was a hotshot junior golfer in the mid-to-late 1960s. Many claim he was among the best junior golfers to come out of the Garden City, pre-Howell. He won the Augusta Junior, the city's most prestigious junior tournament, in 1965 and 1966 at ages fifteen and sixteen. In other state and regional tournaments, he was always among the best players in the field and led Richmond Academy's high school team to a state Class AAA title.

"From the time I was eight years old till I was fourteen, I played every day," Laurence said. "In the summer, my father would drop me off at 'the Patch' at 7:30 in the morning and I'd play eighteen holes in the morning, mess around, and then play eighteen in the afternoon. I remember my mother and some of the other mothers would shine the headlights of their cars on the eighteenth green just so we could finish the last round."

Many compared his mannerisms to those of Palmer, his hero, and Laurence took that to heart. Laurence grimaced, slashed at the golf ball, putted knock-kneed on many occasions, and hitched up his pants just like Arnie. As an early teen, Laurence was known as a club thrower until his father saw him break a club and threatened to take his clubs if he didn't get rid of that temper, much as "Deacon" Palmer lectured a young Arnie on proper golf etiquette during the 1940s in Pennsylvania. Laurence even chose to attend Wake Forest University, Arnie's alma mater, in the late 1960s without a scholarship, at about the same time as Joe Inman and Leonard Thompson, future professional stars, were getting started at the Winston-Salem, North Carolina, school. After one year, Laurence dropped out, disillusioned about his game and college.

"It was like the world was coming to an end if I missed a putt," Laurence said in an early 1970s interview with the *Augusta Chronicle*. "I guess people just didn't expect me to miss."

He resurfaced in the navy in 1968, first stationed in Norfolk, Virginia, and then in Honolulu. He was the navy's best golfer, earning all-navy three times. His duty on an in-base submarine in Norfolk helped him "learn how to hit it straight." In Hawaii, the workload was more rigid, but he jumped around the Hawaiian Islands as a successful amateur and played in his only PGA Tour event, the 1971 Hawaiian Open, where he shot 77-80 to miss the cut.

Through all this time, Augusta still beckoned. His first wife, the former Gail Evans of Augusta, had delivered a son, Louis Jr. Augusta College, now Augusta University, soon offered a full ride for golf, which the twenty-three-year-old Laurence accepted following his four-year navy stint. For three years, Laurence played the No. 1 or No. 2 position for the Jaguars, whose home course was Forest Hills.

But that's about as far as his competitive game reached. He worked in various jobs outside of the game until becoming an assistant golf professional at Forest Hills in 1979. He was an assistant at Goshen Plantation Country Club and gave lessons at a driving range in North Augusta, South Carolina. In the meantime, he got a divorce, and his son died in a 1999 automobile accident in Massachusetts.

More than twenty years later, the lure of Augusta National finally got him.

He took the unusual turn of becoming a caddie at Augusta National in his early forties in the late 1980s. Freddie Bennett, a good friend, convinced him to try caddying there.

"You ought to try it as much as you know about golf and love it," said Bennett, who used to live near Laurence.

"I didn't know Augusta National was taking on caddies," Laurence said.

"Sure, we've got lots of white boys out there," Bennett said with a laugh.

By January 1989, Laurence was hooked. His first bag at Augusta National was Donny Anderson, the former Green Bay Packers halfback. He would later tote for former Miami Dolphins coach Don Shula and Atlanta Braves pitcher John Smoltz and carried in the same group as pop singer Celine Dion and her husband. He has a picture with Celine as they stood on the tee of the par-3 twelfth hole. In the early 2000s, when he was laid off from his full-time job at Augusta's Thermal Ceramics for a second time, he asked Van Dorn if a summer job was available elsewhere to make caddying his year-round occupation.

He caddied at Augusta National from the club's opening in early October until it closed for the summer in late May. He would then trek to Kohler, Wisconsin, in the summer to caddie at another CaddieMaster Enterprises course, Whistling Straits Golf Club, a top-flight club which was the site of the 2004 PGA Championship. That tradition of traveling from Augusta National in the offseason dated back to the 1960s when a large group of Augusta National caddies would spend the summer in Atlantic City, New Jersey, as everything from caddies to cooks to bellhops. Laurence arrived at Whistling Straits at sunrise during the long Wisconsin summers and carried twice a day for as many days as possible. Laurence also remarried in 1998 to Judith, a woman he had met twenty years before when he helped tutor her son in golf at Forest Hills.

"Being away from her is tough," Laurence said. "But she understands this is what I do and love. Plus, she doesn't mind the checks coming back in the mail."

Two months before the 2002 Masters, Laurence's connection with his childhood dream course became even more of a reality. He was picked to caddie for Aaron, who came into town to check out the massive changes made to the course since 2001.

Aaron had picked an Augusta National caddie for the last few years, using Collins in 2000 and even allowing *Sports Illustrated* writer Rick Reilly to step in for Augusta National regular Freddie Robertson for one round in 2001 as Reilly researched a book on various caddie duties.

"I used my Tour caddie until the last few years," Aaron said in 2000, when at age sixty-three he became, at the time, the oldest player in Masters history to make the cut. "But it's so hard for my regular guy to find accommodations. He lives in Arizona and would have had to come all the way back here to caddie. So, I just decided to use a local caddie."

Aaron's magical 2000 Masters included a first-round, even-par 72 that was one of only twelve rounds of par or better and three better than Woods's first-round 75. Aaron followed with a 74 to make the cut, then tired on the weekend with 86-81 for a 313 total, last in the field of weekend finishers, but good enough to earn $10,488. Aaron was one of the few players in the field who had experience with an Augusta National caddie, using Cleveland Randolph on the way to a victory in the 1973 Masters.

"Joe is all I know," Aaron said of Collins in 2000 when asked about his Augusta National caddie. "He didn't hit a bad shot or a bad putt all week. I asked Joe for some advice on a putt on the first hole, just to get his opinion, just to see what he'd have to say. But I read most all my putts and clubbed myself."

Aaron, a Gainesville, Georgia, native, was among the dying breed of aging Masters winners still willing to walk the steep hills of Augusta National and possibly embarrass themselves by shooting rounds in the 80s. Aaron had rarely played on the Champions Tour over the previous few years, but coming to Augusta reminded him of his youth and his most brilliant golf moment. A caddie who gets Aaron's bag, and some others such as Seve Ballesteros, Charles Coody, Billy Casper, Gay Brewer, or Doug Ford, was virtually assured—barring a great start like Aaron had in 2000—of watching golf from behind the ropes on the weekend and making a lesser payday.

But that didn't matter to Laurence. He and Aaron hit it off quickly during the February practice round, and Aaron asked if Laurence would be available to caddie in the Masters.

The request shocked Laurence. He quickly accepted the offer and wrote his name and address on a scorecard for Aaron's reference.

As the Masters moved closer, no follow-up came from Aaron. Laurence figured that the 1973 Masters champion's plans had changed, so Laurence opted to spend the week as a lowly forecaddie at Augusta Country Club, a job where he would search for errant drives instead of toting a bag. His only view of the Masters would be over the fence that separates Augusta Country Club's ninth fairway from Amen Corner.

However, two days before Masters week, as Laurence completed caddie duty for an Augusta National member, he was approached by Dale Fryer, the head of outside services for Augusta National. Aaron had finally called to make his final request for Laurence to work during the Masters.

"I lived my whole life to get here," Laurence said. "Actually, to play here. But I'm not going to make it playing. This is a dream come true for me."

Laurence caddied in practice-round groups that included Phil Mickelson, Mark Calcavecchia, Fred Couples, and Jim Furyk. Aaron and Coody, the 1971 Masters champion, were paired together for the first two rounds.

It didn't matter that Aaron shot 79-78-157 to miss the cut. The experience was priceless. Whether it was the sixty-five-year-old Aaron acting like a nervous rookie on the first tee or carving a fairway wood into one of Augusta National's newly lengthened par-4s, Laurence was in heaven. On occasion, Laurence thought he saw an opportunity to offer a suggestion on club selection or the subtle break of a putt. Then he remembered this wasn't just a high-handicap member he was working with.

"It's intimidating to be in someone's presence who has won the Masters," Laurence said. "They have a confidence on the golf course that is just unnatural."

Laurence earned $700 for his five-day stint with Aaron. The relationship went so smoothly that when Aaron returned in 2003, Laurence was back on the bag. The sixty-six-year-old Aaron sloshed around soggy Augusta National, beginning the tournament bogey, triple bogey, double bogey on the way to a front-nine 47 and 92-80 thirty-six holes, the highest halfway total in the tournament.

Laurence was one of the final caddies of Aaron's Masters career. In 2002, Augusta National chairman Hootie Johnson announced that past champions would have to meet minimum playing requirements during the year to participate after age sixty-five, precluding their previous lifetime invitation. However, the week before the 2003 Masters, Nicklaus and Palmer met with Johnson, and the policy was rescinded to "play as long as they like, so long as they feel they remain competitive." Aaron's final Masters appearance came in 2005.

"He can still play," Laurence said of Aaron after the second round was completed in 2002. "When the gallery claps for him, like they did when he finished his round today, it sends chills up your spine. When he manufactures a shot into these greens with a fairway wood or long iron, you realize that this man has some kind of game. You forget it sometimes, but these guys were the best at one time."

Laurence caddied at Augusta National until 2018 when he was beset by memory issues. A doctor at Augusta National was told about Laurence's difficulty and suggested a visit to a specialist. He was diagnosed with dementia and was unable to caddie at Augusta National any longer, a real disappointment in addition to his diagnosis. In July 2022, Laurence died from Alzheimer's Disease at age seventy-three.

As the calendar turned to 2022, the Augusta National caddie ranks' historic connections had diminished further. Most of the caddie corps today is white, with a sprinkling of Black caddies, some from the Sand Hills, but very, very few with any Masters experience. The focus is now on member play, which has always been the club's cornerstone for its caddies to develop a regular bag, notable connections, and increased weekly income, and the addition of the Augusta National Women's Amateur has added a new level of caddie-player interaction.

The Women's Amateur began in 2019 and consists of two rounds off-site at Champions Retreat in nearby Columbia County, a practice round for the entire field at Augusta National on the Friday before Masters week, and the final round for those who made the cut at Augusta National on Saturday with NBC televising. In the practice round on Friday, the women amateurs are "encouraged" to use Augusta National caddies so that they can get a quicker read on the intricacies of the course. All participants have Augusta caddies at their disposal during the practice round, and many of the thirty final-round qualifiers secure Augusta National caddies. At tournament's end, each participant is presented with the cloth nameplate that is attached to the back of their caddie's jumpsuit as a keepsake.

Even today, the caddie corps' daily routine still resides at 2604 Washington Road. A daily lottery determining the next day's caddies remains quite a sight, with a 5:00 p.m. listing of the next day's arriving members and guests to decipher. The following morning begins shortly after 8:00 a.m. with all caddies prepared for their assigned duties. Sometimes, members and guests have been encouraged to watch the process before they are paired the following morning. Learned caddies know the members who pay the most, and those are most often the first off the board in the lottery.

Prominent among today's caddie collection are two fifty-plus-year-old white men, Steve Kling and Brian McKinley.

A native Southern Californian from Torrance, the sixty-one-year-old Kling made his mark as a baseball coach, most notably as an assistant college coach to Hall of Famer Andy Lopez at Pepperdine University, the University of Florida, and the University of Arizona and remains connected to the sport via scouting and camps. The Pepperdine Waves won the 1992 College World Series, and the University of Florida Gators reached two World Series in Omaha, Nebraska. But by the early 2000s, Kling was tiring of the long seasons and busy summers coaching college kids and realized that an opportunity to guide a Division I program was probably fading.

So Steve and his wife Diana, along with young son Joseph, decided to seek a different path in 2005. Diana was an athletic administrator and searched out possible job opportunities before landing a position with the Peach Belt Athletic Conference, based in Augusta. The Klings drove cross-country from Arizona the day after Hurricane Katrina and settled in neighboring Columbia County as Steve enjoyed golf, dabbled in baseball, and helped to raise their kindergarten-age son Joseph as Diana rose to deputy commissioner of the conference by 2019. Joseph became a college golfer at Georgia College in Milledgeville, Georgia, where he graduated in 2022, worked some as a caddie at Champions Retreat and Augusta National, and currently holds a role with IMG Academy in Bradenton, Florida, while pursuing a master's degree in sport management at the University of Florida.

Kling played casual golf at various courses around the Augusta area, which is rich in accessible quality courses such as Forest Hills Golf Club, Palmetto Golf Club, Aiken Golf Club, and the River Club. One day he was playing Goshen Plantation, an Ellis Maples design in south Augusta, and questioned a playing partner from Augusta about the long odds of playing at Augusta National. He was told that caddies get an opportunity to play on caddie day in late May just as the club closes for the summer. Kling had previously toted for a player at a lower-level Hooters Tour event and was intrigued.

His caddie tutelage began as he got a foot in the door at Augusta National in 2006 and went through CaddieMaster Enterprises' stringent testing method of understanding the role and the rules by looping in front of and with trainers at the River Club in North Augusta, South Carolina, en route to becoming a vaunted Augusta National caddie.

"I was in the old caddie house, the one before the current facility; some guys were friendly and others weren't," Kling said. "There was definitely a learning curve. I did a lot of watching, listening, and learning, especially early on. I learned how to dress, to not wear too much under the uniform. Being a coach, I can observe things and learn from it."

Kling's experience includes earning the bag of Mexican amateur Álvaro Ortiz in the 2019 Masters as the two teamed to shoot the fourth-lowest amateur score in tournament history, 2-under-par 286. A bogey on their final hole, the par-4 ninth, dropped Ortiz one shot behind Low Amateur Viktor Hovland.

A bigger connection came in early 2005 when Kling drove two hundred miles south to Sea Island, Georgia, to caddie in the Jones Cup Invitational, a prestigious amateur event. He was assigned a tall, raw sophomore golfer from Coastal Carolina University, Dustin Johnson. That started a relationship that grew stronger as Johnson began to play in the Masters in 2009. Johnson has traveled to Augusta the week before the Masters for years and uses Kling as his caddie to understand the course and its changes since the previous year. Johnson's regular caddie, first Bobby Brown and then younger brother Austin, tagged along during the practice rounds to take notes alongside Dustin and meet with Kling afterward to document changes in their yardage books and ask further questions as Augusta National caddies are required for rounds prior to the weekend before the Masters. Using veteran Augusta National caddies to prepare both the player and his regular Tour caddie before the tournament was a practice started in the mid-1980s after the caddie ranks were opened.

That process led to Johnson winning the fall 2020 Masters after an unusual preparation period to understand the different grasses, softened greens, and course conditioning and prevalent November wind directions for the only time the Masters has been held other than spring. Kling also serves as one of four on-site caddies on call during Masters week in case there's a need for a marker, a last-minute sub, or someone to work the Wednesday Par 3 Contest.

"It's a routine for Dustin," Kling said. "You learn something new every year, and there's so much for the player to learn that you can't do it in just one or two days here during the practice rounds when it's so busy, especially on the greens. He takes us out to dinner and has been so gracious. I'm happy to just be a little part of the team."

Another tie-in was added to Kling's resume in 2022 when Ted Scott won his third Masters as a caddie in eleven years—the first two with Bubba Watson and this one on Scottie Scheffler's bag. Scott and Kling had developed a friendship during the Masters, and Scott boarded with the Klings during the 2022 tournament victory.

McKinley, a Wheeling, West Virginia, native, is a caddie lifer, carrying for more than twenty years at Augusta National as of 2022 and then working summers at various midwestern and northeastern clubs. At age fifty-one, McKinley has become the gravelly voiced, wise veteran who members and Women's Amateur participants value.

That was evident at the first Women's Amateur in 2019. McKinley was assigned Annabell Fuller, an English amateur headed to the University of Florida. Fuller had difficulty getting through the second round at Champions Retreat, and McKinley was replaced by Fuller's father to help his daughter finish with her head up as she missed the cut to play at Augusta National. An Augusta National member on-site at Champions Retreat who was familiar with McKinley heard about the situation and suggested to second-round leader Jennifer Kupcho that a reputable Augusta National caddie was available should Kupcho need an alternative to her father, Mike. McKinley had worked with Kupcho in the fall of 2018 when the Wake Forest women's team visited Augusta National for a casual round.

After a Friday practice round with McKinley, Kupcho opted—with her father's full blessing—for the Augusta National caddie, a choice that paid off during a Saturday crisis. Deep in a final-round friendly battle with Mexico's María Fassi, the final group left the par-5 eighth green, and things turned dark.

"Brian, I'm having a migraine, and I can't see out of my left eye," Kupcho said.

"You've got to be kidding me," McKinley recounted to masters.com in 2021. "It turned into exactly how to help her out. How to find her brother. How to find a Coca-Cola as fast as possible to help activate the migraine medicine."

Kupcho closed her eyes as she walked the ninth and tenth holes, opening them only to hit a shot. At the tenth tee, McKinley asked an Augusta National member, Danny Yates, to get a drink for Kupcho. Five Cokes showed up on the tee box. At the eleventh tee, Kupcho relaxed on one of Augusta National's sawed-in-half log benches and then took a restroom break at the private player restroom just left of and below the tee.

"I don't care who you are, you are thinking about history, the majesty of it all," McKinley said of Amen Corner—the eleventh, twelfth, and thirteenth holes. "You're at the beginning of three of the greatest golf holes that God ever created. Those holes can bring some of the greatest moments or destroy people's lives."

After swallowing the medication and taking in fluids and with the headache subsiding, Kupcho finished the eleventh hole and spotted Wake Forest friends and her coach, Kim Lewellen, as she approached the devilish par-3 twelfth. She held up four fingers, indicating the number of birdies needed over the last seven holes to overcome Fassi and a two-stroke deficit. She made an eagle on thirteen and three birdies to go 5-under par over the final six holes to complete a final-round 67 for a four-stroke victory.

"We're two down to the female Tiger Woods [Fassi] at thirteen," McKinley said. "For the second shot on thirteen, we had 199 yards to the hole. Jennifer has two hybrids in the bag. She hadn't touched the hybrid with the monkey head cover on it all day. Growing up as a child, my whole thing was monkeys, so my god, we're hitting the monkey. She said that was her favorite club."

The rush of under-par scoring secured the win, but the ability to overcome an illness was the crucial element.

"I think on those holes when I couldn't see, I was able to lean on him and trust him to tell me the yardage, tell me the up/down and to read the green," Kupcho said. "On nine green, I said, 'I can't see anything, so just tell me where to hit it.'

"I think that takes a lot of trust in him, and obviously I had seen him the last, how many holes? Twenty-seven holes, twenty-six holes [counting Friday's practice round], how he was reading the greens, and I knew he had it. So I just had to trust him and go with it."

The caddie ranks for the women that week also included Kling, veteran loopers Moore and Bud Jackson, the younger brother of Carl Jackson and a decades-long Augusta National veteran. In the second playing of the Women's Amateur in 2021, another Augusta National caddie landed in the winner's circle, Florida resident Chad Lamsback, with seventeen-year-old Japanese sensation Tsubasa Kajitani. Lamsback piggybacked off helping other Japanese players navigate Augusta National in previous years.

McKinley took the 2019 victory in and reflected on his experience at Augusta National, including multiple seasons wearing the caddie uniform and walking golf's most famous property: "The best part of this job is I get to meet presidents, senators, congressmen, great baseball and football players, actors, and the best golfers in the world," McKinley said. "I'll see somebody on TV and realize, hey, I caddied for him before.

"Being a part of this club's history is something I wouldn't trade for anything in the world. The place means more to me than anything in my life."

That assertion was never more evident than in early 2023 as the old guard stepped forward one last time. Jariah Beard, the heart, soul, and spirit—and mainly the voice—of the Black Augusta National caddie corps, was besieged with cancer as time for the Masters crept closer. Beard's condition worsened, and despite going through multiple rehabilitations and keeping his always positive disposition, it was necessary for Beard to enter hospice care by late February.

Fuzzy Zoeller received word at his Sellersburg, Indiana, home and called to speak with his old sidekick about their ultimate success forty-four springs before. It would be the last conversation they ever had.

"Jariah was a very special person not only to me but to his family and so many people," Zoeller told *Golfweek*, noting that he let Beard know "how much I enjoyed our times together."

Other caddie acquaintances, neighborhood friends, and a long list of other friends and family called or stopped by to hopefully encourage the ultimate motivator.

Beard passed away on Friday morning, March 3, at age eighty-two, leaving five children, eleven grandchildren, and eight great-grandchildren.

A celebration of life service was held on Saturday, March 11, at Gilbert-Lambuth Chapel on the campus of Paine College in downtown Augusta, officiated by Beard's brother, Reverend Dr. R. F. Telester Leverett of Olive Grove Baptist Church in Decatur, Georgia. More than seven hundred people gath-

The funeral program for Jariah Beard's service in early 2023. The gathering brought back memories for many caddies at Augusta National, just about all associated with Beard and the Sand Hills neighborhood. *Photo by Ward Clayton*

ered in the large chapel, which is located approximately two miles from Sand Hills. An empty golf bag was stationed next to Beard's casket at the front of the pulpit, a tradition that has been carried on for former Augusta National caddies' final rites through the years, alongside an orange Powerbilt-branded large Tour bag, like the one Beard carried for Zoeller in 1979. A letter from Zoeller was read to the gathering. An eight-page, full-color, magazine-style program touting Beard's career and life with an image of Beard playing golf in his signature panama hat on the cover was handed out to all attendees.

It was a full-on display for the respect that Augusta and the golf community held for Beard and his support of the Black Augusta National caddies through the years.

The Reverend Martris Mims offered a story during a time early in the service that involved golf. The younger man indicated that he knew Beard's background, had been on Beard's case to play golf with him, and professed that his own golf skills were growing. This bit of gesturing came from a minister to a golfer who had bettered his age for eighteen holes well into his eighties and was known to have an appetite for wagering on the golf course, particularly at the Patch.

"He easily beat me that day, and I just wanted to get back out there to play him again," Reverend Mims said. "I kept asking him, 'When are we going to play again? I need another chance. I'll be ready then.'"

When Mims asked again, Beard smiled, paused, and quickly stated, "Don't worry. I've got your number."

Beard's frank assessments of the Masters, precise memory, and friendly nature will be sorely missed since he was proud to be a spokesperson for the caddies' history and plight. His work ethic and time commitment have become the embodiment of the ideal Augusta National caddie and are instrumental in properly remembering the impact of the Black caddies over the years.

The potential that the Patch could develop into a respected and amply funded golf course was on the horizon. Tangible steps were being taken to place a historic marker in the Sand Hills community. New programs and buildings in downtown Augusta were enlivening the Black community, with Augusta National's input and financing.

Due out in late 2023 or early 2024 is a documentary from the award-winning, Chicago-based studio Sheridan Road Productions titled *Rise Above: The Carl Jackson Story*, a film that will explore Jackson's life and the controversial time in American history from the 1950s to the 1970s. The Lucy Laney Museum debuted a play titled *Augusta's Black Caddies: The Men on the Bag Experience* in May 2023, scheduled to play throughout the year, where local actors from the Augusta Mini Theatre, dressed in caddie uniforms provided by Daitch, brought to life late icons Pappy Stokes, Cemetery Perteet, and Willie Peterson with portrayals and characteristics drawn from this book and archived photos. Pimento cheese sandwiches and Arnold Palmers were served at the end of the performances, and former caddies and family members were on hand to watch the play, sign autographs, and participate in a Q and A with attendees.

The skill, personality, camaraderie, and persistence among the Black Augusta National caddies continue to resonate with all the recounting and celebrating. What began as a group of Black teenagers simply looking to make a wage became a cadre of iconic figures whose story should hold a prominent place in not only golf history, but also southern and civil rights lore.

Augusta National caddies were known for their attire—the all-white jumpsuit trimmed in green topped by a baseball cap with the cursive "Caddy" lettering on the front, most often worn during member play. The tournament logo was on the caps during Masters play.

Masters Champions and Caddies

Year	Champion	Caddie	Number
1934	Horton Smith	NA	NA
1935	Gene Sarazen	John H. "Stovepipe" Gordon	NA
1936	Horton Smith	NA	NA
1937	Byron Nelson	Fred Searles	NA
1938	Henry Picard	Willie "Pappy" Stokes	12
1939	Ralph Guldahl	NA	NA
1940	Jimmy Demaret	Banny Smalley	NA
1941	Craig Wood	Pearly Dawsey	30
1942	Byron Nelson	Fred Searles (2)	12
1946	Herman Keiser	Thomas Evans	41
1947	Jimmy Demaret	Banny Smalley (2)	69
1948	Claude Harmon	Willie "Pappy" Stokes (2)	12
1949	Sam Snead	O'Bryant Williams	35
1950	Jimmy Demaret	Banny Smalley (3)	37
1951	Ben Hogan	Willie "Pappy" Stokes (3)	6
1952	Sam Snead	O'Bryant Williams (2)	42
1953	Ben Hogan	Willie "Pappy" Stokes (4)	2
1954	Sam Snead	O'Bryant Williams (3)	62
1955	Cary Middlecoff	Clarence "Eight-Ball" Harris	7
1956	Jack Burke Jr	Willie "Pappy" Stokes (5)	8
1957	Doug Ford	George "Fireball" Franklin	57
1958	Arnold Palmer	Nathaniel "Iron Man" Avery	85
1959	Art Wall	Henry Hammond	83
1960	Arnold Palmer	Nathaniel "Iron Man" Avery (2)	13
1961	Gary Player	Ernest "Snipes" Nipper	52
1962	Arnold Palmer	Nathaniel "Iron Man" Avery (3)	13
1963	Jack Nicklaus	Willie Peterson	49
1964	Arnold Palmer	Nathaniel "Iron Man" Avery (4)	82
1965	Jack Nicklaus	Willie Peterson (2)	90
1966	Jack Nicklaus	Willie Peterson (3)	90
1967	Gay Brewer	Johnny Frank Moore	6
1968	Bob Goalby	Frank "Marble Eye" Stokes	21
1969	George Archer	Frank "Skinny" Ware	63
1970	Billy Casper	Matthew "Shorty Mac" Palmer	34
1971	Charles Coody	Walter "Cricket" Pritchett	7
1972	Jack Nicklaus	Willie Peterson (4)	16
1973	Tommy Aaron	Cleveland Randolph	68
1974	Gary Player	Eddie "E.B." McCoy	39
1975	Jack Nicklaus	Willie Peterson (5)	76
1976	Ray Floyd	Fred "Hop" Harrison	36
1977	Tom Watson	Leon McCladdie	26
1978	Gary Player	Eddie "E.B." McCoy (2)	52
1979	Fuzzy Zoeller	Jariah Beard	48
1980	Seve Ballesteros	Marion Herrington	10
1981	Tom Watson	Leon McCladdie (2)	32
1982	Craig Stadler	Ben Bussey	41

(continued)

Year	Champion	Caddie	Number
Outside Caddies Allowed 1983			
1983	Seve Ballesteros	Nick DePaul	6
1984	Ben Crenshaw	Carl Jackson	52
1985	Bernhard Langer	Peter Coleman	9
1986	Jack Nicklaus	Jack Nicklaus II	89
1987	Larry Mize	Scott Steele	72
1988	Sandy Lyle	Dave Musgrove	63
1989	Nick Faldo	Andy Prodger	36
1990	Nick Faldo	Fanny Sunesson	1
1991	Ian Woosnam	Phillip Morby	9
1992	Fred Couples	Joe LaCava	70
1993	Bernhard Langer	Peter Coleman (2)	11
1994	Jose Maria Olazabal	Dave Renwick	54
1995	Ben Crenshaw	Carl Jackson (2)	16
1996	Nick Faldo	Fanny Sunesson (2)	67
1997	Tiger Woods	Mike "Fluff" Cowan	71
1998	Mark O'Meara	Jerry Higginbothem	73
1999	Jose Maria Olazabal	Brendan McCartain	17
2000	Viay Singh	Dave Renwick (2)	19
2001	Tiger Woods	Steve Williams	71
2002	Tiger Woods	Steve Williams (2)	1
2003	Mike Weir	Brennan Little	57
2004	Phil Mickelson	Jim "Bones" Mackay	53
2005	Tiger Woods	Steve Williams (3)	67
2006	Phil Mickelson	Jim "Bones" Mackay (2)	84
2007	Zach Johnson	Damon Green	56
2008	Trevor Immelman	Neil Wallace	38
2009	Angel Cabrera	Ruben Yorio	53
2010	Phil Mickelson	Jim "Bones" Mackay (3)	58
2011	Charl Schwartzel	Greg Hearmon	77
2012	Bubba Watson	Ted Scott	15
2013	Adam Scott	Steve Williams (4)	17
2014	Bubba Watson	Ted Scott (2)	5
2015	Jordan Spieth	Michael Greller	80
2016	Danny Willett	Jonathan Smart	89
2017	Sergio Garcia	Glen Murray	89
2018	Patrick Reed	Kessler Karain	83
2019	Tiger Woods	Joe LaCava (2)	54
2020	Dustin Johnson	Austin Johnson	62
2021	Hideki Matsuyama	Shota Hayafuji	78
2022	Scottie Scheffler	Ted Scott (3)	39
2023	Jon Rahm	Adam Hayes	49

ACKNOWLEDGMENTS

I can't present the story of the Augusta National caddies without mentioning some people who lent me a hand.

The *Augusta Chronicle*, where I worked as sports editor from 1991–2000, was extremely helpful in the research on photographs and old stories when an earlier version of this book was first published in 2004.

Of note is sportswriter David Westin, now retired, who has surely written more words about Augusta National and the Masters than anyone else in the world during his forty-plus years at the *Chronicle*. David goes by the nickname "Ghost," perhaps because he moonlighted as a caddie at Augusta National in the late 1980s. But more likely, David earned his nickname because of his quiet demeanor. The *Chronicle* had a policy that disallowed employees to hold second jobs, but David wanted to caddie and worked during the day at the National when time permitted. One day, David found himself in the same foursome as Billy Morris, an Augusta National member and the newspaper's longtime former owner and publisher. Remembering the no-moonlighting rule, David tried to lay low, pulling his green caddie cap down over his eyes, and planned to stay on the opposite sides of fairways and greens from Morris as often as possible. But Morris spotted him from the outset and strolled over with a smile on his face.

"You know, David, it's very industrious of you to be out here caddying," Morris said, surprising David.

Also, kudos to Rob Carr, the newspaper's former director of photography. Rob was understanding about my frequent requests for photos of old and current caddies. Dennis Sodomka, the longtime executive editor of the *Chronicle*, also lent his support for this project when I worked for him in Augusta and beyond. The newspaper's archived website, https://augustachronicle.newsbank.com, is also quite an innovation in online research, allowing viewers to step back in time to the early 1800s without sitting in front of a microfilm machine.

That website and other technological innovations the newspaper made were the work of longtime college friend and newspaper colleague John Fish, who was way ahead of most folks in that business in realizing the internet's importance to news gathering's future. The newspaper's coverage of the tournament and the invention of the website were cutting edge in the 1990s. Fish also gave me my most important jobs—the first in Lumberton, North Carolina, at the *Robesonian* when I was right out of school from the University of North Carolina and the most impactful in Augusta in 1991. Sadly, in September 2021 we lost Fish to a twelve-year brain cancer battle, the loss of a pal and communications professional whose catchphrase was, "What ya say, ol' dude?" Fish's humor and spunkiness is sorely missed.

Other thanks goes to good friends Donna and Stan Byrdy, with Stan being a former sportscaster in Augusta and a current successful author of golf history in Augusta and neighboring Aiken, South Carolina; Glenn Greenspan, who served as director of communications at Augusta National and then with Tiger Woods; Kathleen Beasley, who helped look after Pappy along with his sisters and brother; the Willie Peterson family (Vanessa and brother Russell); Will Kennedy, my former associate and boss in Augusta; Skip Dewall and the folks at the former Ann Arbor Media Group for encouraging the completion of this original book; and now to Lynn York and Robin Miura of Blair—which has as its home base my own hometown of Durham, North Carolina—for publishing this extensive update on all the characters and situations.

This book carried forward even further over the last few years. In 2015, I received a cold call from a golf fanatic and film executive, Jim Packer, at Lionsgate in Los Angeles. He was interested in doing a documentary on caddies, based on his wonderful experience with various caddies at the regal Bel-Air Country Club. Most notably inspiring for Packer among the Bel-Air caddies is Mike Pope, who has caddied for Packer for a quarter century. Even after transitioning to a full-time job in the trucking industry, Pope still comes back on many weekends to tote at Bel-Air. Another was veteran caddie Roosevelt Richardson, who has been an inspiration for many Bel-Air members and stole the show in the documentary with his homespun caddie perspective. However, Packer's film idea was stuck until David Gang, a technology executive and golf enthusiast, passed along the original, 2004 version of this book to him. Thank you, David. I hesitated, as I had heard similar "this should be a movie" pitches before, but my wife, Elizabeth, was curious, and googled Packer, quickly saying, "I think you ought to call him back." Jim and I spoke at length then and over the course of four years, the film *Loopers: The*

Caddie's Long Walk, with former caddie Bill Murray as the narrator, came out in 2019. Filmmakers Jason Baffa, Michael Murphy, Clark Cunningham, David Brookwell, Mei-Ling Hom, Chris Brown, Carl Cramer, Tyler Emmett, and Packer were enthusiastic and thorough in producing a documentary that has drawn great reviews.

The Augusta National caddie story—from Pappy to Carl and to Jordan Spieth's caddie, Michael Greller—serves as the centerpiece storyline carrying through Scotland and Ireland, St. Andrews, Pebble Beach, Bandon Dunes, professional golf, everyday golf, the Evans Scholars, and showing the true spirit of spending a day with a caddie.

There has come a realization in society that recognizing those who struggled for equity is just as important—maybe more so—as recognizing those who oversee corporations or governments from on high.

Also, love goes out to Elizabeth and our cherished children (now adults), Monica and Will, who put up with my late nights and hour upon hour of research and writing to complete a project that I had only dreamed about previously. That same love goes to in-laws Bill (who passed in 2022), Monica, William, and John Patterson, who share my enthusiasm for all sports. And to my parents, the late Edith and Elmo Clayton, I cannot express enough gratitude for their encouragement to explore writing as a career.

My Masters experience was introduced by the late Buddy Whitfield in Durham, who showed me his passion for the Masters starting in 1985. Beginning in the 1950s, Buddy traded country hams for tickets to the Masters, coaxed ministers to let him use their tickets, wrote Augusta National yearly to check his status on the waiting list, finally received his own tickets in 1993, and became a fifty-six-year Masters attendee before passing away in 2010. His son, David, has gone to Augusta for more than fifty-two years, and good friend David Chapman has often been alongside. We call Augusta the Promised Land, a reference to Moses leading the Israelites out of bondage in Egypt to their fertile promised land to be called Israel. Buddy was our golf and Masters version of Moses. Several other Durham golfers also paid heed to Buddy's Masters vibe, including longtime golf pals Joe Dobson, "Wormy" Rich, Jeff Robinson, Zack Veasey, Karl Blackwell, Charlie Overby, and Alan Stephenson. Hillandale pro Luke Veasey taught many of us how to play and act on a golf course, and Cole Huckabee at Durham's Croasdaile Country Club guided me through my first job in golf as a cart washer, beer server, greens-fee taker, and range picker when I was in high school and college. I first put hands on a golf club in the early 1970s with an introduction from Durham legend Bill Cozart (the grandfather of a dear friend, Mike Woodall) and my mother's boss, Russell Barringer Sr., so they are responsible for getting me hooked on the game. Oakland Avenue neighborhood pals also stoked my interest in sports, led by Mark and Charles Upchurch, Woodall, George Walsh, and anybody else who resided in the shadow of Duke University and thrived on sports.

Thanks also go to Hall of Fame coaches who dipped into the golf world when I was a Durham High student and golf team member—Dave Odom (Wake Forest and South Carolina basketball), who was my first golf coach, and Hal Stewart (multiple state titles in North Carolina prep football), the best motivator I have ever seen in athletics. Coach James "Bump" Elliott also stole over from the football field to lend a helping hand. Our golf team didn't compete for titles, but our squad of Donnie "Wormy" Rich, the late William "SWAT" Gunter, Ernie Simpson, Lawrence Newton, Jeff Cole, Arthur McDonald, and Arthur Whitfield all had a good time trying, whether it be at Hillandale or a night out at the Westwood Par 3.

Another inspiration was the late Dean Smith, the legendary basketball coach at the University of North Carolina. Coach Smith's passion for golf and his competitive spirit were just as intense on the course as on the hardwood.

Members of the Pi Kappa Alpha house at UNC were also key cogs as lifelong friends. They include Jim "J. C." Corbett, Dave "Cosmo" Costner, David "Nipper" Colquitt, Randy "R. C." Day, Gary Edge, Greg Allen, Donnie "Double D" Douglas, Rolo T. Lassiter, Eric "Brahma" Henry, Zack Touloupas, Mark "The Big O" Steliotes, Mac "Hawkeye" Purcell, Mike Perry, Steve Flinn, Mike Cox, Calvin Coghill, Barney Spooner, A. J. Belt, Mike Amos, "Dirty" Don Milligan, Frank Hart, Andy Bills, Page Singletary, Cal Wood, Wayne "Trigger" Rogers, and the ringleader, Sammy "the King" Batten.

I also borrowed insight from Augustans Lowell Dorn, Dan O'Shea, Fred Palmer, and John Boyette, great friends and golf companions. They stand alongside my pal Walter Clay, the owner of my favorite Augusta restaurant, Rae's Coastal Café, as terrific historical and current-day resources for all things Augusta.

Finally, and most of all, thanks go to the Augusta National caddies who told the tales of their cohorts. Carl Jackson is a rock of a man who has persisted during his life and is dedicated to his family, foremost. Tall and quiet, I'm sure he was very easy for Ben Crenshaw to lean on in the challenging times that they have spent on and off the course. Jariah Beard had a passion for golf and caddying, creating great memories, and the brotherhood that collaborated and bickered with each other to form the world's greatest caddie corps. Also, thanks to Joe Collins, Pappy Stokes, Bennie Hatcher, Buck Moore, Louis Laurence, Tommy Bennett, Billy Ricks, Marion Herrington, Robert Bass, Lawrence Bennett, caddie supporters Leon Maben and Joyce Law, and anyone who has ever carried a golf bag at Augusta National—and beyond.

All you must do is sit for a few minutes with some of these former caddies and you'll be hooked. Their deep passion for the sport and a competitive fire second to none is evident from the outset despite most of society's discouragement. They knew more than just the golf games of Jones, Hogan, Snead, Nicklaus, Palmer, and Woods. They can recite the mannerisms and the personality traits that created an ability to win the Masters.

Playing Augusta National would be a dream day for any golf fan. Having a caddie with such great knowledge and instinct increases the joy immeasurably. Remember their names and impact.

BIBLIOGRAPHY

Alexander, Jules, Martin Davis, Ken Venturi, Dave Anderson, Ben Crenshaw, and
   Dan Jenkins. *The Hogan Mystique*. Greenwich, CT: The American Golfer, 1994.
Augusta Chronicle, The. https://augustachronicle.newsbank.com.
Champions Tour Media Guide, 2003
Christian, Frank. *Augusta National and the Masters*. Ann Arbor, MI: Sleeping
   Bear Press, 1996.
Concannon, Joe. "Augusta National's First Caddie Recalls Early Days," *Augusta
   Chronicle*, August 28, 1990.
Crenshaw, Ben, with Melanie Hauser. *A Feel for the Game: To Brookline and Back*.
   New York: Doubleday, 2001.
Crenshaw, Ben, and Carl Jackson, with Melanie Hauser. *Two Roads to Augusta:
   The Inspiring Story of How Two Men from Different Backgrounds Grew to Be-
   come Best Friends and Capture the Biggest Prize in Golf*. Greenwich, CT: The
   American Golfer, 2013.
Golf Digest, April 1993; December 1998; May 2002.
Green, Ron, Sr. *Shouting at Amen Corner: Dispatches from the Masters, the
   World's Greatest Golf Tournament*. Champaign, IL: Sports Publishing, 1999.
Loopers: The Caddie's Long Walk (documentary film). Gravitas Ventures, 2019.
Masters Journal, The. 1994.
Masters Media Guide, 2023
Masters Tournament Player and Caddie List, 1984–2023.
Masters.com
Nicklaus, Jack, with Ken Bowden. *My Story*. New York: Simon & Schuster, 1997.
Owen, David. *The Making of the Masters*. New York: Simon & Schuster, 1999.
Palmer, Arnold, with James Dodson. *A Golfer's Life*. New York: Ballantine, 1999.
PGA Tour Media Guide, 2003.
Price, Charles. *A Golf Story: Bobby Jones, Augusta National, and the Masters Tour-
   nament*. New York: Atheneum, 1986.
Reilly, Rick. "Once More, with Feeling," *Sports Illustrated*, April 17, 1995.
Rushin, Steve. "Out of the Woods," *Sports Illustrated*: April 20, 1998.
Sampson, Curt. *Hogan: A Biography*. Nashville, TN: Rutledge-Hill, 1996.
Sarazen, Gene. *Thirty Years of Championship Golf*. New York: Prentice-Hall, 1950.
Shipnuck, Alan. "Vijay Day," *Sports Illustrated*, April 17, 2000.
Sports Illustrated Vault, https://vault.si.com.

Van Natta, Don Jr. *First Off the Tee: Presidential Hackers, Duffers, and Cheaters from Taft to Bush*. New York: Public Affairs, 2003.

Zimmerman, John G. "Two Shots That Won the Masters," *Sports Illustrated*, April 15, 1957.

Printed in the USA
CPSIA information can be obtained
at www.ICGtesting.com
JSHW051347030324
58329JS00004B/4